# Dark Shadows
# Almanac

## MILLENNIUM EDITION

foreword by
**DAVID SELBY**

edited by
**KATHRYN LEIGH SCOTT & JIM PIERSON**

POMEGRANATE PRESS LTD.

LOS ANGELES   LONDON

This is a Pomegranate Press, Ltd. book.

*Dark Shadows Almanac:Millennium Edition*

Copyright ©2000 Pomegranate Press. All rights reserved.

*Dark Shadows*© Dan Curtis Productions, Inc.
All rights reserved.

Library of Congress Card Number: 00-101705

Softcover: ISBN 0-938817-18-3

Cover and Interior Design:
*Cheryl Carrington*


Second Printing 2002

2 4 6 8 10 9 7 5 3


Printed and bound in the United States of America

POMEGRANATE PRESS, LTD.
P.O. Box 17217
Beverly Hills, CA 90209
fax: 310•271•4930
http://www.pompress.com

# Acknowledgments

Nancy Barrett, Leigh Beery, Dave Brown, Tim Choate, Dale Clark, Melody Clark, Robert Cobert, Dan Curtis, Dan Damiano, Yvonne David, Roger Davis, George DiCenzo, Yvette Dilworth, Louis Edmonds, Dennis Eger, Charles Ellis, Richard Estep, Robert Finocchio, Jonathan Frid, Stuart Goodman, Darren Gross, Mary McKinley-Haas, Guy Haines, Craig Hamrick, Philip Hansen, Pam Jarman, Nina Johnson, John Karlen, David Kennedy, Nancy Kersey, Barbara Keyes, Richard Levantino, Michael Lipowski, Stuart Manning, Cary Mansfield, Dan Markell, Malcolm Marmorstein, Ben Martin, Todd McIntosh, Mary McKinley-Haas, Paul Michael, Diana Millay, Geoff Miller, Walter Miller, Alexandra Moltke, MPI Home Video, Jay Nass, Kristi Nelson, Denise Nickerson, Chris Nokes, Mary Overstreet, Lara Parker, Dennis Patrick, Chris Pennock, Lilo Raymond, Kathy Resch, Kathleen Reynolds, Richard Photo, Lisa Richards, Marcy Robin, Helen Samaras, Michael Seggie, David Selby, Michael Sheridan, Dick Smith, Mary Spooner, Jeff Thompson, Sy Tomashoff, Kelly Wade, Marie Wallace, Donna Wandrey, Thomas Weisser, Dean Wilson

# Contents

# A Foreword

## by David Selby

URING THE SUMMER OF 1965, WHILE THE LOS ANGELES RIOTS WERE raging, I was a graduate student at Southern Illinois University, performing the role of Abraham Lincoln in *Prologue To Glory* in a New Salem, Illinois summer stock company production.

By the summer of 1966, the Vietnam War was going strong. I was an apprentice at the Barter Theatre in Abingdon, Virginia. I passed my physical for the army that summer but was told I could not join the 300,000 troops in Vietnam because I had too much education and because I was married. So it was off to the Cleveland Playhouse, where I was instructed not to leave my hotel because of the riots. Violence was dominating the stage again in the world of human affairs.

The Civil Rights Movement was in full force as was the Free Speech Movement, with its upheavals at Berkeley and Columbia. I was reading Robert Lowell, Ezra Pound, Anne Sexton, Sylvia Plath, and Sam Shepard, as well as Eldridge Cleaver. Like so many others, I listened to Dylan and Joplin. But unlike so many others, I was not aware of a particular television show that premiered in June 1966, the same month and year that Stokeley Carmichael used the slogan "Black Power" for the first time.

*Dark Shadows* was a Gothic romance that took on other dimensions and higher ratings when a character named Barnabas Collins appeared. How could I have missed it? Did it have something to do with my being caught up in the riots of Detroit, the worst of this century? Or being stunned on a subway where I heard that Martin Luther King had been assassinated? Or being shocked a couple of months later at the killing of Robert Kennedy, which brought back an earlier nightmare? Were these events more overwhelming to me than to others who were horrified by them?

In the Sixties there were many wars going on, including the War on Poverty. The one thing I never considered when deciding to become an actor was money. The idea of making money, of being paid to act, had never occurred to me. I was very innocent and foolish. Fortunately, my wife was more grounded, and it was she who kept us out of poverty while I went merrily on finding my way as an actor in an increasingly violent world.

It was my good fortune that an agent saw me in a scene from Tennessee Williams' *Summer and Smoke*. That agent sent me to see New York casting director Marion Dougherty, who put me in a cab and accompanied me to see a producer named Dan Curtis. After he removed a few golf balls from his plush carpet, I performed a scene from *Dark Shadows*, auditioning for the role of Quentin Collins. A few days later, Dan tested me on camera, and a few days after that my saga with *Dark Shadows* began. It continues today, some twenty-seven years later.

*Dark Shadows* was a creative product of Dan Curtis. Even someone in a Sixties' drug-induced trance would not have been immune to the vibrations of Dan's energy. I liked it and I liked Dan, although I was never sure where I stood with him. Perhaps it was the Sixties. I was never certain where I stood with the Sixties either, although I knew I was lucky just to be alive in the decade, when things were happening.

Andy Warhol was shot and almost killed in 1968. It was he who said, "In the future, everyone will be famous for fifteen minutes." Those of us on *Dark Shadows* have had our fifteen minutes—plus. For this hill child from West Virginia, it was all a little overwhelming. I'm sure Andy Warhol was a fan. Goodness, Joanne Woodward's mother was even a fan! It seemed fitting that *Dark Shadows* was part of the Sixties, when there was a certain craziness in the air. *Dark Shadows* was not low-keyed drama; it didn't reflect the ordinary man's conception of the world. Although its style of acting could be indulgent and downright hammy, *Dark Shadows* was true to life—true to its life, its universe. *Dark Shadows* created its own world, a world that millions of television viewers decided to enter. And once they did, they would not let it go. The Sixties would end, but *Dark Shadows* would endure.

My mind is still haunted by the newspaper photograph of the Kent State slaughter. We were of that time. Each of us was moved, numbed, angered, and heartbroken by man's inhumanity to man. But those of us in the *Dark Shadows* family were lucky, all of us—cast, crew, writers, directors, producers, makeup, hair, reception, and, of course, the viewers, the fans. We were lucky because we had a place we could escape to, the world of *Dark Shadows*. Those of you who joined us in that world must know we worked hard, we played, we touched each other, we became close. I see your faces, hear your voices—you are in my heart.

My son was born in 1969. We named him Jamison. He is now a young actor in New York. Take care of him; he is one of yours. And if he is lucky, he too will get to have a bubblegum card with his name on it. ☞

# Maggie Comes Home

### by Kathryn Leigh Scott

ON A SPARKLING, UNSEASONABLY WARM LATE OCTOBER AFTERNOON, I stood on the bluffs in front of the Carey Mansion, as it's known by locals in Newport, Rhode Island, and looked at waves crashing against a rocky shore. Yes, *those* waves, the ones that made their debut more than 33 years ago under the opening credits of the premiere episode of *Dark Shadows*. I couldn't stop myself from humming the opening bars of Robert Cobert's famous theme music and recalling those wistful words spoken by the young governess, Victoria Winters . . . *My journey is beginning . . . a journey to link my past with my future* . . . on her way to the mysterious Collins Mansion.

But what I was experiencing in nature's glorious technicolor, we in early 1966 viewed in grainy shades of gray, lending even more ghostly shadows to the mansion on the hill with the haunting glow of light in a single upstairs window. And therein lies a story I was to discover in October 1999 as a guest author attending Haunted Newport Hallowe'en celebrations.

Seaview Terrace, as the Carey mansion was originally known, had been built in the 1920s for a wealthy Washington D.C. distiller (producer of Old Crow Whisky) who requested that his architect, Howard Greenley, pattern the summer home after a particular chateau in France. The family stayed in their vacation house with the ocean view only about three times. As often happened, after the Great Depression and the introduction of federal income taxes during the 1930s, the wealthy owners could no longer afford the luxury of the huge household staffs necessary to the upkeep of these lavish summer homes that were not built for year-round living. Seaview Terrace had not been inhabited for a decade prior to World War II, when it was used as barracks for naval personnel. Windows were broken, the lawns overgrown when the mansion was purchased for back taxes in 1949 and converted for use as a summer school, Burnham-by-the-Sea.

In early May of 1966, Dan Curtis arrived in Newport with his set designer, Sy Tomashoff, to scout exterior locations for ABC's new afternoon soap, *Dark Shadows*. The Gothic architecture of Seaview Terrace had caught Tomashoff's discerning eye as a suitably brooding facade for the Collins mansion which was set in the mythical town of Collinsport, Maine. Curtis negotiated to film the opening credits at Seaview Terrace for the sum of $500, with the owner's stipulation that filming would have to be completed before school opened in late June. However, to the consternation of the school's staff, Dan Curtis arrived unannounced with a film crew at noon the day before the summer term was to begin. The crew set up their cameras and spent the afternoon filming on the grounds of Burnham-by the-Sea. By late afternoon, the weary headmaster asked if they were finally finished shooting. No, Curtis told him, they would also be shooting that night and would need to have the entire mansion dark except for one light shining in a window. The headmaster protested that with school beginning in the morning, he had a lot of work to do and needed the lights on. After considerable persuasion (Curtis, after all, had a television series to launch!) the school master was relegated to a room in the turret where he worked by candlelight with a blanket covering the window.

Curtis later returned to film exterior scenes on the grounds of the school with Alexandra Moltke, Louis Edmonds, Thayer David and David Henesy. Since 1976, the mansion has housed Salve Regina College.

That October evening in 1999, after a lecture and book signing, my hosts introduced me to The Black Pearl on Bannister's Wharf. Not only is the charming restaurant and tavern famous for its New England chowder, but, with its rustic black lacquer interior and red-checkered tablecloths, it's easily recognizable to any *Dark Shadows* fan as the prototype for the Blue Whale. The very long, very narrow building is about 100 years old and was originally used as a rigging shop in the days when the only way to get off the island was by ship. During the winter months, the ships would dock at Bannister's Wharf and the masts would be hauled into the shop for repairs.

The rigging shop was converted into a restaurant in the early 1960s. The wharf area was once known as Blood Alley, a rough neighborhood with colorful strip joints and bars that catered to sailors and fisherman—and certainly would have lured "Pop," Maggie's dear old dad, Sam Evans. I can picture him, sketchpad in hand, roaming the waterfront and then nipping into the Blue Whale for a convivial whisky with Bob the bartender.

Today the wharf is a quaint promenade with restaurants, shops and galleries. As we strolled the moonlit wharf after a wonderful meal at the Black Pearl, I couldn't help but imagine myself as the young Maggie Evans walking hand-in-hand with Joe Haskell after a hamburger and a dance or two at the Blue Whale. Once again, as I looked out over the water at the bobbing sailboats, I found myself humming a few bars of Robert Cobert's nostalgic Blue Whale music and remembering my good friend Joel Crothers.

And surely somewhere in this evocative setting, lurking in the *Dark Shadows* of the wharf, Barnabas Collins was watching us, a sinister gleam in his eye. ☞

*The Blue Whale set.*

# Program History

ARK SHADOWS DEBUTED JUNE 27, 1966, ON THE ABC-TV NETWORK as the first Gothic daytime drama. The program was the creation of producer Dan Curtis, who would later gain critical acclaim with the monumental television mini-series *The Winds of War* and *War and Remembrance*.

The original plot of *Dark Shadows* centered on a young woman named Victoria Winters who becomes the governess of a ten-year-old boy in Collinsport, Maine, a small and stormy fishing village. She was employed by the wealthy Collins family, who reside in a mysterious old mansion overlooking the ocean.

Veteran motion picture actress Joan Bennett was featured in the role of Elizabeth Collins Stoddard, matriarch of the Collins family and mistress of the great house called Collinwood. After several months on the air, the show was failing to attract a large enough audience with its traditional Gothic suspense formula. In a dramatic effort to save the show from cancellation, Dan Curtis decided to introduce one of the most unusual characters in daytime television history.

In April of 1967, Shakespearean actor Jonathan Frid joined the cast as Barnabas Collins, a 175-year-old vampire. Frid's portrayal of Barnabas was a surprise success when he added humanity to his characterization and made Barnabas a tragic figure.

After more supernatural elements were added to *Dark Shadows*, it became the most popular daytime series on ABC. Numerous ghosts, a werewolf, and a witch named Angélique appeared as the show alternated its stories between the present day Collins family and their ancestors in the past In 1970, Metro-Goldwyn-Mayer released a theatrical film based on the series entitled *House of Dark Shadows*. Many of the television cast members reprised their roles, but they were surrounded by more explicit displays of horror that were not suitable for the daytime television program.

On April 2, 1971, while still a respectably popular attraction, *Dark Shadows* ended its five-year network run. At that time, production commenced on a second MGM film, *Night of Dark Shadows*, released later in the year.

Since ending production, *Dark Shadows* has retained a devoted following through reruns and home video releases. Regular cast reunions and an active fan network continue to celebrate *Dark Shadows'* unique and timeless appeal. Thirty-five years after its debut, *Dark Shadows'* reputation as a television classic remains firmly intact. ☞

# Dark Shadows Through the Years

1966 *Dark Shadows* debuts as an ABC-TV afternoon soap opera on June 27. The first of 32 Paperback Library novels is issued, starting a *Dark Shadows* merchandising blitz.

1967 Jonathan Frid joins the cast as reluctant vampire Barnabas Collins.

1968 David Selby makes his first appearance as the ghost of Quentin Collins.

1969 *Dark Shadows* achieves its highest ratings ever with the 1897 storyline. *Original Music from Dark Shadows* reaches #18 on the *Billboard* album chart, and the single *Quentin's Theme*, by the Charles Randolph Grean Sounde, hits the Top 20.

1970 The MGM motion picture *House of Dark Shadows* is released. *Quentin's Theme* is nominated for a Grammy Award.

1971 After 1,225 shows, *Dark Shadows* ends its run on April 2. The MGM motion picture *Night of Dark Shadows* is released.

1973 Jonathan Frid tours South America to promote Spanish language broadcasts of *Dark Shadows*.

1975 *Dark Shadows* reruns debut in U.S. syndication with 260 episodes, starting with Barnabas' introduction. *The World of Dark Shadows* fanzine begins publishing.

1979 The first issue of *ShadowGram*, the *Dark Shadows* current events newsletter, is published.

1982 *Dark Shadows* reruns air for the first time on PBS stations.

1983 The first *Dark Shadows* Festival is held in Newark, New Jersey. An additional 260 episodes are released in syndication.

1985 New Jersey Network airs the first *Dark Shadows* Special. An additional 260 episodes are released in syndication.

1986 The book *My Scrapbook Memories of Dark Shadows* and *Original Music from Dark Shadows Volume 2* are issued.

1987 WNYC-TV airs the special *Casting Shadows*. *Original Music from Dark Shadows Volume 3* is released.

1988    *Dark Shadows* stage play presented by Dance Theatre Workshop in New York. *Original Music from Dark Shadows Volume 4* is released.

1989    *Dark Shadows* debuts on home video.

1990    MGM's primetime revival of *Dark Shadows* goes into production. *The Dark Shadows Companion* book is issued. *Quentin's Theme* is given Broadcast Music Incorporated's one-million radio performances award.

1991    *Dark Shadows* revival series airs for 12 episodes on NBC-TV. The 25th Anniversary is celebrated at the *Dark Shadows* Festivals in Los Angeles and New York.

1992    *Dark Shadows* reruns begin on the Sci-Fi Channel national cable station. The revival series debuts on home video.

1994    The revival series reairs for the first time on the Sci-Fi Channel.

1995    *The Dark Shadows Almanac*, original edition, is issued.

1996    The 30th Anniversary is celebrated at the The *Dark Shadows* Festival in Los Angeles.

1998    HarperCollins issues first *Dark Shadows* novel in 26 years, *Angélique's Descent*, written by Lara Parker.

1999    *Dark Shadows Special Edition*, the show's first DVD is released. *Original Music from Dark Shadows* is reissued on CD in a deluxe edition with bonus cast radio interviews.

2000    Dan Curtis prepares a *Dark Shadows* stage musical. Restoration of *Night of Dark Shadows* is proposed.

# 𝔅𝔯𝔬𝔞𝔡𝔠𝔞𝔰𝔱 𝔥𝔦𝔰𝔱𝔬𝔯𝔶

D ARK *SHADOWS* DEBUTED JUNE 27, 1966 AT 4:00 P.M. EASTERN & Pacific Standard Time (3:00 p.m. Central Time.) It followed another soap opera, *The Nurses*. An afternoon teenage music series, *Where The Action Is*, followed *Dark Shadows*.

When *The Nurses* was cancelled, *Dark Shadows* moved to 3:30 p.m. Eastern/Pacific on April 2, 1967, and *General Hospital* was its new lead-in program. *The Dating Game* was now the program that aired immediately after *Dark Shadows*.

As *Dark Shadows* became a popular attraction with school kids, ABC received thousands of requests to move the show to a later time period. As a result, the show returned to its original time period of 4:00 p.m. Eastern/Pacific on July 15, 1968. On this day, the serial *One Life To Live* debuted, airing in *Dark Shadows'* old time slot. *Dark Shadows* remained at this time until it went off the air on April 2, 1971. It was replaced by a revival of the game show *Password*.

# Dark Shadows Origins

I N 1965, UPSTART TELEVISION PRODUCER DAN CURTIS HAD A DREAM which led to the eventual birth of *Dark Shadows*. His nocturnal vision involved a beautiful young woman riding on a train, with her destination being a brooding old mansion.

Writer Art Wallace was commisioned to develop a story outline for Curtis' proposed series, which was tentatively named *Shadows on the Wall*. Wallace drew heavily from one of his previous works—an original teleplay entitled *The House*, which had been seen as an episode of NBC-TV's *Goodyear TV Playhouse* on September 8, 1957.

According to *TV Guide*, *The House* was set in a New England fishing village where middle-aged Caroline Barnes has lived the life of a recluse since her seafaring husband disappeared years ago. The only people she sees are her daughter Elizabeth and her piano pupils. In an attempt to change her life of seclusion, Caroline plans a dinner party.

For *Dark Shadows*, the New England fishing village from *The House* became Collinsport, Caroline Barnes became Elizabeth Collins Stoddard, the missing husband became Paul Stoddard, and daughter Elizabeth became daughter Carolyn. The piano teacher aspect was dropped for *Dark Shadows*, although Elizabeth Collins Stoddard was depicted as playing the piano in early episodes.

*The House*, directed by Paul Stanley, was a one-hour color program broadcast live from New York. Videotape was not yet commonly used, so the program was recorded via the kinescope method on black-and-white film. Hope Emerson portrayed Caroline, and Frances Sternhagen portrayed Elizabeth. Other cast members included Jay C. Flippen as Jeb, Peter Mark Richman as Larry, Ford Rainey as Walt, and Paula Trueman as Martha. ☞

# Lara's Descent Into Gothic Romance

### by Lara Parker

OW IN THE WORLD DOES AN ACTRESS END UP WRITING A NOVEL? Actresses are those vain, frivolous creatures who bask in the limelight and would never think of holing up in a dark office for months struggling to produce a piece of fiction. Actresses spend all their time waiting for that big break taking acting classes, maybe dance classes, voice classes—but not English, not Composition, not World Lit.

I was sure the editor from HarperCollins, Caitlin Blasdell, who invited me to lunch at the Marriott Marquis in New York City's Times Square was thinking along these lines. I was there for the 1997 *Dark Shadows* convention and she had come over from her Fifth Avenue office to meet me and to discuss the possibility of my writing the first of a series of novels based on the television show. She was young and soft-spoken, wore a dove colored business suit, and her shiny ash-blond hair was cut short. Jim Pierson, who had been working for months putting together this meeting, was with us. These book spin-offs were his idea, and he had succeeded in getting Caitlin and HarperCollins interested.

I appreciated the opportunity but I really didn't believe I'd be able to do it. Granted, I had taken some screen writing courses at UCLA. In fact I had written three unsold screenplays. But a novel? Well, no, I had never written a novel. I had never written a short story. I was neither foolish enough nor presumptuous enough to assume that I would have the ability to generate hundreds of pages that in any way that would resemble the many fascinating, intriguing novels I had read in my life—the twists and turns of the plot, the complexities of character. I had great respect of the craft of writing and I knew how difficult it was to write even one cohesive paragraph. Needless to say I was resistant to the whole idea.

But as Caitlin and I talked over our Caesar salads, I realized she was much more optimistic than I was, and I wondered why. She said she had a lot of faith in me. I told her, hesitantly, that I might like to write the story of Angélique's childhood, and she was very pleased with that idea. Then she cleared up the whole mystery of her confident demeanor. Dropping her voice to a conspiratorial tone, she confided gently, "Please don't worry, Lara. Just write it the best you can. We have professional writers at Harpers who will take what you do, fix it up,  and make it into a real book."

They would do what? I bristled at the very idea. Ahhhh . . . of course: "ghost writers . . ." That's how those "celebrity writers" become authors. A ghost writer . . . how in keeping with *Dark Shadows*, I thought with a grim chuckle. But Caitlin's proposition, meant to reassure me, to ease my panic, had the absolute opposite effect. Make it into a real book? She meant someone would re-write my writing, change what I had agonized over for months without my being able to stop them. (You realize I had yet to write a single word.) I was insulted, my pride was injured, and I could think of nothing but how much I resented her offer.

I remember mumbling something like, "But how could some hack writer at Harpers know as much about Angélique as I do?" Caitlin smiled, asked me to send her an outline, and said we would go from there.

My "outline" was a re-hash of a letter I had sent to the *Dark Shadows* writer, Sam Hall, when he was working on the new *Dark Shadows* series. Trying to remember how Angélique had become a witch, he called me to see whether I knew. I had no recollections from the show, but luckily, I had just returned from a trip to Nepal.

In Katmandu I had seen the "Living Goddess," a lonely little girl with dark kohl around her eyes, dressed in colored silks, dripping with jewels.  She sat in an upstairs window of a house on a public square,  and stared blankly down at the crowd. My tour guide said she had been chosen at nine years of age in an ordeal which tested her composure. A group of little girls were placed in a room with rabid dogs who tore apart a slaughtered buffalo. The little girl who did not cry became the "Living Goddess", and as an idol of worship, she remained in seclusion until she reached puberty. At times she was carried through the streets in a curtained chaise to the temple, but most of the time was kept alone. She grew up with no friends, no real childhood. I remember feeling deeply sorry for her.

In my letter to Sam Hall, I co-opted this amazing story. I had always wondered what series of events could transform an innocent child into someone as evil as Angélique. What complex experiences would shape a woman who loved so compulsively and hated with such intensity?

The Living Goddess in Katmandu also seemed the perfect place to begin my scenario for HarperCollins. My outline was accepted and Caitlin told me to start writing the book.

But how? Too terrified to actually begin writing, I started reading. Trying to discover the vocabulary and sentence structure which gave Gothic Literature its lush, emotional tone, I read Daphne du Maurier, Robert Louis Stevenson, Charles Dickens, Henry James, the Bronte sisters, Edgar Allan Poe, Bram Stoker, to name only a few. I read *Interview with a Vampire* and *Gone With the Wind*, digging beneath the stories to focus on structure and point of view. I was determined to steep myself in the romantic style.

The months slipped by and still I didn't write a page. I spent many hours perusing history books on the Caribbean and taking notes. I studied plans of sugar plantations, read about the sufferings of the slaves. I found a five hundred page diary kept by a sugar planter in Martinique in 1801 which detailed his day-to-day difficulties and inconveniences, and I experienced them all with him. I was thrilled to discover, since any horror story demands a dark and gloomy mansion, that many great houses, even castles, were built in the islands by the plantation owners homesick for their European homelands, the stones shipped from the continent as ballast on the schooners. I found a book written by a Jesuit priest who had lived for a time in Martinique and I was able to procrastinate for another week trudging through his life story. And of course it was necessary that I become familiar with the history of the French and English conquest of the islands as well as the history of America in those early days of the new nation.

Whenever anyone asked how the novel was going, I said, "Oh, fine . . . I'm . . . uh . . . doing a lot of research."

Naturally, it was important that I learn about voodoo, the pagan religion of Haiti brought over from Africa by the slaves. I read of the ceremonies, possession by the spirits, and I found Erzulie, the Voodoo goddess of sensuality who seemed perfect as Angélique's spiritual guardian.

Immersed in these rich discoveries, I began to feel intriguing ideas emerging, and I told myself that when I did begin to write I would have a wealth of material to draw from. Most time consuming of all was the need to watch hours and hours of the original series again and this time to imagine what all the characters were thinking, especially my own. Writing Angélique's interior dialogue, I told myself, would be my chance to reveal her emotional identity, her torturous indecision and her increasing obsession with Barnabas.

I do remember being amazed at how well the shows were written, how skillfully the tension was sustained and how well the conflict grew out of the characters. Once again I was paralyzed with feelings of inadequacy. More and more I realized what a hard job I had ahead of me, especially if I kept putting it off.

Finally, one day after I had finished listening to *Dr. Jekyll and Mr. Hyde* on my car stereo, and been inspired by the language, almost on a whim I pulled over into a parking lot and began to scribble a few lines on a piece of scrap paper: "Barnabas woke trembling, his heart pounding, his breath coming in gasps."

A week or so later, with great trepidation, I sent fifty pages off to Caitlin at Harpers and sat back to wait for her reply. I would say I had butterflies in my stomach every time I thought of her reading my manuscript, but it was more like huge frogs leaping around in there. When I thought about what I had written I felt sick. Who was I kidding? This was all a huge mistake. I was humbled and humiliated and very embarrassed.

But to my amazement, she responded right away. She said she had enjoyed the story very much so far, that she thought everything was going to be fine, and that, perhaps, there was just a little too much "moonlight." Stung by this criticism, I nevertheless breathed a huge sigh of relief that she had not rejected everything out of hand. I took out a few adjectives describing the moon, and kept writing. I knew I had some problems. I had always believed that Angélique was a victim of seduction and abandonment. One of the first lessons in acting is to find a way to believe you are right to do what you do, even if you are playing the villain. Therefore, as I was doing the part on the television show, I always searched for deeper motivations whenever Angélique became insanely jealous, or unleashed her ruthless vengeance on others. People are not born evil, I reasoned, experiences turn them evil. Hearts are not hard at first; betrayal and disillusionment turn hearts to stone.

Also, I realized that if Angélique were to be the protagonist of the novel, she would have to be sympathetic on some level. The reader does not remain involved if he can't identify with the main character. I wanted Angélique to be a tragic heroine, doomed by fate, twisted by envy, and tortured by unrequited love. But on the show she had always seemed to be pure evil, "the witch you loved to hate." How could I make her more complex— even vulnerable?

I began to imagine ever more heartbreaking events which would harden Angélique. Her hopes would soar, only to be shattered against the rocks. Love would come to her and she would see it slip through her fingers. But a succession of rotten breaks would grow tedious if the bad luck was simply arbitrary and came out of nowhere. There had to be some unseen hand behind her misfortunes, and that is how the idea of the devil came to me. I decided that if he had been seeking control of her from the very beginning and she had never been able to escape him, then she would be struggling against powers greater than her own. Something would be driving her besides her jealousy and willful vanity, and that struggle, requiring resiliency and courage, would make us sympathize with her more.

Most startling of all, the writers—I can only imagine in an effort to make the show more scary—had included several scenes where Angélique seemed to be bewildered by magic she had not herself invented: the skull, for instance, with a wig like Josette's hair, which Barnabas opened as a wedding present; the appearance of Jeremiah as a walking corpse; the wedding champagne turning to blood. These events which so tortured and terrified Angélique could now be explained by the existence of the devil lurking in the background.

Looking closely at the many heroines in novels, I realized they all were flawed, and their talents and their faults arose from the same source. For instance, Angélique was drawn to magic because she was intelligent and curious and because her instinct for survival urged her to find any means of escape. But as she developed her skills, she doomed herself, since, in pursuing magic, she tied herself inexorably to the devil. Practice of witchcraft became an addiction; she was never able to give it up. The more desperate she became, the more she clung to those depraved techniques which made her the devil's handmaiden. I found this irony fascinating.

Caitlin suggested that Angélique and Barnabas meet by page fifty. (Apparently this is a structural rule in romance novels.) Obedient to her guidelines, I decided to have them see each other for the first time as children, and, in my imagination, even then they were drawn to one another. He gave her a moonstone which she kept her whole life. I had them meet again aboard ship when Angélique was disguised as a boy, and finally in the marketplace where he noticed her for the first time and was attracted to her. She, of course, remembered him, and still kept the moonstone in the charm at her neck. I worked very hard on these scenes, writing them over and over, paring them down. I wanted to leave the reader aching for more.

At last I was able to write about "those nights in Martinique" which Angélique so often implored Barnabas to remember. Angélique's misplaced trust in Barnabas, her shattered dreams and her bitter disappointment, suggested the background scenes I had always imagined when I was acting on the show, forcing the witchy little serving maid to play her bad-tempered tricks. Caitlin also suggested the title, *Angélique's Descent*, which I resisted at first until I found the story of Inanna, the first recorded goddess myth, and the fragment of poetry, "Inanna abandoned heaven, abandoned earth, to the nether world she descended." At that point the Living Goddess in Katmandu, Erzulie, and Inanna all began to fall into place as rich sources for Angélique.

The writing was long and arduous. Caitlin was a steady hand and a constant encouragement. Jim Pierson attempted to keep my characters true to the originals on the television show. The pages began to pile up and I began to think I might actually find a way to meet this challenge. I finally began to find the process enjoyable.

Any student of literature will recognize the obvious symbolism I struggled to put in place. Since Angélique was a child of the sea, water was her emotional center—her passionate love of the ocean, the loss of her mother in the hurricane, her first sexual experience in the rain. Likewise, since the vampire was a creature of the night, the moon is a symbol for Barnabas. When, from all the jewels, he chooses the moonstone to give Angélique, it is a gift of himself. When the moonstream flows across the water, in my mind the two lovers embrace, and when the moon's refection falls into the lake it's . . . well, you know . . . .

Another interesting symbol for me was the mirror. The image and the reflection represent, for instance, the two sides of Angélique's nature—

innocent and corrupt, as when she looked in the mirror and saw her wedding dress covered in blood. The mirror reflects what was seen clearly but then becomes vague or opaque, revealing what was hidden. The duality of lovers who come together as one, suggests the narcissism of seeing oneself, one's own reflection, in the eyes of one's beloved. In many ways the mirror became a reoccurring theme throughout the book, the reflected image always offering a deeper truth, even as shadows are mirrors of sorts, darker shapes of what is real. That the vampire has no mirror image, and that he casts no shadow, makes him even more mysterious. The vampire is the essential enigma, death disguised as life, and the living side has vanished. As the Bokor, Angélique's voodoo master, pointed out to her in the chapter which is my personal favorite, "The power is in the mirror." The essential truth is what we can only glimpse.

Any reader of that particular chapter who is reminded of Carlos Castaneda should look no further. Don Juan's teaching that "the greatest power is in desiring nothing," is a familiar one. It worked for me because the Bokor sees that Angélique will never become a great sorceress, that she will always be thwarted by her own selfish nature and that she will never achieve indifference. He says to her, "You will always be obsessed with something. You will seek love and it will turn to jealously, then revenge, because deep beneath all your rainbow colors is a deep pool of despair and because your way is the way of desire." This was my way of explaining why so many of Angélique's spells went awry.

I played with these elements, only because, despite what I said about actresses in the beginning, I was an English minor in college, and these were the things that interested me. Also, since Angélique was a good student as a child, and the priest, who recognized her longing for understanding, gave her a book of Shakespeare, I was unable to resist threading a few lines from Shakespeare through her thoughts.

And so I continued on the tedious day by day process of drawing out the story. I was naive and inexperienced, but I came to enjoy the task and to feel happy with some of the things I had written. I worked for over a year, and I could have worked much longer. In the end Harpers' deadline forced me to stop. I was bound by my outline and the decision made at Harpers, to keep "the curse" as the ending of the book in order to tie it to the television show. For this reason, there was a lot of story to tell and I had to cover a huge amount of material in a short amount of space. At times I thought I would still be writing in my grave,

The book was published as I wrote it, and I believe that Caitlin was relieved she did not have to have that "ghost writer" brought in. Hopefully, I will have the opportunity to write another novel in the series, and the next tale will be both more leisurely and more original. I learned a lot, mostly through my mistakes. Of course, as with any other writer, there are things I would like to go back and change.

*Dark Shadows* has given me many firsts in my life: my first professional engagement as an actress, my first feature film, and now my first job as a professional writer. But then for all of us, this enduring television saga with its many intriguing characters is a continuing and replenishing source of fascination and dreams. ☞

# SHADOWS FACTS

✠ The original 1965 agreement between ABC-TV and Dan Curtis Associates, later Dan Curtis Productions, reveals that the original name intended for *Dark Shadows* was *The House on Storm Cliff*. Later, Art Wallace's bible for the show was titled *Shadows on the Wall*.

✠ *Dark Shadows* was the first daytime drama to attract a substantial following of young viewers, a trend that continued with other soap operas such as *The Young and the Restless*, *All My Children*, and *General Hospital*.

✠ *Dark Shadows* is one of only a few television series to spawn two theatrical motion pictures (*House of Dark Shadows* and *Night of Dark Shadows*), and the only daytime drama to do so.

✠ Several of the male stars from *Dark Shadows*, particularly David Selby and Jonathan Frid, were recognized as major teen idols of the late 1960s and early 1970s. Along with David Henesy, Don Briscoe, Michael Stroka, Chris Pennock, and Roger Davis, they were heavily featured in publications such as *16* and *Tiger Beat* as well as numerous soap opera and TV/movie magazines.

✠ *Dark Shadows* was the only new network soap opera to debut in 1966. It replaced the cancelled teen serial *Never Too Young*. It was also ABC-TV's first color soap opera.

✠ *Dark Shadows* was the first daytime drama to feature supernatural themes and the first to utilize special effects. The production budget, excluding actor and producer salaries, for the series was approximately $70,000 for a week's worth of five shows.

✠ *Dark Shadows'* storyline covered several centuries. In addition to the 1966-1971 present day time periods, sequences set in the years 1795/1796, 1897, 1840, 1949, and 1692 were featured. Portions of the series were also devoted to the science fiction concept of parallel time, set in the years 1970, 1841, and 1680.

✠ *Dark Shadows* was the first daily network soap opera to be offered in domestic syndication.

✠ *Dark Shadows* was the first series purchased by the Sci-Fi Channel cable service. The program debuted on the Sci-Fi Channel's second day of broadcast, September 25, 1992.

# My Shadowy Past

by Chris Pennock

Y TWO YEARS ON *DARK SHADOWS* WERE SIMPLY THE RICHEST, most stimulating, challenging, and terrifying of my life as an actor. At least, so far. Imagine going from an "under five" (speaking lines) spot on *Guiding Light* to suddenly . . . "you're Chris!"—a big, juicy role as a fiendish, dominating, seductive Leviathan on *Dark Shadows*! ("Remember, Chris, he's got to be likeable." "But he's a monster." "Yeah, but he's got to be a likeable, sexy Monster". "Okay, no problem. I can do that." "Try to act like Roger Davis!")

I did have talent for shameless, over-the-top, quasi-Shakespearean-chewing-the scenery acting. No problem there. When I finally got a handle on Jeb Hawkes' outrageous villainy, "zap!" they tried to make him remorseful, sympathetic, loving and depressed about it all. Well, all those elements were simply too much for my limited scope as a 24-year-old actor. (But James Dean was 24, I'd think to myself.) I mean I barely knew my lines! By the time I was flung off Widows' Hill, screaming to my death, I wanted to say, "But, I've got him! I've got the handle! I can do Jeb!"

Splat! I went onto the jagged rocks.

But then, lo and behold, Dan Curtis—who kept the faith—said to me, "Chris how about doing *Dr. Jekyll and Mr. Hyde?*" I was stunned! Me? Playing the greatest roles in history? I immediately went into a soaring manic state of actor ecstasy! The only problem was actually acting the role.

During rehearsals, I was attacked savagely for still being "too much like Jeb!" Panicking, I locked myself in my dressing room hoping they would forget about me and replace me with Christopher Walken. But the Stanislavski thunderbolt struck! I became Cyrus Longworth, babbling shyly in the mirror, his sweet and cerebral character stayed with me forever.

But then, the menacing John Yaeger appeared. I tried imitating all kinds of savage, villainous actors, to no avail. (Spencer Tracy, Jack Palance, Al Pacino) But a deep, booming voice saved me. A big, happy murderous gorilla! James Earl Jones, in a nameless and forgotten movie, was my inspiration for Yaeger.

Yaeger celebrated evil! It was his opiate! He was having too much fun! And he couldn't understand why Cyrus didn't loosen up and wreak havoc too! What else was there?

It all became chillingly real one day in the studio when I thrust the wrong knife-edged cane upon Elizabeth Eis' neck. One twitch on my part would slice through her jugular vein! We kept on with the scene, sweat breaking out on our faces, acute achycardia thundering in our chests, eyes locked in silent communication. "Sorry Liz!" "You're an ******* Chris!" followed by, "OK, moving on." Then all hell broke loose! "Hey props! Who put the wrong cane here?"

"I could have killed her!" "He could have killed me!" "What idiot did this?" Just another day on the set of *Dark Shadows*.

My next character, Sebastian Shaw, hippie astrologer, was totally forgettable. I really do not remember a single day playing him. I must have been wishing I were someone else. In what seemed like a few days later, I was someone else! Gabriel Collins, the fabulous, evil, self-pitying, fake cripple in his wheel chair. The inspiration this time was Geraldine Page in *Sweet Bird of Youth* . . . Princess Alexandra de Lago. A strange choice? I have never allowed gender bending to interfere with my creativity. After all, I was about to portray a siamese twin who loses his twin, forgets his sexual identity and becomes a man/woman in James Ivory's film *Savages* (with Thayer David!)

Gabriel was such a treat. There was so much fun to be had playing in a wheel chair, a great dramatic device. The writers endowed Gabriel with a very witty, sarcastic tongue, so I could insult literally everyone at Collinwood with impunity. Gabriel even had some tender, vulnerable scenes with Louis Edmonds, who portrayed his father. What more could an actor ask for?

Unless the muse returns to strike Dan Curtis with an inspiration as daring as *Dark Shadows*, I am unlikely to have the joy of such characters to play again. It was the time of my life.

# Shooting Shadows

## by Stuart Goodman

I N 1966, I WAS ON STAFF AT THE ABC-TV NETWORK AS A CAMERA-
man. I had just finished an afternoon dramatic series directed by
Lela Swift. She admired my talent and we worked very well
together. Lela mentioned to me that in the summer ABC would be starting
*Dark Shadows*, the first Gothic daytime drama. She wanted me to be one of
the cameramen and I accepted the exciting offer.

That spring, I worked on various shows where I met other cameramen
who said they were also being considered for the new soap opera. In May,
Ross Skipper, John Woods and myself assembled at ABC to begin what is
now a legend in daytime programming, *Dark Shadows*. We met the cast and
the other tech people who would make up the team that would put this
unusual show on the air. Being a movie buff I was quite impressed meeting
Joan Bennett. I didn't know any of the other actors, and at the time I don't
think anyone else did either. Most of them were newcomers; some had theater experience, but most of us were quite young and eager to get a break,
including me. The mysterious premise of the show sounded wonderful.

We did the first episode in June of 1966. The sets were so large and the
cameras (initially black and white) were so bulky that we kept banging into
props, walls and furniture. Live television was not easy. Those of you who
have some of the cassette releases of the episodes will probably hear the
noises we made behind the scenes while the show was in performance.

During the first year the show was not received by as large an audience as Executive Producer Dan Curtis and ABC had hoped for. In early 1967, there was rumors that we were going to be canceled. Then came a day that I will never forget. We finished taping the show in the afternoon and Lela and Dan asked me if I would stay and work overtime. They had some new characters they wanted to audition on tape. My wife was pregnant and due any day, but Lela insisted it was something special and that she really wanted my personal opinion as well. I agreed to stay. We subsequently auditioned about six or seven actors who read text that sounded like it was from a horror movie. I didn't understand it, but kept shooting. Afterward, I told Lela that one actor made such an impression on me. "Whatever you are looking for, I believe you'll get it from this actor." His name was Jonathan Frid. He was hired to play vampire Barnabas Collins and started work in early April, right after my daughter Julie was born.

The entire show started to take a different slant after Barnabas arrived on the scene. I couldn't believe what was happening; characters were changed, the sets got spookier and suddenly I had cobwebs all over my camera.

In the late summer of 1967, the head of engineering at ABC came to visit our set and notified us we would be getting brand new color cameras! That sounded terrific—until they came. They were much smaller than the black and white machines, which was great, but they were all electronically powered zoom cameras. They scared the living daylights out of us. If you think you heard noise on the early shows! In August of 1967, we not only banged into things, we had a hard time finding focus. Once we got the hang of things, the new color cameras brought life to the show, and were much easier to use than the old ones.

As the show progressed, and the stories took on a darker and more mysterious edge, we started to experiment with visual effects. Remember, this long before *Star Wars* and computer effects captivated the world. I found that if I put Saran Wrap around my lens and then coated the edges with Vaseline petroleum jelly and made small zooms in and out I created a scary image of the character. Well, this combined with cobwebs scared the audience no end. It was a tremendous success. As I started to perfect my special effects skills, I found that if I put a contained bucket of fire in front of my lens it made Angélique look like she is jumping out of an actual fire.

We had a lot of fun in those early days of *Dark Shadows*. I didn't think that it would catch on the way it did. After awhile, we couldn't leave the studio without a mob of teenagers hounding us for autographs. They didn't care if I was an actor, just as long I was part of *Dark Shadows*. That was enough. I must have given out hundreds of autographs.

I remained on *Dark Shadows* until sometime in 1969, when ABC assigned me to shoot major dramatic specials and *Wide World of Sports*. I received six Emmy nominations for my camerawork during my aegis at the network. In 1978, I left to form my own production company, and finally started to direct and produce, something I longed to do for many years. I am now an award-winning (Emmy, CableAce) producer with offices in New York and Toronto. Interestingly, I recently teamed up with *Dark Shadows* alumni Kathryn Leigh Scott to produce the two-hour special *The Bunny Years* for the A&E Network.

I often look back on *Dark Shadows* and fondly reminisce. I was very fortunate to have worked with such gifted people and to have honed my craft with an exceptional talent like Dan Curtis. ☞

# A Profile of Dan Curtis

---

D AN CURTIS WAS BORN AUGUST 12 IN BRIDGEPORT, CONNECTICUT. He began his entertainment career in the 1950s, working for years as a top sales executive at NBC and MCA. After creating and selling *The Arnold Palmer-Gary Player Challenge Golf Show*, he created and produced *The CBS Golf Classic*—his first show as an independent producer. The program ran for ten years, winning an Emmy along the way.

Curtis burst into television drama in 1966 with the creation of the legendary Gothic daytime serial *Dark Shadows* for ABC-TV. That supernatural soap opera launched Curtis' international reputation as a leading producer/director of first-rate thrillers.

Curtis is equally comfortable whether working in the adventure, drama or horror genres. His horror credits include: *Burnt Offerings*, starring Bette Davis, Oliver Reed and Karen Black; *The Turn of the Screw*, starring Lynn Redgrave; *Dracula*, starring Jack Palance; *The Night Stalker* and *The Night Strangler*, both starring Darren McGavin; *Trilogy of Terror*, starring Karen Black; *Trilogy of Terror II* starring Lysette Anthony; *Dead of Night*, three stories starring Joan Hackett, Ed Begley Jr. and Patrick Macnee; and *The Strange Case of Dr. Jekyll & Mr. Hyde*, starring Jack Palance, which received six Emmy nominations including Best Dramatic Special.

He has also directed *When Every Day Was the Fourth of July*, a poignant, yet suspenseful drama set in his native Bridgeport, Connecticut; and the quasi-sequel, *The Long Days of Summer*. Both were based on his boyhood reminiscences.

Curtis has also produced and directed a diverse collection of television films ranging from comedy and drama to adventure. These include: *The Last*

*Ride of the Dalton Gang*, selected Outstanding Fictional Television Program in the National Cowboy Hall of Fame's Western Heritage Awards; *Mrs. R's Daughter*, a tense, dramatic tour-de-force for Cloris Leachman; and such capers as *The Great Ice Rip Off*; *Melvin Purvis, G-Man*; *The Kansas City Massacre* and *Me and the Kid*.

Curtis spent most of the 1980s directing, co-writing and executive producing the critically acclaimed miniseries *The Winds of War* and *War and Remembrance*.

Curtis' three-way creative involvement with *The Winds of War* and *War and Remembrance* was honored with an Emmy from the television industry; as well as by the Directors Guild of America (DGA Award); the Hollywood Foreign Press Association (Golden Globe); and by the public itself with the People's Choice Award. He also received the Anti-Defamation League's Torch of Liberty Award; the Simon Wiesenthal Center's Distinguished Service Award; and the American Film Institute's Producers Award.

In 1991, Curtis executive produced, co-wrote and directed a primetime revival of *Dark Shadows* for NBC-TV. The following year, he executive produced and directed *Intruders*, a four hour mini-series about aliens and UFOs. He most recently received critical raves and high ratings for *The Love Letter*, a Hallmark Hall of Fame presentation for CBS.

Curtis' work has also brought him awards from the Mystery Writers of America, the Academy of Science Fiction, Fantasy & Horror, the Count Dracula Society, the Southern California Motion Picture Council, and the International Film Festival of Fantasy & Horror. ☞

*Alexandra Moltke as Victoria Winters.*

*Joan Bennett as Elizabeth Collins Stoddard.*

*Louis Edmonds as Roger Collins.*

*Sandy (Katherine Bruce) and Mrs. Hopewell (Elizabeth Wilson). The original
Matthew Morgan (George Mitchell) and Victoria Winters (Alexandra Moltke).
Carolyn Stoddard (Nancy Barrett) and Burke Devlin (Mitchell Ryan).*

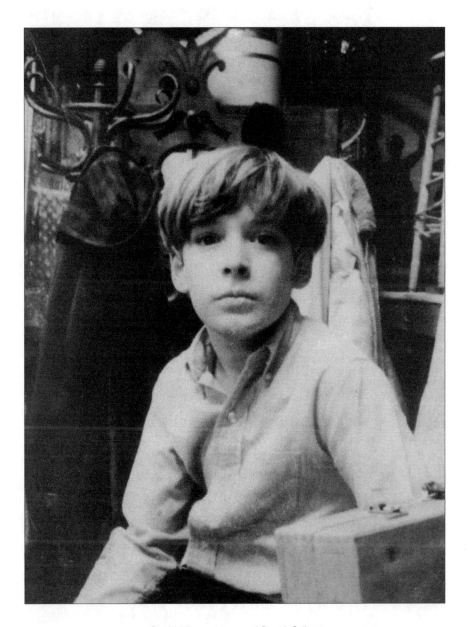

*David Henesy portrayed David Collins.*

*Rehearsal with Joan Bennett and Dennis Patrick who portrayed Jason McGuire.*

*Jonathan Frid as vampire Barnabas Collins.*

*Director John Sedwick in the studio rehearsal hall with Sharon Smyth and David Henesy; David, Robert Gerringer and Jonathan Frid.*

*An aged Barnabas.*

*Jonathan Frid adjusts his fangs.*

*Séance at Collinwood:
Elizabeth Collins Stoddard
(Joan Bennett) Carolyn Stoddard
(Nancy Barrett), Roger Collins
(Louis Edmonds), Phyllis Wick
(Margot Head), Dr. Julia
Hoffman (Grayson Hall),
Barnabas Collins (Jonathan Frid).*

1795: Angélique (Lara Parker), Abigail Collins (Clarice Blackburn) and jailors (James Shannon and Howard Hemig).

*Lara Parker and Jerry Lacy rehearse; Professor Stokes (Thayer David) and Roger Collins (Louis Edmonds).*

*Kathryn Leigh Scott (Maggie Evans).*

# Characters

The name of each *Dark Shadows* character is followed by the episode numbers in which each character appeared and, in parenthesis, the total number of episodes in which each character appeared.

Adam 475-636 (83)
Adlar 915-915 (1)
Ezra Ahern aka Herne 89-99 (2)
Andreas 826-826 (1)
Aristede 791-881 (34)
Audrey 915-915 (1)
Sophie Baker 704-704 (1)
Lorna Bell 1142-1145 (2)
Mr. Best 922-932 (3)
Adam Bilodeau 89-89 (1)
Garth Blackwood 878-883 (5)
James Blair 42-95 (4)
Nicholas Blair 521-979 (62)
Reverend Bland 396-397 (2)
Wilfred Block* 1003-1003 (1)
Peter Bradford 404-968 (30)
Ezra Braithwaite 684-764 (3)
Tim Braithwaite 1126-1126 (1)
Tim Braithwaite* 1214-1215 (2)
Reverend Brand 969-969 (1)
Stuart Bronson 27-27 (1)
Reverend Alton Brook 380-380 (1)
Maude Browning 439-512 (4)
Bruno 942-976 (13)
Crystal Cabot 663-664 (2)
Constable Carter 23-32 (5)
Zeb Cartwright 89-89 (1)
Larry Chase* 1006-1020 (5)
Beth Chavez 646-880 (57)
Jeff Clark 465-637 (48)
Victoria Winters Clark 1-665 (348)
Abigail Collins 367-442 (14)
Alexis Stokes Collins* 984-1001 (15)
Amadeus Collins 1140-1144 (2)

Amanda Collins* 1231-1236 (2)
Amy Collins* 983-1049 (11)
Angélique Bouchard Collins aka
    Cassandra Collins aka Angélique
    DuBois aka Angélique duVal aka
    Valerie Collins aka Miranda duVal
    368/9-1198 (176)
Angélique Stokes Collins* 1000-1056
    (44)
Barnabas Collins 210-1198 (573)
Bramwell Collins* 1197-1245 (28)
Brutus Collins* 1225-1245 (5)
Carl Collins 706-780 (11)
Chris Collins* 977-1001 (5)
Catherine Harridge Collins* 1186-1245
    (39)
Daniel Collins 431-1191 (23)
Daniel Collins* 979-1028 (10)
Daphne Harridge Collins* 1186-1238
    (16)
David Collins 4-1109 (225)
Desmond Collins 1117-1198 (26)
Edith Collins 701-1186 (13)
Edward Collins 705-870 (50)
Flora Collins 1086-1198 (16)
Flora Collins* 1188-1245 (18)
Gabriel Collins 1110-1191 (27)
Gabriel Collins* 1189-1237 (14)
Harriet Collins 1131-1131 (1)
Jamison Collins 702-838 (35)
Jenny Collins 716-897 (15)
Jeremiah Collins 367-862 (22)
Josette DuPres Collins 70-948 (48)
Josette Collins* 1206-1238 (5)

Joshua Collins 367-661 (37)
Joshua Collins* 1008-1012 (3)
Julia Collins* 1187-1245 (37)
Justin Collins* 1196-1215 (3)
Laura Collins aka Laura Radcliff
   Collins aka Laura Murdock Collins
   aka Laura Stockbridge Collins
   123-760 (63)
Maggie Evans Collins* 981-1060 (38)
Morgan Collins* 1186-1245 (40)
Naomi Collins 366-467 (37)
Nora Collins 716-859 (16)
Quentin Collins aka Grant Douglas
   (1897, 1969-1970, 1995) 646-1113
   (204)
Quentin Collins* (1970PT) 981-1060
   (51)
Quentin Collins (1840) 1086-1197 (48)
Quentin Collins* (1841PT) 1195-1230
   (15)
Roger Collins 1-979 (204)
Roger Collins* 975-1055 (17)
Sarah Collins 255-415 (37)
Tad Collins 1065-1165 (14)
Lieutenant Costa 174-174 (1)
Judge Crathorne 270-271 (2)
Sheriff Davenport 917-961 (8)
Charles Dawson 1141-1196 (14)
Burke Devlin 1-346 (145)
Diabolos 628-629 (2)
Randall Drew 1143-1154/5 (5)
Roxanne Drew 1081-1177 (25)
Roxanne Drew* 1039-1061 (25)
Samantha Drew* 1192-1193 (2)
Rachel Drummond 705-776 (24)
Andre DuPres 370-394 (10)
Natalie DuPres 368/9-886 (30)
Minnie Duval* 997-997 (1)
Ed the Records Clerk 1062-1062 (1)
Dameon Edwards* 994-1006 (6)
Leona Eltridge aka Danielle Roget
   594-595 (2)
Maggie Evans 1-1108 (197)

Sam Evans 5-530 (105)
Eve 595-633/4 (16)
Leticia Faye 1113-1198 (21)
Pansy Faye 771-778 (4)
Laszlo Ferrari 1130-1158 (3)
Mrs. Fillmore 810-810 (1)
Janet Findley 647-649 (3)
Thomas Findley 962-966 (5)
Doctor Fisher 335-335 (1)
Amos Fitch 89-89 (1)
Portia Fitzsimmons 193-193 (1)
Victor Flagler 1062-1062 (1)
Millicent Collins Forbes 373-886 (25)
Nathan Forbes 366-666 (47)
Suki Forbes 419-512 (5)
James Forsythe* 1231-1236 (2)
Doctor Franklin 191-191 (1)
Deputy Fred 323-329 (3)
Donna Friedlander 674-674 (1)
Frank Garner 92-180 (19)
Richard Garner 92-246 (6)
Noah Gifford 439-455 (5)
Horace Gladstone* 987-1010 (8)
Otis Greene 1124-1124 (1)
Jeremy Grimes 1163-1185 (4)
Mordecai Grimes 1154/5-1184 (2)
Nelle Gunston 951-951 (1)
Lawrence Guthrie 949-949 (1)
Doctor Peter Guthrie 160-186 (25)
Buzz Hackett 252-262 (4)
Michael Hackett 913/4-929 (9)
Insp. Hamilton* 1040-1057 (5)
Kitty Hampshire 844-885 (19)
Evan Hanley 708-878 (24)
Judge Hanley 427-452 (5)
Buffie Harrington* 996-1023 (11)
Second Coachman-Harris* 1245-1245
   (1)
Amanda Harris aka Olivia Corey
   812-934 (24)
John Harris 44-44 (1)
Harry 2-2 (1)
John Hart 963-965 (3)

Carrie Stokes 1066-1185 (20)
Carrie Stokes* 1215-1237 (12)
Hallie Stokes 1070-1109 (27)
Hannah Stokes* 992-1014 (7)
Prof. T. Eliot Stokes 464-1198 (66)
Timothy Stokes* 1027-1060 (11)
Strak 899-900 (2)
Wilbur Strake 1-2 (2)
Ned Stuart 687-698 (6)
Sabrina Stuart 692-978 (13)
Sabrina Stuart* 987-1033 (15)
Susie 22-91 (7)
Charles Delaware Tate aka Harrison
    Monroe 804-938 (30)
Ruby Tate 414-512 (2)
Doctor Thornton 371-371 (1)
Alexander Todd 905-912 (6)
Megan Todd 888-971 (34)
Philip Todd 888-968 (23)
Charity Trask 727-887 (47)
Gregory Trask 725-884 (38)
Judith Collins Trask 702-884 (50)
Lamar Trask 1114-1198 (26)

Minerva Trask 733-791 (7)
Mr. Trask* 994-1049 (7)
Reverend Trask 385-1126 (23)
Dorcas Trilling 751-766 (2)
Judge Vail 1165-1197 (9)
Constable Jim Ward 1156-1157 (2)
Mrs. Mildred Ward 1157-1161 (3)
Doctor Welles 1147-1147 (1)
Mr. Wells 1-632 (4)
Werewolf 640-976 (27)
Phyllis Wick 365-461 (2)
Judge Wiley 1162-1162 (1)
Dirk Wilkins 709-776 (20)
Doctor David Woodard 219-362 (43)
John Yaeger* 995-1035 (21)
Kendrick Young* 1191-1245 (23)
Melanie Collins Young* 1190-1245 (31)
Stella Young* 1188-1204 (4)
Judah Zachery 1117-1142 (16)

*Denotes character in a *Dark Shadows*
Parallel Time storyline.

# Actors

This listing contains the names of all the peformers who are known to have appeared on *Dark Shadows*. Each actor's name is followed by the number of episodes in which the actor appeared (in parenthesis), the name(s) of the character(s) portrayed and the year each character's storyline took place (in parenthesis). PT denotes a Parallel Time storyline.

MART ALDRE: (1) Stand-in for Paul Stoddard (1969)
MARK ALLEN: (7) Sam Evans (1966)
PHILLIP R. ALLEN: (1) Policeman (1970PT)
ANDREW AMIC-ANGELO: (1) Blue Whale Customer (1967)
CALVIN ANDER: (1) Collinsport Inn Hotel Clerk (1966)
ARTHUR ANDERSON: (1) Cab Driver (1966)
MICHAEL ANN: (1) Collinsport Inn Restaurant Customer (1966)
FRAN ANTHONY: (2) Stand-in for Doctor Julia Hoffman (1967)
WALTER ARNOLD: (1) Blue Whale Customer (1966)
CAMILA ASHLAND: (3) Mrs. Hutchins (1970), Minnie Duval (1970PT),
    Mrs. Purdy (1840)
MARC ASHTON: (1) Stand-in for Gregory Trask (1897)
HUMBERT ALLEN ASTREDO: (100) Nicholas Blair (1968, 1970), Evan Hanley
    (1897), Ghost of Nicholas (1970), Charles Dawson (1840)
BEVERLY ATKINSON: (1) Collinsport Hospital Nurse (1968)
CONRAD BAIN: (4) Collinsport Inn Hotel Clerk-Mr. Wells (1966, 1968)
HENRY BAKER: (4) Istvan (1897)
KATHARINE BALFOUR: (1) Collinsport Hospital Nurse (1968)
DIANE BALL: (2) Blue Whale Customer (1966)
JOHN BARAGREY: (4) James Blair (1966)
LESLIE BARRETT: (5) Judge Hanley (1795)
NANCY BARRETT: (403) Carolyn Stoddard Hawkes (1966-1970), Millicent
    Collins Forbes (1795, 1796), Charity Trask (1897), Carolyn Loomis (1970PT),
    Carolyn Stoddard Hawkes aka Carolyn Fredericks (1995), Leticia Faye (1840),
    Melanie Collins Young (1841PT), Amanda Collins (1680PT, 1841PT)
EMORY BASS: (5) Mr. Best (1897, 1970), Minister (1841PT)
DODIE BAUER: (1) Bangor Pine Hotel Restaurant Customer (1966)
JOANN BAYES: (1) Blue Whale Customer (1967)
JOHN BEAL: (9) Judge Vail (1840)
BETTY BEAIRD: (2) Ghost (1966)
LEE BEERY: (10) Ghost of Joanna Mills (1840), Joanna Mills (1840)

THEODORE BENIADES: (2) Policeman (1967)

JOAN BENNETT: (391) Elizabeth Collins Stoddard (1966-1971, 1949), Naomi Collins (1795), Ghost of Naomi (1968), Judith Collins Trask (1897), Elizabeth Collins Stoddard (1970PT), Flora Collins (1840), Flora Collins (1841PT)

MAGGIE BENSON: (1) Ghost of Maude Browning (1968)

CHRISTOPHER BERNAU: (23) Philip Todd (1969-1970)

JACQUELINE BERTRAND: (2) Ghost (1966)

DAN BISHOP (1) Blue Whale Customer (1967)

CLARICE BLACKBURN: (79) Ghost (1966-1967), Mrs. Sarah Johnson (1966-1970, 1995), Abigail Collins (1795), Ghost of Abigail (1795), Minerva Trask (1897), Ghost of Minerva (1897), Mrs. Sarah Johnson (1970PT)

ANITA BOLSTER: (3) Bathia Mapes (1795)

ROBERT BONDS: (2) Blue Whale Customer (1966-1967)

JEAN PIERRE BORU: (1) Bartender (1949)

MARLIN BRADLEY: (3) Blue Whale Customer (1967)

MARTIN BRENT: (2) Johnson (1840)

AMBER BRIE: (1) Stand-in for Alexis Stokes (1970PT)

DONALD BRISCOE: (96) Tom Jennings (1968), Chris Jennings (1968-1970), Timothy Shaw (1897), Chris Collins (1970PT)

ANGIE BROWN: (1) Deputy (1968)

BARBARA BROWNELL: (1) Stand-in for Laura Collins (1897)

KATHERINE BRUCE: (1) Sandy (1966)

JANET BURTIS: (1) Ghost of Widow (1966)

ANGUS CAIRNS: (2) Sheriff George Patterson (1967)

STEPHEN CALDER: (2) Executioner (1840)

AUDREY A. CAMPBELL: (3) Blue Whale Customer (1966-1967)

RAY CARLSON: (2) Blue Whale Customer (1967), Aldon Wicks (1970PT)

VALA CLIFTON: (3) Maude Browning (1795)

RICHARD COATE: (3) Blue Whale Customer (1966-1967)

KATHY CODY: (49) Ghost of Carrie Stokes (1995, 1970), Hallie Stokes (1970), Carrie Stokes (1840), Carrie Stokes (1841PT)

DAVID COLUMBIA: (2) Stand-in for Nathan Forbes (1795)

JOHN CONNELL: (2) Lieutenant Dan Riley (1967)

MARY COOPER: (5) Josette Collins (1841PT)

ALEXANDER CORT: (3) Tate's Creation (1897)

DON CRABTREE: (3) Sheriff (1995)

PAUL CRAFFEY: (2) Spectator (1795)

TERRY CRAWFORD: (63) Ghost of Beth Chavez (1968-1969, 1897), Beth Chavez (1897), Edith Collins (1840)

CAROL CRIST: (4) Collinsport Inn Restaurant Waitress-Susie (1966)

JOEL CROTHERS: (166) Joe Haskell (1966-1969), Lieutenant Nathan Forbes (1795, 1796), Ghost of Forbes (1968, 1795)

ED CROWLEY: (2) Policeman (1967)

DAVID CRYER: (1) Ghost in Woods (1795)

CLIFF CUDNEY: (4) John Hart as a zombie (1970), Victor Flagler (1995)

MICHAEL CURRIE: (5) Constable/Sheriff Jonas Carter (1966)

KEENE CURTIS: (2) Voice of Judah Zachery (1840, 1692)

PHILIP CUSACK: (1) Ghost of Abraham Howell (1897)

JANI DARNAGLO: (1) Nurse Packard (1967)

TONI DARNAY: (1) Ghost of Widow (1966)

THAYER DAVID: (225) Matthew Morgan (1966), Ben Stokes (1795, 1796, 1840), Professor Timothy Eliot Stokes (1968-1971, 1897, 1995, 1840), Sandor Rakosi (1897), Victor Fenn-Gibbon aka Count Pefoti (1897), Sandor as a zombie (1897), Count Andreas Petofi (1897), Ghost of Sandor (1897), Timothy Stokes (1970PT), Mordecai Grimes (1840), Ben Stokes (1841PT)

DIANA DAVILA: (4) Julianka (1897), Ghost of Julianka (1897)

ANN DAVIES: (1) Miss Jackson (1968)

ROGER DAVIS: (128) Peter Bradford (1795, 1796, 1968), Jeff Clark (1968), Ned Stuart (1969), Dirk Wilkins (1897), Charles Delaware Tate aka Harrison Monroe (1897, 1969-1970), Ghost of Peter (1970)

FRANK DAWNING: (1) Bangor Pine Hotel Restaurant Customer (1966)

RONALD DAWSON; (2) Professor Henry Osmund (1969), Ed, the Records Clerk (1995)

STEVE DAWSON: (1) Blue Whale Customer (1967)

JOE DELLA SORTE: (1) Ghost of Sergio (1897)

GEORGE DiCENZO: (4) Hand of Sheriff Davenport (1970), Stand-in for Judah Zachery (1840), Body of Judah (1840)

ALFRED DILLAY: (2) Stand-in for Barnabas Collins (1967)

BEVERLY DIXON: (1) Blue Whale Customer (1967)

CHRISTINE DOMANIECKI aka Domaneck: (1) Barmaid (1840)

JAMES DONAHUE: (1) Pirate (1970)

LYNN DOVEL: (1) Blue Whale Customer (1967)

WILLIS DOWNSING: (1) Blue Whale Bartender (1966)

JANE DRAPER: (5) Suki Forbes (1795), Ghost of Suki (1968)

ALICE DRUMMOND: (4) Nurse Jackson (1967)

BETSY DURKIN: (10) Victoria Winters Clark (1968)

ELIZABETH EARL: (1) Blue Whale Customer (1966)

GAYE EDMOND: (5) Ghost of Harriet Collins (1840), Stella Young (1841PT)

LOUIS EDMONDS: (323) Roger Collins (1966-1970), Joshua Collins (1795, 1796), Edward Collins (1897), Roger Collins (1970PT), Ghost of Joshua (1970PT), Daniel Collins (1840), Amadeus Collins (1692), Ghost of Amadeus (1840), Ghost of Daniel (1840), Ghost of Brutus Collins (1841PT), Brutus Collins (1680PT)

JENNY EGAN: (1) Hortense Smiley (1840)

ELIZABETH EIS: (15) Nelle Gunston (1970), Buffie Harrington (1970PT), Mrs. Mildrd Ward (1840)

DANA ELCAR: (35) Sheriff George Patterson (1966-1967)

LENORE ELLIN: (8) Blue Whale Customer (1966-1967), Bangor Pine Hotel
Restaurant Customer (1966)
ANDREW ELLIOT: (1) Collinsport Inn Restaurant Customer (1966)
JOEL FABIANI: (1) Paul Stoddard (1949)
CHARLOTTE FAIRCHILD: (1) Maid (1795)
MARY FARRELL: (1) Mrs. Fillmore (1897)
ALAN FEINSTEIN: (1) Mike (1966)
JOHN FELTON: (1) Blue Whale Customer (1967)
ERICA FITZ: (2) Ghost of Danielle Roget aka Leona Eltridge (1968)
BOB FITZSIMMONS: (1) Mr. Jarret (1968)
TOM FORAL: (3) Blue Whale Customer (1967)
DAVID FORD: (108) Sam Evans (1966-1968), Andre DuPres (1795), Ghost of
Sam (1968)
FRED FORREST: (1) Blue Whale Customer (1967)
CONARD FOWKES: (19) Frank Garner (1966-1967)
MILLICENT FRANCE: (2) Blue Whale Customer (1967)
IVOR FRANCIS: (1) Doctor Franklin (1967)
HUGH FRANKLIN: (6) Richard Garner (1966-1967)
JONATHAN FRID: (593) Barnabas Collins (1967-1971, 1795, 1796, 1897,
1970PT, 1995, 1840), Bramwell Collins (1841PT)
KAY FRYE: (4) Pansy Faye (1897), Ghost of Pansy (1897)
JEFF GALD: (2) Blue Whale Customer (1966)
PAUL GEIER: (2) Amos Ross as a zombie (1970)
ANTHONY GEORGE: (48) Burke Devlin (1967), Jeremiah Collins (1795)
ROBERT GERRINGER: (29) Doctor David Woodard (1967)
PAUL KIRK GILES: (10) Reverend Alton Brook (1795), Reverend Bland (1795),
Judge (1840)
BILL GISH: (2) Blue Whale Customer (1966)
CHARLES GOFF: (3) Bangor Pine Hotel Restaurant Waiter (1966)
ANTHONY GOODSTONE: (3) Blue Whale Customer (1967), Bailiff (1795, 1796)
TIMOTHY GORDON: (31) Bangor Pine Hotel Restaurant Customer (1966),
Blue Whale Customer (1966-1967), Hand of Barnabas Collins (1967, 1795),
Body of Ghost of Jeremiah Collins (1795, 1968, 1897), Stand-in for Riggs
(1795), Minister (1968), Spectator (1796), Hand of Count Petofi (1897)
TOM GORMAN: (18) Blue Whale Customer (1967), Blue Whale Bartender
(1967-1968), Servant (1795), Mr. Prescott (1795), Judge (1795), Ghost of Ezra
Simpson (1968)
JAY GREGORY: (1) Blue Whale Customer (1967)
DAVID GROH: (2) Ghost of One-Armed Man (1968), Hangman Assistant (1796)
STANLEY GROVER: (1) Frank Paxton (1970PT)
CAROLYN GROVES: (3) Victoria Winters Clark (1796)
MICHAEL HADGE: (4) Buzz Hackett (1967)
JIM HALE: (3) Executioner (1897), Hand Holding Scimitar (1897)

GRAYSON HALL: (474) Doctor Julia Hoffman aka Doctor Julia Hoffman Collins (1967-1971, 1897, 1970PT, 1995, 1840), Countess Natalie DuPres (1795, 1796), Magda Rakosi (1897), Julia Hoffman (1970PT), Ghost of Hoffman (1970PT), Julia Collins (1841PT)

JAMES HALL: (4) Willie Loomis (1967)

JOHN HALLOW: (1) Railroad Station Master (1897)

COLIN HAMILTON: (5) Inspector Hamilton (1970PT), Doctor (1841PT)

ROGER HAMILTON: (2) Constable Jim Ward (1840)

TOM HAPPER: (4) Jeremy Grimes (1840)

JOHN HARKINS: (16) Lieutenant Costa (1966), Ghost of Garth Blackwood (1897), Strak (1969, 1949), Horace Gladstone (1970PT)

LLOYD HARRIS: (1) Doctor Welles (1840)

SARA HARTE: (1) Bangor Pine Hotel Restaurant Customer (1966)

EDMUND HASHIM: (1) Wilfred Block (1970PT)

BEVERLY HAYES: (1) Donna Friedlander (1969)

MARGOT HEAD: (1) Phyllis Wick (1968, 1795)

FRANCES HELM: (2) Collinsport Hospital Nurse (1967)

DAVID HENESY: (277) David Collins (1966-1970), Daniel Collins (1795), Jamison Collins (1897), Daniel Collins (1970PT), Ghost of Tad Collins (1995, 1970), Tad Collins (1840)

ALFRED HINCKLEY: (2) Train Conductor (1966), Doctor Ian Reade (1897)

HERB HOLCOMBE: (1) Adam Bilodeau (1966)

BARBARA HOLLIS: (1) Blue Whale Customer (1967)

JERED HOLMES: (6) Ghost of Dameon Edwards (1970PT)

HOWARD HONIG: (3) Gaoler (1795)

ISABELLA HOOPES: (5) Edith Collins (1897), Ghost of Edith (1897)

DONALD HOTTON: (1) Reverend Brand (1970)

PAT HOUSE: (2) Blue Whale Customer (1967)

CAVADA HUMPHREY: (3) Janet Findley (1968)

BARNARD HUGHES: (1) Stuart Bronson (1966)

DAVID HURST: (3) Justin Collins (1841PT), Ghost of Justin (1841PT)

ELAINE HYMAN: (1) Ruby Tate (1795)

LIZ INGLESON: (1) Bangor Pine Hotel Restaurant Customer (1966)

KATE JACKSON: (70) Ghost of Daphne Harridge (1995, 1970), Daphne Harridge Stiles (1970, 1840), Daphne Harridge Collins (1841PT)

CHARLES JAMES: (1) Bangor Pine Hotel Restaurant Customer (1966)

HOUSE JAMESON: (2) Judge Crathorne (1967)

BILL JAMESEND: (1) Blue Whale Customer (1967)

DAVID JAY: (6) Alexander Todd (1969)

PAUL JENKINS: (1) Blue Whale Customer (1967)

DENNIS JOHNSON: (3) Deputy Fred (1967)

PAGE JONES: (1) Collinsport Inn Restaurant Customer (1966)

MARILYN JOSEPH: (2) Lorna Bell (1840)

JOSEPH JULIAN: (2) Wilbur Strake (1966)
JEANNE KAPLAN: (1) Blue Whale Customer (1966)
JOHN KARLEN: (180) Willie Loomis (1967-1970), Carl Collins (1897), William
    Hollingshead Loomis (1970PT), Desmond Collins (1840), Kendrick Young
    (1841PT)
RUSS KARSEN: (2) Blue Whale Customer (1966)
DORRIE KAVANAUGH: (6) Stand-in for Maggie Evans (1967), Phyllis Wick
    (1967), Stand-in for Josette duPrés Collins (1795)
JORDAN KEAN: (2) Second Guard (1840)
HARVEY KEITEL: (2) Blue Whale Customer (1966)
DANIEL F. KEYES: (9) Caretaker (1967)
COLLEEN KELLY: (3) Collinsport Inn Restaurant Waitress-Susie (1966)
JOHN KUHNER: (2) Body of Tim Braithwaite (1841PT)
MARGO LACEY: (1) Bangor Pine Hotel Restaurant Customer (1966)
JERRY LACY: (109) Tony Peterson (1967-1968), Reverend Trask (1795), Ghost
    of Trask (1968), Gregory Trask (1897), Mr. Trask (1970PT), Lamar Trask
    (1840), Lamar Trask (1841PT)
JOHN LA MOTTA: (1) Ghost of Marco (1897)
ROBIN LANE: (2) Haza (1796)
JAMES LANGRALL: (1) Pirate (1970)
AUDREY LARKIN: (2) Crystal Cabot (1796)
JOHN LASELL: (25) Doctor Peter Guthrie (1967)
JUDD LAURENCE: (3) Blue Whale Customer (1966)
PAULA LAURENCE: (7) Hannah Stokes (1970PT)
CAROL ANN LEWIS: (1) Barmaid (1968)
GENE LINDSEY: (5) Randall Drew (1840)
ALLEN LINDSTROM: (3) Blue Whale Customer (1966)
PETER LOMBARD: (4) Oberon (1796, 1969)
DEBORAH LOOMIS: (3) Tessie Kincaid (1897), Ghost of Tessie (1897)
JUDITH LOWRY: (1) Stand-in for Cassandra Collins (1968)
BENNETT LUBIN: (1) Blue Whale Customer (1967)
AL LUST: (1) Pirate (1970)
KAREN LYNN: (1) Wanda Paisley (1897)
PAT LYSINGER: (2) Blue Whale Customer (1966)
MICHAEL MAITLAND: (9) Michael Hackett (1969-1970)
MICHELE MANTVIDAS: (1) Blue Whale Customer (1967)
GRETA MARKSON: (1) Nurse (1968)
TOM MARKUS: (5) Judge (1840)
RICHARD MARR: (2) Bangor Pine Hotel Restaurant Customer (1966)
LEO MARRELL: (1) Zeb Cartwright (1966)
EDWARD MARSHALL: (2) Harry Johnson (1969), Ezra Braithwaite (1897)
PIERRINO MASCARINO: (1) Adlar (1969)
MARSHA MASON: (1) Audrey (1969)

TOM MASTERS: (2) Blue Whale Customer (1967)

GEORGE MATHEWS: (1) Amos Fitch (1966)

GEORGE McCOY: (21) Blue Whale Customer (1966-1967), Eagle Patron (1795), Spectator (1795)

KEN McEWEN: (5) Larry Chase (1970PT)

MICHAEL McGUIRE: (11) Head of Judah Zachery (1840), Judah Zachery (1692), Body of Judah (1840)

DONNA McKECHNIE: (24) Amanda Harris aka Olivia Corey (1897, 1969-1970)

KENNETH McMILLAN: (2) Jack Long (1969), Eagle Bartender (1970PT)

PAT McNAMARA: (1) Bangor Pine Hotel Restaurant Customer (1966)

ROSEMARY McNAMARA: (3) Ghost of Josette duPrés Collins (1967)

PATRICK McVEY: (1) John Harris (1966)

MARYANN MERRICK: (1) Blue Whale Customer (1966)

PAUL MICHAEL: (5) King Johnny Romano (1897)

JERED MICKEY: (1) Lawrence Guthrie (1970)

DIANA MILLAY: (61) Laura Radcliff Collins (1966-1967, 1897), Laura Murdock Collins (1897), Ghost of Laura Stockbridge Collins (1897)

HARRY ELDON MILLER: (1) Blue Whale Customer (1967)

JOHN MIRANDA: (1) Policeman (1897)

GEORGE MITCHELL: (3) Matthew Morgan (1966)

SANDY MITCHELL: (1) Stand-in for Josette duPrés Collins (1795)

TOM MIXAN: (2) Blue Whale Customer (1966)

VIC MOHICA: (1) Ghost of Stefan (1897)

RICHARD MOLICH: (1) Pirate (1970)

ALEXANDRA MOLTKE: (335) Victoria Winters (1966-1968, 1795)

CHUCK MORGAN: (3) Emory Page as a zombie (1970), Pirate (1970)

DAN MORGAN: (4) Riggs (1795)

DUANE MORRIS: (9) Monster (1968), Ghost of Headless Man (1968), Diabolos (1968)

JOSEPH MOSCA: (2) Hanging Man (1970PT)

PETER MURPHY: (14) Caretaker (1967), Blue Whale Customer (1967), Body of Ghost of Doctor David Woodard (1967), Stand-in for Burke Devlin (1967), Stand-in for Barnabas Collins (1967, 1795), Doctor Thornton (1795), Guard (1795), Gaoler (1795), Gravedigger (1968)

T. J. MURPHY: (3) Footsteps (1966), Blue Whale Customer (1966)

TOM MURPHY: (3), Chauffeur (1966), Blue Whale Customer (1967), Deputy (1968)

CARL NICHOLAS: (2) Judge (1840)

JOY NICHOLSON: (4) Ghost of Widow (1967), Blue Whale Customer (1967)

DENISE NICKERSON: (71) Amy Jennings (1968-1970), Nora Collins (1897), Amy Collins (1970PT)

NATALIE NORWICK aka Natalie Norwich: (7) Ghost of Ruby Tate (1968), Ghost of Josette duPrés Collins (1968-1969), Stand-in for Edith Collins (1897), Stand-in for Judith Collins Trask (1897)

VINCE O'BRIEN: (10) Lieutenant Dan Riley (1967), Sheriff George Patterson (1967-1969)

BOB O'CONNELL: (58) Bob Rooney aka Andy (1966-1967, 1970), Mr. Mooney (1795), Bartender (1897)

BRIDGET O'DONNELL: (3) Ghost of Widow (1967)

SHO ONODERA: (1) Mr. Nakamura (1969)

LARA PARKER: (269) Angélique Bouchard Collins (1795, 1968, 1796), Ghost of Angélique (1795), Cassandra Blair Collins (1968), Angélique DuBois aka Angélique Duval (1897), Angélique Rumson (1970), Alexis Stokes (1970PT), Angélique Stokes Collins (1970PT), Miranda Collins aka Valerie Collins (1840), Miranda duVal (1692), Catherine Harridge Collins (1841PT)

NORMAN PARKER: (5) Figure in Vision (1897), Judah Zachery's Headless Body (1840)

WENDY PARKER: (1) Blue Whale Customer (1967)

WOODY PARKER: (1) Blue Whale Bartender (1967)

DENNIS PATRICK: (66) Jason McGuire (1967, 1949), Paul Stoddard (1969-1970, 1949)

CLIFFORD PELLOW: (1) Deputy (1968)

CHRISTOPHER PENNOCK: (126) Jeb Hawkes (1970), Cyrus Longworth aka John Yaeger (1970PT), Sebastian Shaw (1970), Gabriel Collins (1840), Gabriel Collins (1841PT)

DEAN PERCHALL: (1) Stand-in for Willie Loomis (1967)

JACK PICKETT: (1) Bangor Pine Hotel Restaurant Customer (1966)

ADDISON POWELL: (39) Voice of Ghost of Jeremiah Collins (1795, 1968), Judge Matigan (1795), Doctor Eric Lang (1968), Ghost of Eric (1968), Judge Wiley (1840)

LOVELADY POWELL: (1) Portia Fitzsimmons (1967)

KEITH PRENTICE: (40) Morgan Collins (1841PT), James Forsythe (1680PT, 1841PT)

KATHERINE QUINT: (7) Blue Whale Customer (1966-1967), Hand of Carolyn (1967)

SHEILA RAY: (1) Laura Collins' Scream (1966)

DIANN REDFORD: (1) Blue Whale Customer (1966)

DOUGLAS REED: (2) Collinsport Inn Restaurant Customer (1966), Blue Whale Customer (1967)

FRANK RERCH: (1) Blue Whale Customer (1967)

CHARLES REYNOLDS: (2) Reverend Johnson (1841PT)

LISA RICHARDS: (28) Sabrina Stuart (1969-1970), Sabrina Stuart (1970PT)

NORMAN RIGGINS: (1) Ghost of Pedor (1897)

ED RILEY: (8) Voice of Harrison Monroe aka Charles Delaware Tate (1969), Sheriff/Deputy Davenport (1970), Sheriff Davenport as a zombie (1970)

MARIN RILEY: (4) Ghost of Widow (1967)

ROBERT RODAN: (78) Adam (1968)

VICTOR ROMANO: (1) Pirate (1970)

JANE ROSE: (1) Mrs. Mitchell (1966)

LISA ROSS: (1) Carolyn Stoddard as a Child (1969)

HANSFORD ROWE: (3) Judge (1795)

ANN RUGGIERO: (1) Blue Whale Customer (1967)

CHARLES RUSH: (4) Stand-in for Grant Douglas (1969), Hand of Thomas Findley (1970), Stand-in for Daniel (1840), Guard (1840)

GORDON RUSSELL: (1) Second Coachman-Harris (1841PT)

MITCHELL RYAN: (107) Burke Devlin (1966-1967)

DICK SABOL: (1) Tim Braithwaite (1840)

ANTHONY SACCO: (1) Stand-in for Ghost of Joshua Collins (1970PT)

ARLENE SAND: (2) Stand-in for Angélique Bouchard (1795)

ALFRED SANDOR: (1) Sheriff George Patterson (1968)

LILIANE SANDOR: (4) Stand-in for Roxanne Drew (1970)

ED SAUTER: (1) Deputy (1967)

FRANK SCHOFIELD: (15) Bill Malloy (1966), Ghost of Malloy (1966)

GEOFFREY SCOTT aka Geoffery Scott: (13) Schuyler Rumson (1970)

KATHRYN LEIGH SCOTT: (310) Maggie Evans (1966-1970), Ghost of Josette duPrés Collins (1966, 1795, 1970), Josette duPrés Collins (1795, 1796), Rachel Drummond (1897), Kitty Soames aka Lady Hampshire (1897), Maggie Evans Collins (1970PT)

DAVID SELBY: (311) Ghost of Quentin Collins (1968-1969), Quentin Collins aka Grant Douglas (1897, 1969-1970, 1995), Quentin Collins as a zombie (1897), Quentin Collins (1970PT), Quentin Collins (1840), Quentin Collins (1841PT)

JOHN SERVETNIK: (1) Ezra Ahearn (1966)

JAMES SHANNON: (13) Hangman (1795, 1796), Policeman (1968), Deputy (1968), Guard (1795), Gaoler (1795), Thomas Findley as a zombie (1970)

LANA SHAW: (1) Widow Romano (1897)

REBECCA SHAW: (2) Doxy (1795)

MARY LYNN SHIELDS: (1) Blue Whale Customer (1967)

WILLIAM SHUST: (1) Doctor Fisher (1967)

MEL SIGAN: (1) Bangor Pine Hotel Restaurant Customer (1966)

CRAIG SLOCUM: (17) Noah Gifford (1795), Harry Johnson (1968-1969)

AL SMITH: (1) Blue Whale Customer (1966)

SHARON SMYTH: (37) Ghost of Sarah Collins (1967), Sarah Collins (1795)

THOMAS SPRATLEY: (1) Justice of the Peace (1968)

JACK STAMBERGER: (1) Doctor (1795)

FLORENCE STANLEY: (4) Ghost (1966-1967), Voice of Ghost of Josette duPrés Collins (1968)

ALEX STEVENS: (25) Werewolf: Chris Jennings (1968-1969), Stunt Double (1968), Werewolf: Quentin Collins (1897), Stand-in for Claude North (1970PT)

FRED STEWART: (2) Doctor D. Reeves (1966-1967)

JESSICA STEWART: (2) Blue Whale Customer (1967)

RAY STEWART: (1) Bangor Pine Hotel Restaurant Customer (1966)
JAMES STORM: (81) Ghost of Gerard Stiles (1970, 1995), Ivan Miller aka
    Gerard Stiles (1840), Gerard Stiles (1841PT)
GAIL STRICKLAND: (2) Dorcas Trilling (1897), Ghost of Dorcas (1897)
MICHAEL STROKA: (64) Aristede (1897), Bruno (1970), Bruno Hess (1970PT),
    Laszlo Ferrari (1840)
BRIAN STURDIVANT: (4) Bellboy (1970), Claude North (1970PT)
GEORGE STRUS: (2) Steve (1970PT)
SUSAN SULLIVAN: (1) Ghost (1967)
ELIZABETH SWAIN: (1) Ghost of Widow (1966)
LARRY SWANSON: (1) Blue Whale Customer (1966)
DOLPH SWEET: (1) Ezra Herne (1966)
INGRID SWENSON: (1) Blue Whale Customer (1967)
ANN TEEMAN: (3) Blue Whale Customer (1966)
TED TINLING: (1) Collinsport Inn Restaurant Customer (1966)
K. C. TOWNSEND: (1) Sophie Baker (listed on credits as "Sophie Barnes") (1897)
PAUL TRAHAN: (1) Blue Whale Customer (1967)
BARBARA TRACEY: (3) Stand-in for Ghost of Joanna Mills (1840), Stand-in for
    Samantha Collins (1840)
PETER TURGEON: (11) Doctor David Woodard (1967), Voice of Ghost of
    Woodard (1967)
SCOTT UPRIGHT: (8) Blue Whale Customer (1967), Spectator (1795)
GWEN VAN DAM: (2) Miss Hopewell's Secretary (1966), Blue Whale Customer
    (1967)
PETER VAN NIEL: (1) Spectator (1796)
VIRGINIA VESTOFF: (29) Samantha Drew Collins (1840), Samantha Drew
    (1841PT)
ABE VIGODA: (3) Ezra Braithwaite (1969), Otis Greene (1840)
ROBERT VIHARO: (1) Harry (1966)
PAUL VINCENT: (1) Policeman (1897)
RAY VON ORDEN: (1) Ghost of Andreas (1897)
DIANA WALKER: (1) Carolyn Stoddard (1968)
MARIE WALLACE: (64) Eve (1968), Danielle Rogét aka Eve (1795), Jenny
    Collins (1897), Ghost of Jenny (1897, 1969), Megan Todd (1969-1970)
DONNA WANDREY: (34) Roxanne Drew (1970PT), Roxanne Drew (1970,
    1840), Ghost of Roxanne (1840)
ROBERT WARLOCK: (1) Policemen (1897)
HAL WHITE: (1) Judge (1795)
ELIZABETH WILSON: (2) Mrs. Hopewell aka Miss Hopewell (1966)
RICHARD WOODS: (2) Doctor Woodard (1967)
BOBBI ANN WORONKO: (1) Nurse Pritchett (1968)
AMY YAEKERSON: (1) Young Woman (1897)
BARBARA YOUNG: (1) Blue Whale Customer (1966)

## CREDITS TRIVIA

First credit for "Miss Scott's Clothes" in episode 1018

Credit for "Christopher" Pennock changed to "Chris" Pennock in episode 1073

First credit for "Mary McKinley Costume Design" in episode 1144

First credit reading "Starring Jonathan Frid" in episode 905

First credit reading "Mostoller" in episode 579

The scenic designer credit is misspelled "Thomashoff" in episode 5

Cast credits follows production credits on screen in episode 573

"Ghost of Daniels Collins" is a credit appearing at the end of episode 1191

The credit for Louis Edmonds is misspelled "Louis Edmunds" in episode 1140

Violet Welles, writer, is spelled "Wells" in the credits for episode 944

Elizabeth Collins Stoddard is billed as "Judith Collins" in episode 968

Kathryn Leigh Scott was billed as Kathryn "Lee" Scott in episodes 844 & 846

The wording "Fashions from Ohrbach's" appears only at the end of episode 1

The first episode with the Dan Curtis copyright as the only closing credit is episode 46

Jerry Lacy's name is misspelled "Lacey" in episodes 358 and 359

In episode 618, the writer credit appears as "Gordon Sproat," partially combining the names of writers Gordon Russell and Ron Sproat. The rolling credits were originally typed on a paper roll attached to a background material not seen by the camera. In this episode, part of the paper became detached revealing the name underneath.

*Michael Stroka.*

At the end of episode 520, the rolling credits stopped between Harriet Rohr and Robert Cobert so that both showed on screen. After a few seconds they cut out and were followed by five seconds without credits; then the Dan Curtis Productions copyright notice appeared, but for the year 1966 instead of 1968.

## CHARACTERS PLAYED BY DIFFERENT ACTORS

During the nearly five-year run of *Dark Shadows*, many characters were played by more than one actor. New actors took over roles, and stand-ins (with their faces not clearly visible and no lines of dialogue) were used for brief appearances. The following entries give details.

Nancy Barrett was Carolyn Stoddard Hawkes, although Diana Walker played the role in one episode during 1968 when Nancy was ill. Katherine Quint supplied the hand of Carolyn as she prepared to shoot Jason McGuire. Lisa Ross played Carolyn as a child, evading Paul Stoddard while he was threatened by the Leviathans.

In 1840, Daphne and Quentin held a seance to summon the spirit of Joanna Mills. In response, Barbara Tracey appeared as the silent ghost of Joanna; later Lee Beery was Joanna when she began to haunt Samantha, played by Virginia Vestoff. Later still, Barbara Tracey substituted as Samantha when she almost killed Daphne Harridge.

Natalie Norwich substituted for Joan Bennett briefly as a stand-in when Judith Collins Trask returned from Rushmore Sanitarium, to which she had been committed in 1897.

Donald Briscoe played Chris Jennings, but Alex Stevens played Chris whenever he turned into a werewolf.

Maude Browning, a victim of Barnabas in 1795, was played by Vala Clifton. When the ghost of Maude was revived by Trask's ghost in 1968, she was played by Maggie Benson.

Joel Crothers played Lieutenant Nathan Forbes; David Columbia was his stand-in during the scene at the end of 1795 in which Barnabas takes his revenge on Nathan.

Matthew Morgan was played by George Mitchell for the character's first three episodes, including one in which his home-baked muffins were enjoyed by Victoria Winters. He was replaced by Thayer David, who went on to play a record-setting eight different roles during the remainder of *Dark Shadows'* run. Thayer David played Count Andreas Petofi in 1897, but his disembodied hand was represented by Timothy Gordon, before it was reunited with Petofi's body.

Among the many roles played by Roger Davis was the eccentric Charles Delaware Tate, who arrived in 1897 to paint a portrait of Quentin. In 1969, Julia asked Harrison Monroe about Tate and heard his voice, spoken by Ed Riley. Later she learned it was the aged Tate who had told her to go away.

While Maggie Evans was confined in Windcliff Sanitarium, her nurse, Miss Jackson, was played by Alice Drummond. Later, when Willie was released from Windcliff, Miss Jackson was played by Ann Davies.

At the end of the first episode in 1840, Julia Hoffman was nearly strangled by Charles Rush as her unknown attacker. In the next episode, her attacker was revealed as the aged Daniel Collins, played by Louis Edmonds. Louis Edmonds appeared as the ghost of Joshua Collins in 1970 Parallel Time; Anthony Sacco substituted for him in one episode.

From 1966 to 1968, Sheriff George Patterson was played by Dana Elcar and three other actors: Vince O'Brien, Alfred Sandor, and Angus Cairns. At the end of one episode, Vince O'Brien as the sheriff watched Willie come out of his coma, but when the same scene was repeated the next day, the Sheriff was again played by Dana Elcar.

In the fifth episode of *Dark Shadows*, Sam Evans, played by Mark Allen, met Victoria Winters on Widows' Hill. After seven episodes, David Ford took over the role, when Burke tried to learn about the connection between Sam and Roger.

The day before the arrival of Jonathan Frid as Barnabas Collins, Timothy Gordon played the hand of Barnabas as it reached out from the coffin to choke Willie Loomis. During the next year, Peter Murphy and Alfred Dillay stood-in as Barnabas in brief appearances. Tim Gordon also played the hand of Barnabas when it threatened Trask in 1795.

Anthony George played Jeremiah Collins until the character died in 1795, after which the part of his ghost was shared by Timothy Gordon, as the body, and Addison Powell, who provided the voice of the ghost.

Richard Woods was the first actor to play Dr. Woodard, when he was called in to examine Willie Loomis. Later, Robert Gerringer played Dr. Dave Woodard, until an AFTRA strike led to Peter Turgeon taking over the role. Woodard's ghost was played by Peter Murphy, and Peter Turgeon supplied the voice which terrified Julia Hoffman.

Dr. Julia Hoffman was played by Grayson Hall for nearly four years. Shortly after her arrival, Fran Anthony stood-in as Dr. Hoffman twice when she appeared in a dream to David.

"Grandmama" Edith Collins was played by Isabella Hoopes in 1897, and Natalie Norwich provided Edith's hands which indicated the position of the will hidden in her coffin. Terry Crawford played Edith Collins in 1840.

The first victim of Barnabas Collins was Elaine Hyman as Ruby Tate. When the ghosts of his victims were summoned to line up in the cellar of the Old House, Ruby Tate was played by Natalie Norwich.

James Hall played Willie Loomis for four episodes. He was then replaced by John Karlen before Willie released Barnabas. After Willie was shot while trying to warn Maggie Evans, Dean Perchall played an obscured Willie lying in the hospital, groaning as he recovered from a coma.

During the seance that sent Victoria Winters back to 1795, her place in 1967 was taken by Phyllis Wick, played by Dorrie Kavanaugh. When Victoria returned from 1795, Margot Head played Phyllis Wick.

While Maggie Evans had days off in the Collinsport Inn Restaurant, the waitress there was played by Colleen Kelly and Carol Crist. Both girls were called "Susie."

In 1897, Evan Hanley conducted a ceremony to call up the Devil. While he and Quentin Collins watched apprehensively, a figure appeared—but it was Gregory Trask, played by stand-in Marc Ashton. Otherwise, all the Trasks were played by Jerry Lacy.

Michael McGuire played the head of Judah Zachery, brought to Collinwood by Desmond Collins as a gift for Quentin. Norman Parker played the headless body, searching for its head. George DiCenzo also made two uncredited appearances as the body. The voice of the head was supplied by Keene Curtis.

Diana Millay was Laura Collins in all her different manifestations. Barbara Brownell was a stand-in as Laura when she returned in 1897 to greet Nora, and Sheila Ray supplied a scream by Laura in 1966.

From the beginning of *Dark Shadows*, Alexandra Moltke starred as Victoria Winters. After she left the show in 1968, Betsy Durkin took over the role, and Victoria was finally married to Jeff Clark, who was really Peter Bradford, her 1795 sweetheart. After she and Peter returned to 1795, Barnabas returned to save her from the gallows, and at that time Victoria was played by Carolyn Groves.

Dan Morgan, as the servant Riggs in 1795, guarded the door to Josette's room. Later, when he and another servant carried out the body of Barnabas on orders from Joshua, the role was played by Timothy Gordon.

During the investigation of Laura in 1967, Lt. Dan Riley was played by John Connell, and later by Vince O'Brien, who later still played Sheriff Patterson.

Angélique was played by Lara Parker throughout *Dark Shadows*. When the ghost of Jeremiah carried her to his grave just before her marriage to Barnabas, Arlene Sand was an Angélique stand-in. Amber Brie appeared as an Alexis Stokes stand-in(also played by Lara Parker) when she was forced to replace her twin sister, Angélique, in her coffin, during the 1970 Parallel Time sequence. And Judith Lowry played Angélique as Cassandra's aged hands in 1968.

Dennis Patrick was Paul Stoddard when he returned to Collinwood, only to be threatened by the Leviathans. Just before his return, Mart Aldre substituted as a stand-in. But back in 1967, when Dennis Patrick returned as Paul's friend Jason

McGuire to blackmail Elizabeth Stoddard, she recalled the events of 1949, in which Joel Fabiani played Paul Stoddard.

In 1970, Jeb Hawkes revived Sheriff Davenport, played by Ed Riley, as a zombie. As the victim was called up from its grave, its hand appeared, clutching at the air; the hand belonged to George DiCenzo.

While Dr. Eric Lang assembled the body that became Adam, the creature was played by Duane Morris. Robert Rodan became Adam shortly before he was brought to life.

Mitchell Ryan was Burke Devlin from the first episode but was replaced by Anthony George in 1967. Peter Murphy stood in as Burke when Vicki confronted him in a dream.

Kathryn Leigh Scott was Maggie Evans starting with the very first episode, and she also played the ghost of Josette duPrés beginning with its first appearance in 1966. Since that time, other actresses who substituted as the ghost were Rosemary McNamara, in 1796, Florence Stanley, in 1968, and Natalie Norwich in 1968 and 1969. Dorrie Kavanaugh substituted for Josette in the dream in which Naomi saw Josette embrace Jeremiah; Dorrie Kavanaugh also was a stand-in for Maggie Evans briefly while Barnabas tried to turn her into Josette in 1967. When Barnabas raised Josette from the dead in 1795, Sandy Mitchell played the ghost as she walked through the cemetery.

In 1897, David Selby was Quentin Collins; when he turned into the werewolf, he was played by Alex Stevens, stunt coordinator. Seen lurking outside the antique shop, Charles Rush stood in once for David Selby when Quentin Collins reappeared, briefly known as Grant Douglas.

The Leviathan leader, Jeb Hawkes, called up four dead men to help him against Barnabas Collins. The hand of Charles Rush rose out of a grave, representing Thomas Findley. In the next episode four zombies arose, and Thomas Findley was played by Jim Shannon.

Mrs. Johnson's wayward son, Harry, was played by Craig Slocum, but in one episode Edward Marshall substituted for him.

During 1970 Parallel Time, a mysterious man appeared, looked for Roxanne. Alex Stevens played the man, whose face was not visible. In the next episode, his face revealed him to be the even more mysterious Claude North, then played by Brian Sturdivant.

After his arrival in Collinsport, Burke Devlin planned to take over Collins Enterprises. He offered four Collins employees, old friends from the cannery, good jobs and high pay to desert the Collinses. The fourth man, Ezra Ahearn, was played by John Servetnik. Later the character, now renamed Ezra Herne and played by Dolph Sweet, returned to Burke to tell him the men had turned down his offer.

Abe Vigoda was Ezra Braithwaite when Barnabas visited him in 1969 to learn about the pentagram he made long ago. In 1897, Edward Marshall played Ezra as a young man who had just made the pentagram.

Donna Wandrey played Roxanne Drew. In 1970, Roxanne as a vampire went to attack Maggie. Later, Liliane Sandor stood in as Roxanne when the children saw the vampire rise from its coffin, and when Julia and Willie went to the coffin to destroy the vampire.

## CHARACTER REPLACEMENTS

Joel Crothers' character of Joe Haskell replaced Mitch Ryan's character of Burke Devlin in Episode 252. Ken McEwen's character of Larry Chase replaced Don Briscoe's character of Chris Collins in five episodes when Briscoe left the series. The character of James Blair, played by John Baragrey, replaced the character of Stuart Bronson, played by Barnard Hughes. Both characters served the same function, but Bronson was written out when Barnard Hughes was no longer available.

## CHARACTER RENAMINGS

Victoria Winters was originally named Sheila March in the series' bible.

Jason McGuire was originally named Walt Cummings in the series' bible.

Barnabas Collins was originally to be named Jeremiah Collins or Jered Collins.

Julia Hoffman was originally named Julius Hoffman, but was changed when the decision was made to hire an actress for the part.

Riggs, the Collins family servant in 1795, was originally to be named Briggs.

Noah Gifford was originally to be named Rex Butler.

Professor Stokes was originally refered to as Timothy Stokes and later, Eliot Stokes —eventually resulting in T.E. Stokes.

Amy Jennings was originally to be named Molly Jennings.

Chris Jennings was originally to be named Bob Jennings.

Diabolos was originally to be named Balberith.

Edward Collins was originally to be named Oscar Collins.

Sandor was originally to be named Zoltan.

Daphne Harridge was originally to be named Lavinia.

Valerie Collins (alias Angélique) was originally to be named Natasha.

*Amy (Denise Nickerson) and Chris Jennings (Don Briscoe).*

John Karlen; Joel Crothers; Anthony George; Roger Davis; David Henesy;
Daniel Keyes; Timothy Gordon; Robert Rodan; Dennis Patrick.

*Kathy Cody; Clarice Blackburn; Alexandra Moltke; Lee Beery; Donna McKechnie; Nancy Barrett; Terry Crawford; Virginia Vestoff; Marie Wallace.*

*Jonathan Frid; Opposite: David Selby; Michael Stroka; Thayer David; Jerry Lacy;*
*Louis Edmonds; Humbert Allen Astredo.*

# 𝔇ark 𝔖hadoᴡs 𝔖torylines

### VICTORIA'S ARRIVAL (EPISODES 1-6)

Victoria Winters comes to Collinwood to serve as governess to David Collins. She is an orphan and hopes to find clues to her identity. She finds a reclusive matriarch, Elizabeth Collins Stoddard; a disturbed child, David Collins; and a town full of mysterious and frightening legends.

### THE REVENGE OF BURKE DEVLIN (EPISODES 1-201)

Despising the Collins' power and influence, Burke Devlin returns to Collinsport after spending time in prison. He befriends Victoria, manipulates Carolyn Stoddard, Elizabeth's daughter, and interrogates others to discover the truth about the accident which led to his conviction.

### MATTHEW MORGAN KILLS BILL MALLOY AND KIDNAPS VICTORIA (EPISODES 46-126)

Collins fishing fleet manager Bill Malloy is killed by Collinwood caretaker Matthew Morgan after Matthew learns Malloy wants Roger Collins to confess to the car accident which sent Burke to prison. Matthew kidnaps Victoria when she discovers he was responsible for Malloy's death. Victoria is saved by the ghost of Josette Collins who joins the ghost of Malloy in scaring Matthew to death.

### LAURA THE PHOENIX (EPISODES 123-191)

Laura Collins, Roger's wife and David's mother, schemes to reclaim her son. Laura is a creature of the supernatural, an immortal Phoenix who almost succeeds in taking David with her as she is consumed by flames.

### THE BLACKMAILING OF ELIZABETH (EPISODES 193-275)

Jason McGuire, a friend of Liz's missing husband Paul Stoddard, returns to Collinwood. Victimized by his blackmail, Liz agrees to marry Jason, but at the last moment reveals the truth. Eighteen years before, Jason led her to believe she killed Paul and then allowed Jason to bury the body in the basement of Collinwood. An investigation uncovers no body; Paul did not die. Jason is killed after he enters the Old House to search for jewels.

### THE INTRODUCTION OF BARNABAS (EPISODES 202-220)

Jason's drifter friend Willie Loomis joins Jason as an unwelcome guest at Collinwood. Fascinated by the portrait of Barnabas Collins and the legend he was buried with his jewels, Willie opens the coffin of Barnabas and accidentally releases the 200-year-old vampire. Barnabas introduces himself at Collinwood as a descendant of the Barnabas in the portrait. With Liz's permission, Barnabas moves into the Old House and begins its restoration.

### THE KIDNAPPING OF MAGGIE (EPISODES 221-261)

Barnabas meets waitress Maggie Evans and is struck by her close resemblance to Josette, his love in the distant past. He abducts Maggie and attempts to recreate her as Josette so she may join him as his eternal vampire bride. With the help of a mysterious child, Maggie escapes and is confined at Windcliff Sanitarium.

### THE INTRODUCTION OF JULIA (EPISODES 265-365)

Maggie's doctor, Julia Hoffman, arrives at Collinwood, posing as an historian. She discovers the secret of Barnabas and offers to cure him. When the experiments backfire, Barnabas turns on her. Barnabas attempts to kill those who he believes know his secret, but he is stopped by the ghost of his little sister Sarah.

### 1795 (EPISODES 365-461)

After a seance, Vicki is transported back to 1795. She meets Collins ancestors who resemble present-day family members. The witch Angélique jealously destroys Barnabas' romance with Josette DuPrés and places the curse of the vampire on him. Josette sees a vision of herself as a vampire and leaps to her death from Widows' Hill. Reverend Trask causes Vicki to be tried and condemned as a witch. Vicki falls in love with Peter Bradford. As she is about to be hung as a witch, Vicki is returned to the present.

### THE DREAM CURSE (EPISODES 461-536)

Vicki is haunted by her experiences in the past. Dr. Eric Lang temporarily cures Barnabas. Angélique appears, disguised as Roger's new wife Cassandra. She initiates an evil dream curse to turn Barnabas back into a vampire. At the climax of the dream curse, Barnabas is attacked by a bat, but he does not become a vampire at that time.

### THE CREATION OF ADAM AND EVE (EPISODES 486-626)

Dr. Lang dies. Barnabas and Julia continue his experiments to create a man from human body parts using Barnabas' life force. Adam is brought to life. Warlock Nicholas Blair influences Adam to demand a mate; Eve is created, but she despises Adam for his weakness. Nicholas punishes Angélique by turning her into a vampire. Angélique bites Barnabas in an attempt to place him under her power. Adam kills Eve.

### RETURN TO 1796 (EPISODES 657-667)

Barnabas revisits the past to save Vicki from hanging. By destroying Angélique, he enables Vicki to remain in the past with Peter Bradford.

### THE WEREWOLF AND THE GHOST OF QUENTIN (EPISODES 627-700)

When the moon is full, Chris Jennings transforms into a werewolf. His sister Amy comes to live at Collinwood. Using an old disconnected telephone, Amy and David speak to the ghost of Quentin Collins, which attempts to possess David. After Quentin forces everyone to leave Collinwood, his wild laughter echoes through the empty house. Maggie saves the children after Quentin lures them back to Collinwood.

### 1897 (EPISODES 700-884)

By using the I-Ching wands, Barnabas goes back to 1897 to learn the secret of Quentin and the werewolf. Schoolteacher Rachel Drummond attempts to save the children, Jamison and Nora, from cruel treatment by Reverend Gregory Trask at his school, Worthington Hall. Angered that Quentin was responsible for the death of her sister Jenny, Magda places the curse of the werewolf on Quentin and all his descendants. Count Petofi regains his hand and uses its power to switch minds with Quentin in his attempt to reach the future. Barnabas meets the true reincarnation of Josette, Lady Kitty Hampshire.

### THE LEVIATHANS (EPISODES 885-980)

Barnabas follows Kitty as Josette to 1795 but is returned to the present by the Leviathans. He is used by them in their quest to displace mankind and return their ancient cult to supremacy. Carolyn marries Leviathan leader Jeb Hawkes. Angélique creates a shadow to follow Jeb and destroy him.

## QUENTIN AND AMANDA (EPISODES 904-934)

Quentin appears in the present but has no memory of his past life in 1897. His lost love from that time, Amanda Harris, discovers him and helps him regain his memory. But Quentin loses her in a struggle with Mr. Best—Death.

## 1970 PARALLEL TIME (EPISODES 980-1060)

A room in Collinwood's east wing enables Barnabas to enter Parallel Time, where familiar people have made different choices and live different lives. Angélique, risen from the dead, is determined to regain her husband Quentin, now married to Maggie Evans. Barnabas falls in love with Roxanne Drew, who has provided the life force for Angélique.

## 1995 (EPISODES 1061-1070)

Barnabas and Julia are transported to the future, where they find Collinwood in ruins. They question survivors and follow clues, determined to avert the crisis by returning to the present and changing history.

## THE GHOSTS OF DAPHNE AND GERARD (EPISODES 1070-1109)

David and Hallie Stokes find a sealed-off playroom in Collinwood and become possessed by Tad and Carrie who lived in 1840. Ghost of Daphne Harridge is unable to stop the ghost of Gerard Stiles from summoning an army of the dead to destroy Collinwood.

## 1840 (EPISODES 1110-1198)

Barnabas and Julia use the stairway created by Quentin in 1840 to travel back to that time. Gerard Stiles, possessed by Judah Zachery, becomes master of Collinwood. After Angélique causes the destruction of Judah, Barnabas realizes he loves her, but she is immediately killed by Lamar Trask. Brokenhearted, Barnabas returns with Julia to the present.

## 1841 PARALLEL TIME (EPISODES 1198-1245)

Because of a curse, the Collins family must hold a lottery once in each generation. Only when the person chosen can spend the night in a mysterious room and survive both alive and sane can the curse be broken. Bramwell Collins, son of Barnabas and Josette, returns to town hoping to marry Catherine Harridge. But Catherine marries Morgan Collins, unaware that she is pregnant with Bramwell's child. Morgan attempts to kill the lovers by locking them in the room, but they survive, breaking the curse. Morgan perishes. The ghosts and vampires at Collinwood have been laid to rest.

# Dark Shadows Timeline

| | |
|---|---|
| Episodes 1-365 | Set in Present Time/1966-1967 (a) |
| Episodes 366-460 | Set in 1795 |
| Episode 461 | Set in 1795 and in Present Time/1968 |
| Episode 462-660 | Set in Present Time/1968-1969 (b) |
| Episode 661 | Set in Present Time/1969 and in 1796 |
| Episodes 662-665 | Set in 1796 |
| Episode 666 | Set in Present Time/1969 and in 1796 |
| Episodes 667-700 | Set in Present Time/1969 (c) |
| Episode 701 | Set in Present Time/1969 and in 1897 |
| Episodes 702-884 | Set in 1897 (d) |
| Episode 885 | Set in 1897 and in 1796 |
| Episode 886 | Set in 1796 |
| Episodes 887-980 | Set in Present Time/1969-1970 (e) |
| Episode 981 | Set in Present Time/1970 and in 1970 Parallel Time |
| Episode 982-1060 | Set in 1970 Parallel Time (f) |
| Episode 1061-1070 | Set in 1995 (g) |
| Episode 1071-1108 | Set in Present Time/1970 |
| Episode 1109 | Set in Present Time/1970 and in 1840 |
| Episodes 1110-1197 | Set in 1840 (h) |
| Episode 1198 | Set in 1840, then in Present Time/1971, then in 1841 Parallel Time |
| Episodes 1199-1245 | Set in 1841 Parallel Time (i) |
| (a) | Episode 270 includes scene set in 1949 |
| (b) | Episode 610 includes scene set in 1795 |
| | Episode 623 set in 1795 |
| (c) | Episode 698 includes scene set in 1967 |
| (d) | Episode 815 includes scene set in Present Time/1969 |
| | Episodes 835, 836, 837 include scenes set in Present Time/1969 |
| | Episode 873 includes scene set in Present Time/1969 |

Episode 877 includes scene set in the early 1890s
(e)  Episode 900 includes scene set in 1949
Episode 922 includes scene set in 1897
Episode 938 includes scene set in 1897
Episodes 969-971, 975-980 include scenes set in 1970 Parallel Time
(f)  Episodes 1007, 1012, 1031, 1032, 1035, 1052 include scenes set in Present Time/1970
(g)  Episode 1070 includes scene set in Present Time/1970
(h)  Episodes 1113, 1114 include scenes set in Present Time/1970
Episode 1140 includes scene set in 1692
Episodes 1186-1197 include scenes set in 1841 Parallel Time
(i)  Episode 1231 includes scenes set in 1680 Parallel Time

(Note: Dreams set in different times are not included.)

# Who's Who

A description of *Dark Shadows* characters.

## PRESENT TIME (1966-1971)

ELIZABETH COLLINS STODDARD Collins family matriarch, mother of Carolyn and sister of Roger.

ROGER COLLINS Elizabeth's younger brother and father of David.

DAVID COLLINS Young son of Roger and Laura.

CAROLYN STODDARD Elizabeth's teenage daughter.

VICTORIA WINTERS Governess to David Collins. An orphan uncertain of her identity.

BURKE DEVLIN Ex-convict who returns to town for revenge for being falsely convicted. Becomes Victoria's fiance.

SAM EVANS Widowed artist father of Maggie Evans.

MAGGIE EVANS Daughter of Sam and waitress at Collinsport Inn restaurant. Replaces Victoria as David's governess.

JOE HASKELL Local fisherman. Boyfriend to Carolyn, then Maggie.

MATTHEW MORGAN Caretaker at Collinwood.

BILL MALLOY Manager of the Collins Fishing Fleet.

LAURA COLLINS Estranged wife of Roger and mother of David. Also an immortal creature known as a phoenix.

MRS. SARAH JOHNSON Collinwood housekeeper, formerly employed by Bill Malloy.

CONSTABLE JONAS CARTER Collinsport lawman who investigates Roger's near-fatal car crash.

SHERIFF GEORGE PATTERSON Successor of the constable as Collinsport's head lawman.

DR. PETER GUTHRIE Psychic investigator who explores strange occurances at Collinwood caused by Laura.

RICHARD GARNER Collins family lawyer.

FRANK GARNER Attorney son of Richard and temporary romantic interest for Victoria.

WILBUR STRAKE Private detective hired by Burke to investigate the Collinses.

STUART BRONSON Burke's New York banker .

JAMES BLAIR Successor to Stuart Bronson.

MR. WELLS Primary desk clerk at the Collinsport Inn.

GHOST OF BILL MALLOY Malevolent spirit of Bill.

THE WAILING WIDOWS The spirits of three women who lost their husbands at sea.

DR. FRANKLIN Elizabeth's physician during her Boston hospital stay.

DR. D. REEVES Collins family doctor.

CARETAKER Elderly custodian of the Eagle Hill Cemetery.

MRS. HOPEWELL Director at Hammond Foundling Home, where Victoria grew up.

SANDY Victoria's roommate at the foundling home.

PORTIA FITZSIMMONS Art dealer interested in buying paintings from Sam.

JASON McGUIRE Old friend of Paul Stoddard who returns to blackmail
   Elizabeth.

WILLIE LOOMIS Jason McGuire's travelling companion. Becomes Barnabas
   Collins' servant.

BOB ROONEY aka ANDY Chief bartender and occasional waiter at the Blue Whale.

SUSIE Waitress at the Collinsport Inn restaurant.

AMOS FITCH Loyal captain of the Collins Fishing Fleet.

EZRA AHERN Employee of Collins Enterprises.

ADAM BILODEAU Employee of Collins Enterprises.

ZEB CARTWRIGHT Employee of Collins Enterprises.

LIEUTENANT RILEY Phoeniz police detective who investigates Laura's alleged death.

LIEUTENANT COSTA Associate of Lieutenant Riley.

MRS. MITCHELL Friendly passenger on Victoria's train to Collinsport.

GHOST OF JOSETTE COLLINS Benevolent spirit of Jeremiah Collins' bride
   who leaped to her death from Widows' Hill in 1795.

BARNABAS COLLINS Posing as a cousin from England, the same Barnabas who
   first lived in the eighteenth century. Cursed as a vampire by Angélique in 1795
   and chained in his coffin, he is accidentally released by Willie Loomis.

PAUL STODDARD Elizabeth's long-missing husband and father of Carolyn.

HARRY JONES Collinsport's cab driver.

DR. DAVE WOODARD Physician who treats Willie and Maggie after they are
   attacked by Barnabas.

DR. JULIA HOFFMAN Blood specialist from Windcliff Sanitarium who attempts
   to cure Barnabas of his vampirism.

TONY PETERSON Collinsport attorney who becomes Carolyn's boyfriend.

BUZZ HACKETT Hippie motorcyclist who is briefly Carolyn's boyfriend.

DR. FISHER Psychiatrist called in to examine David.

JUDGE CRATHORNE Local official who performs Elizabeth's and Jason's aborted
   wedding ceremony.

GHOST OF SARAH COLLINS Benevolent spirit of Barnabas' young sister who
   died in 1795.

PHYLLIS WICK Sarah Collins' eighteenth century governess who appears in
   Victoria's place following the seance which sends Victoria to 1795.

NURSE PACKARD Maggie's nurse at the Collinsport Hospital.

NURSE JACKSON Maggie's nurse at Windcliff.

DR. ERIC LANG Physician who instigates the creation of Adam, the man-made creature.

JEFF CLARK Aka Peter Bradford, who has transcended time from the eighteenth century and marries Victoria.

ADAM Created by Dr. Lang from human body parts and brought to life by Dr. Julia Hoffman using Barnabas Collins' life-force.

CASSANDRA COLLINS Roger Collins' second wife who is actually Angélique disguised in a black wig.

PROFESSOR TIMOTHY ELIOT STOKES College professor and occasional confidante of Julia and Barnabas.

GHOST OF REVEREND TRASK Avenging spirit of Reverend Trask.

GHOST OF NATHAN FORBES Avenging spirit of Nathan.

GHOST OF SUKI FORBES Avenging spirit of Suki.

GHOST OF EZRA SIMPSON Avenging spirit of a judge.

GHOST OF MAUDE BROWNING Avenging spirit of Maude.

NICHOLAS BLAIR Warlock who poses as Cassandra's brother.

GHOST OF DR. ERIC LANG Spirit of Dr. Lang.

GHOST OF SAM EVANS Spirit of Sam.

EVE Artificial woman created to be Adam's mate, using the life force of Danielle Roget.

LEONA ELTRIDGE Reincarnation of Danielle Roget from eighteenth century. Life force used to bring Eve to life.

DIABOLOS Demonic leader of the Netherworld.

HARRY JOHNSON Mrs. Johnson's unscrupulous son who becomes a henchman for Nicholas Blair.

TOM JENNINGS Collinsport handyman who becomes a vampire after dying from Angélique's attack.

CHRIS JENNINGS Tom's identical brother who suffers from the werewolf curse.

AMY JENNINGS Tom and Chris Jennings' young sister who comes to live at Collinwood.

SABRINA STUART Chris Jennings' girlfriend.

NED STUART Sabrina Stuart's brother.

MR. JARRET Collinsport undertaker.

DONNA FRIEDLANDER Friend of Carolyn's who is killed by the werewolf.

GHOST OF QUENTIN COLLINS Malevolent spirit of Quentin, who first lived in 1897.

GHOST OF BETH CHAVEZ Benevolent spirit of Beth, who first lived in 1897.

MADAME JANET FINDLEY A psychic who investigates Quentin's haunting of Collinwood.

EZRA BRAITHEWAITE Elderly Collinsport silversmith.

OBERON A Leviathan.

HAZA A Leviathan.

PAUL STODDARD Elizabeth's long-missing husband and Carolyn's father.

MEGAN TODD Collinsport Antique Shop owner and wife of Philip Todd.

PHILIP TODD Collinsport Antique Shop owner and husband of Megan Todd.

GHOST OF JENNY COLLINS Spirit of Jenny.

OLIVIA COREY 20th century alias of Amanda Harris.

MR. NAKAMURA Man who assists Olivia Corey.

PROFESSOR HENRY OSMOND Art specialist.

HARRISON MONROE 20th century alias of an aged Charles Delaware Tate.

JACK LONG Sailor

MR. BEST The physical manifestation of Death.

MRS. HUTCHINS Elderly woman who assists the Leviathans.

AUDREY Leviathan dream vampire.

ALEXANDER Leviathan leader as a young child.

MICHAEL HACKETT Leviathan leader as an older child.

JEB HAWKES Leviathan leader as a full-grown adult, who marries Carolyn Stoddard.

DEPUTY/SHERIFF DAVENPORT Collinsport lawman.

SKY RUMSON Leviathan follower and 20th century husband of Angélique.

BRUNO Deviant Leviathan supporter.

GHOST OF PETER BRADFORD Spirit of Peter.

NELLE GUNSTON Leviathan recruit attacked by Barnabas.

LAWRENCE GUTHRIE State investigator.

GHOST OF GERARD STILES Malevolent spirit of Gerard, who originally lived in 1840.

GHOST OF DAPHNE HARRIDGE Benevolent spirit of Daphne, who originally lived in 1840.

DAPHNE HARRIDGE 1840 governess who transcends time and space to come back to life.

HALLIE STOKES Professor Stokes' teenage niece who comes to live at Collinwood.

SEBASTIAN SHAW Astrologist and romantic interest for Maggie Evans.

ROXANNE DREW Sebastian Shaw's psychic partner who is a vampire.

### 1795-96

BARNABAS COLLINS Son of Naomi and Joshua Collins, brother of Sarah Collins.

NAOMI COLLINS Mother of Barnabas and Sarah Collins. Wife of Joshua Collins.

JOSHUA COLLINS Father of Barnabas and Sarah Collins. Husband of Naomi. Brother of Abigail and Jeremiah Collins.

JEREMIAH COLLINS Brother of Abigail and Joshua Collins. Husband of Josette duPrés.

ABIGAIL COLLINS Sister of Jeremiah and Joshua Collins.

MILLICENT COLLINS Sister of Daniel. A family cousin from New York.

DANIEL COLLINS Brother of Millicent. A family cousin from New York.

JOSETTE duPRÉS Barnabas' fiance from Martinique who marries Jeremiah after being bewitched by Angélique.

ANDRE duPRÉS Josette duPrés' father, a wealthy plantation owner from Martinique.

NATALIE duPRÉS Andre's sister and Josette's aunt from Martinique.

ANGELIQUE BOUCHARD Josette's servant, a witch who marries Barnabas.

PETER BRADFORD Victoria Winters' lawyer who becomes her romantic interest.

BEN STOKES Collins family servant.

LIEUTENANT NATHAN FORBES Naval officer who marries Millicent.

SUKI FORBES Nathan Forbes' first wife.

REVEREND TRASK Fanatical witch-hunting minister.

RUBY TATE First victim of Barnabas Collins after he becomes a vampire.

MAUDE BROWNING A victim of Barnabas Collins.

BATHIA MAPES Good witch summoned to exorcise Barnabas Collins after he becomes a vampire.

REVEREND BLAND Minister who performs wedding of Barnabas Collins and Angélique.

NOAH GIFFORD Helper of Nathan Forbes.

JUDGE HANLEY Main judge at Victoria Winters' witchcraft trial.

JUDGE MATIGAN Judge who refuses to be Victoria Winters' attorney.

GHOST OF JEREMIAH COLLINS Avenging spirit of Jeremiah.

DR. THORNTON Treats Barnabas after Angélique's choking spell.

DANIELLE ROGET One-time lover of Peter Bradford. Reincarnated as Leona Eltridge, used as the life force to bring Eve to life in 1968.

## 1897

EDITH COLLINS Collins family head, grandmother of Edward, Judith, Quentin and Carl Collins.

QUENTIN COLLINS Brother of Edward, Judith and Carl, and husband of Jenny Collins.

JUDITH COLLINS Sister of Carl, Quentin and Edward.

EDWARD COLLINS Brother of Quentin, Judith and Carl. Nominal head of the Collins family.

CARL COLLINS Brother of Judith, Quentin and Edward.

JENNY COLLINS Quentin's estranged and insane wife and Magda Rakosi's sister.

LAURA COLLINS Edward's estranged wife, an immortal phoenix, returns to reclaim her children, Jamison and Nora Collins.

BARNABAS COLLINS Same Barnabas from 1969 who uses the I-Ching wands to go to 1897.

JAMISON COLLINS Son of Edward and Laura Collins and brother of Nora.

NORA COLLINS Daughter of Edward and Laura Collins and sister of Jamison.

SANDOR RAKOSI Gypsy husband of Magda.

MAGDA RAKOSI Gypsy fortune-teller. Wife of Sandor and sister of Jenny Collins.

ANGELIQUE duVal Barnabas' wife—the same Angélique from 1795.

EVAN HANLEY Lawyer and practitioner of black arts.

RACHEL DRUMMOND Worthington Hall teacher. Becomes governess to Jamison and Nora.

GREGORY TRASK Head of Worthington Hall. Husband of Minerva Trask and father of Charity Trask. He marries Judith Collins.

MINERVA TRASK Wife of Gregory Trask and mother of Charity.

CHARITY TRASK Daughter of Gregory and Minerva Trask.

DIRK WILKINS Caretaker at Collinwood.

BETH CHAVEZ Servant at Collinwood, looks after Jenny Collins.

COUNT ANDREAS PETOFI Comes to Collinsport to regain his hand, which was taken by gypsies in exchange for their help 150 years ago.

ARISTEDE Count Petofi's assistant.

JULIANKA Gypsy girl who offers to cure Quentin in exchange for the Hand of Count Petofi.

CHARLES DELAWARE TATE Artist given special abilities by Count Petofi.

DR. JULIA HOFFMAN Same Julia from 1969, uses I-Ching wands to go to 1897 to help Barnabas.

TIM SHAW Teacher at Worthington Hall who befriends Rachel Drummond.

KING JOHNNY ROMANO Gypsy looking for the Hand of Count Petofi.

AMANDA HARRIS Romantic interest of Quentin Collins created by Charles Delaware Tate when he painted her two years earlier.

KITTY SOAMES Lady Hampshire, a widow. Barnabas discovers she is the true reincarnation of Josette duPrés.

GARTH BLACKWOOD Master of Dartmoor Prison, recreated by Charles Delaware Tate.

SOPHIE BAKER Collinsport street walker who is Barnabas' first victim in 1897.

DORCAS TRILLING Worthington Hall teacher who is Quentin's first victim as the werewolf.

EZRA BRAITHWAITE Young Collinsport jeweler from whom Beth orders a silver pentagram.

PANSY FAYE Cockney music hall performer and mentalist.

HAND OF COUNT PETOFI Magical hand severed by the gypsies.

TESSIE KINCAID Woman murdered by Quentin as the werewolf.

MRS. FILLMORE Woman who has been looking after Quentin and Jenny's infant twins.

ISTVAN Gypsy asociate of King Johnny Romano.

GHOST OF ABRAHAM HOWELL Spirit who searches for his hand.

GHOST OF SANDOR RAKOSI Spirit raised by King Johnny Romano during Magda's gypsy trial.

GHOSTS OF ANDREAS, MARCO, STEFAN, PEDOR, SERGIO
Spirits of murderers who comprise a gypsy jury who try Magda for murder.

GHOST OF DORCAS TRILLING Spirit of the murdered school teacher.

GHOST OF EDITH COLLINS Spirit who appears to Quentin.

GHOST OF PANSY FAYE Spirit whose voice is heard by Carl Collins

GHOST OF MINERVA TRASK Spirit who appears to Judith Collins.

TATE'S CREATION Man who comes to life after Charles Delaware Tate draws him.

WANDA PAISLEY Experiment subject during I-Ching wand test by Count Petofi.

GHOST OF JEREMIAH COLLINS Spirit who appears to Kitty when she visits Jeremiah's grave.

GHOST OF JULIANKA Spirit of murdered gypsy.

GHOST OF TESSIE KINCAID Spirit of murdered woman.

DR. IAN READE Collinsport physician who examines Barnabas.

WIDOW ROMANO Gypsy wife of King Johnny Romano.

## 1949

ELIZABETH COLLINS STODDARD Wife of Paul Stoddard and Carolyn Stoddard's mother.

PAUL STODDARD Elizabeth's husband and Carolyn's father.

STRACK Leviathan who makes a bargain with Paul.

## 1995

BARNABAS COLLINS Same Barnabas as in present time.

DR. JULIA HOFFMAN Same Julia as in present time.

CAROLYN STODDARD HAWKES FREDERICKS Same Carolyn as in present time, but aged and insane.

QUENTIN COLLINS Same Quentin as in present time, but insane.

PROFESSOR TIMOTHY ELIOT STOKES Same Stokes as in present time, but aged and insane.

MRS. SARAH JOHNSON Same Mrs. Johnson as in present time, but aged and insane.

GHOST OF GERARD STILES Malevolent spirit from 1840.

GHOST OF DAPHNE HARRIDGE Benevolent spirit from 1840.

GHOST OF DAVID COLLINS Spirit of David from 1970.

GHOST OF HALLIE STOKES Spirit of Hallie from 1970.

VICTOR FLAGLER Local farmer.

ED Clerk at records office.

## 1840

DANIEL COLLINS Survivor from 1795 who is now the aged family head and father of Quentin and Gabriel Collins.

QUENTIN COLLINS Husband of Samantha and father of Tad Collins, son of Daniel and brother of Gabriel.

SAMANTHA COLLINS Wife of Quentin Collins, mother of Tad Collins, and sister of Roxanne Drew and Randall Drew.

TAD COLLINS Young son of Quentin and Samantha Collins.

GABRIEL COLLINS Son of Daniel Collins and husband of Edith Collins.

EDITH COLLINS Wife of Gabriel Collins.

BARNABAS COLLINS Same Barnabas from 1970 who is freed from his coffin by Julia.

DR. JULIA HOFFMAN COLLINS Same Julia from 1970 who pretends to be Barnabas' sister.

BEN STOKES Aged survivor from 1795 who lives at Collinwood. Carrie Stokes' grandfather.

CARRIE STOKES Young granddaughter of Ben Stokes who falls in love with Jeremy Grimes.

FLORA COLLINS Popular novelist who lives in Rose Cottage with her son Desmond Collins.

DESMOND COLLINS Son of Flora Collins.

GERARD STILES Friend of Quentin who becomes fully possessed by Judah Zachery.

LETICIA FAYE Cockney friend of Gerard who becomes partially possessed by Judah Zachery.

LAMAR TRASK Mortician owner of Trask Chapel.

ROXANNE DREW Samantha Collins and Randall Drew's sister. She is courted by Lamar Trask.

HEAD OF JUDAH ZACHERY Demonic relic brought back by Desmond as a present for Quentin.

DAPHNE HARRIDGE Governess to Tad and sister of Joanna Mills. She marries Gerard Stiles.

JUDAH ZACHERY 17th century warlock who has returned for revenge against the Collins family.

VALERIE COLLINS aka ANGELIQUE Same Angélique from 1795, using an alias.

LASZLO FERRARI Gypsy companion of Angélique.

CHARLES DAWSON Lawyer who brings Head of Judah Zachery to Gerard to possess him.

JOANNA MILLS Sister of Daphne Harridge and former lover of Quentin Collins.

RANDALL DREW Brother of Roxanne and Samantha.

OTIS GREENE Antique dealer struck dead after he sees the Head.

TIM BRAITHWAITE Collinsport man bribed by Desmond to help revive Judah Zachery.

HORTENSE SMILEY Collinwood governess killed by Judah.

MRS. PURDY Woman who reveals what happened to Joanna Mills.

GHOST OF AMADEUS COLLINS Spirit who orders Valerie to testify against Judah.

DR. WELLES Physician at sanitarium where Joanna was confined.

CONSTABLE JIM WARD Arrests Quentin for the murder of Randall Drew.

MILDRED WARD Wife of Jim Ward who accuses Quentin of witchcraft.

JEREMY GRIMES Son of Mordecai Grimes who falls in love with Carrie Stokes.

JUDGE VAIL Head of the tribunal which tries Quentin for witchcraft.

GHOST OF JOANNA MILLS Spirit of Daphne's sister who returns for revenge.

GHOST OF DANIEL COLLINS Spirit who returns for revenge against Gabriel.

GHOST OF ROXANNE DREW Spirit raised at a séance.

PROFESSOR TIMOTHY ELIOT STOKES Same Stokes from 1970. Travels to 1840 to help Julia.

MORDECAI GRIMES Collinsport farmer and father of Jeremy.

REVEREND JOHNSON Marries Daphne to Gerard.

GHOST OF HARRIET COLLINS Spirit summoned by Valerie to terrify Harriet's husband Daniel.

LORNA BELL Woman who comes to Trask's chapel to pay her respects to Roxanne.

JUDGE WILEY Holds the inquest involving the death of Randall Drew.

## 1692

AMADEUS COLLINS Judge at the trial of Judah Zachery, convinces Miranda duVal to testify against Judah.

MIRANDA duVal Servant who has come under the influence of warlock Judah Zachery. She later assumes the name of Angélique.

JUDAH ZACHERY Accused as a warlock, he is tried and condemned to be beheaded.

## 1970 PARALLEL TIME

BARNABAS COLLINS Same Barnabas as in present time.

DR. JULIA HOFFMAN Same Julia as in present time.

ELIZABETH COLLINS STODDARD Mother of Carolyn and sister of Roger.

ROGER COLLINS Brother of Elizabeth.

CAROLYN STODDARD LOOMIS Daughter of Elizabeth and wife of William H. Loomis

WILLIAM HOLLINGSHEAD LOOMIS Author husband of Carolyn.

QUENTIN COLLINS Cousin of Elizabeth and Roger. Father of Daniel. Married to Angélique, then Maggie.

MAGGIE EVANS COLLINS Second wife of Quentin and stepmother to Daniel.

ANGELIQUE STOKES A witch. Stepdaughter of Timothy Stokes and identical twin sister of Alexis. Quentin's first wife and mother of Daniel.

ALEXIS STOKES Angélique's identical twin sister and stepdaughter of Timothy.

TIMOTHY STOKES Angélique's and Alexis' stepfather and Hannah Stokes' brother.

HANNAH STOKES Psychic aunt of Angélique and Alexis. Sister of Timothy.

JULIA HOFFMAN Collinwood housekeeper.

DANIEL COLLINS Son of Quentin and Angélique.

AMY COLLINS Family cousin and sister of Chris Collins.

CHRIS COLLINS Family cousin and lawyer. Brother of Amy Collis.

CYRUS LONGWORTH Collinsport scientist and fiancé of Sabrina Stuart.

JOHN YAEGER Evil alter-ego of Cyrus.

SABRINA STUART Cyrus' lab assistant and girlfriend.*

BRUNO HESS Music composer who lives in Collinwood estate cottage.

BUFFIE HARRINGTON Blue Whale barmaid.

HORACE GLADSTONE Chemist supplier from Boston.

ROXANNE DREW Artificial woman created by Timothy and brought to life by Barnabas.

MR. TRASK Collinwood butler.

CLAUDE NORTH Mystery man involved with Roxanne.

GHOST OF DAMEON EDWARDS Spirit of Dameon, a family friend.

LARRY CHASE Successor to Chris Collins as family attorney.

VICTOR FLAGLER Local farmer

INSPECTOR HAMILTON Investigates the death of Angélique.

FRANK PAXTON Police investigator.

MINNIE DUVALL Buffie's apartment landlord.

STEVE Collinwood handyman

WILFRED W. BLOCK Caretaker for William H. and Carolyn Loomis

ALDON WICKS Farm house landlord of John Yaeger.

GHOST OF JOSHUA COLLINS Spirit of Joshua.

## 1841 PARALLEL TIME

MORGAN COLLINS Brother of Gabriel and Quentin Collins, son of Flora and Justin Collins. He marries Catherine Harridge.

JULIA COLLINS Sister of Justin Collins.

CATHERINE HARRIDGE Sister of Daphne Harridge who marries Morgan Collins and becomes pregnant by Bramwell Collins.

DAPHNE HARRIDGE Sister of Catherine Harridge. She marries Bramwell Collins.

FLORA COLLINS Wife of Justin Collins and mother of Gabriel, Morgan and Quentin Collins.

GABRIEL COLLINS Son of Flora and Justin Collins and brother of Morgan and Quentin Collins.

MELANIE COLLINS Adopted daughter of Justin and Flora Collins. She marries Kendrick Young.

STELLA YOUNG Secretary to Flora Collins and sister of Kendrick Young.

KENDRICK YOUNG Brother to Stella Young. He marries Melanie Collins.

QUENTIN COLLINS Son of Justin and Flora and brother of Morgan and Gabriel.

JUSTIN COLLINS Husband of Flora and father of Gabriel, Morgan and Quentin.

BRAMWELL COLLINS Son of Baranabas and Josette Collins. He marries Daphne Harridge and impregnates her sister Catherine Harridge.

SAMANTHA DREW Nurse at Collinwood.

LAMAR TRASK Same Trask from 1840. Shot by Barnabas, he dies in the Parallel Time room after he is caught there when it changes.

JOSETTE COLLINS Widow of Barnabas and mother of Bramwell.

CARRIE STOKES Daughter of Ben Stokes.

BEN STOKES Lives with daughter Carrie on the Collinwood estate.

GERARD STILES Collins family friend with psychic powers.

TIM BRAITHWAITE Local man hired by Gabriel to take his place in the locked room.

HARRIS Second Coachman who carries Melanie after she collapses from being bitten.

GHOST OF JUSTIN COLLINS Spirit who warns Melanie that the lottery must be held again.

GHOST OF BRUTUS COLLINS Spirit who threatens Morgan and Catherine.

### 1680 PARALLEL TIME

BRUTUS COOLINS Husband of Amanda Collins and business partner of James Forsythe.

JAMES FORSYTHE Brutus Collin's business partner who suspects he is embezzling funds.

AMANDA COLLINS Wife of Brutus Collins who shows her lover James Forsythe where to find proof against Brutus.

CONSTANCE COLLINS Sister of Brutus who has always taken his side against James and Amanda.

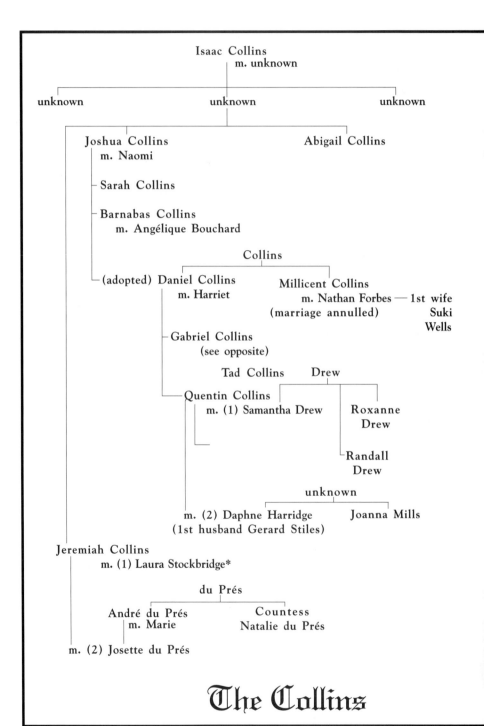

Isaac Collins
m. unknown

unknown       unknown       unknown

Joshua Collins       Abigail Collins
m. Naomi

Sarah Collins

Barnabas Collins
m. Angélique Bouchard

Collins

(adopted) Daniel Collins       Millicent Collins
m. Harriet       m. Nathan Forbes — 1st wife
(marriage annulled)    Suki
Wells

Gabriel Collins
(see opposite)

Tad Collins       Drew

Quentin Collins
m. (1) Samantha Drew       Roxanne
Drew

Randall
Drew

unknown

m. (2) Daphne Harridge       Joanna Mills
(1st husband Gerard Stiles)

Jeremiah Collins
m. (1) Laura Stockbridge*

du Prés

André du Prés       Countess
m. Marie       Natalie du Prés

m. (2) Josette du Prés

𝕿𝖍𝖊 𝕮𝖔𝖑𝖑𝖎𝖓𝖘

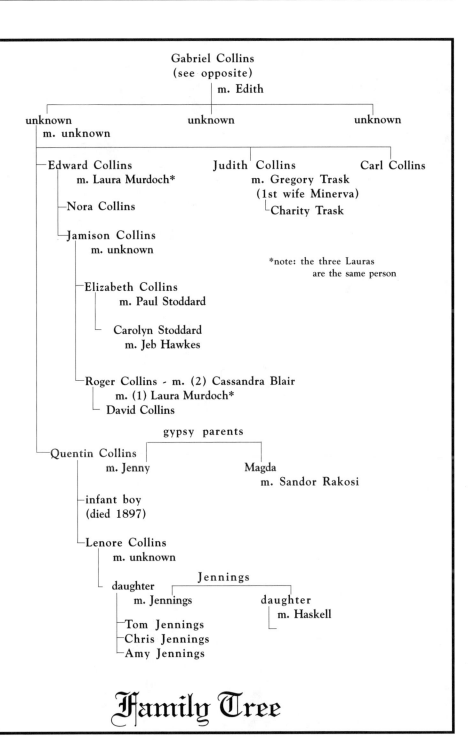

Gabriel Collins
(see opposite)
m. Edith

unknown                    unknown                    unknown
m. unknown

Edward Collins          Judith Collins          Carl Collins
m. Laura Murdoch*          m. Gregory Trask
(1st wife Minerva)
Nora Collins                    Charity Trask

Jamison Collins
m. unknown
*note: the three Lauras
are the same person

Elizabeth Collins
m. Paul Stoddard

Carolyn Stoddard
m. Jeb Hawkes

Roger Collins - m. (2) Cassandra Blair
m. (1) Laura Murdoch*
David Collins

gypsy parents

Quentin Collins
m. Jenny                    Magda
m. Sandor Rakosi

infant boy
(died 1897)

Lenore Collins
m. unknown

Jennings
daughter
m. Jennings                    daughter
m. Haskell
Tom Jennings
Chris Jennings
Amy Jennings

# 𝔉amily 𝔗ree

# Dark Shadows Milestones

Episode 1      Victoria Winters arrives at Collinwood.

Episode 51     Bill Malloy is found dead.

Episode 70     The ghost of Josette duPrés first appears.

Episode 108    Matthew Morgan kidnaps Victoria.

Episode 123    Laura Collins returns to Collinsport.

Episode 170    The first seance is held.

Episode 191    Laura attempts to lure David Collins into the fire.

Episode 193    Jason McGuire arrives at Collinwood.

Episode 201    Burke Devlin forces Roger Collins to admit his guilt.

Episode 210    Willie Loomis unchains Barnabas Collins' coffin.

Episode 212    Barnabas introduces himself at Collinwood as a cousin from England.

Episode 221    Barnabas meets Maggie Evans at the Collinsport Inn restaurant.

Episode 225/6  Barnabas attacks Maggie for the first time.

Episode 235    Barnabas kidnaps Maggie to make her the recreation of his lost love Josette.

Episode 255    The ghost of Sarah Collins appears outside Maggie's cell in the Old House basement.

Episode 270    Elizabeth Collins Stoddard reveals Jason's blackmail scheme.

Episode 284    Dr. Julia Hoffman comes to stay at Collinwood.

Episode 289    Julia discovers that Barnabas is a vampire.

Episode 341    Barnabas kills Dr. Dave Woodard with the help of Dr. Julia Hoffman.

Episode 348    Barnabas ages to 175 years after Julia attempts to cure him of his vampirism.

Episode 365    A seance is held to contact the spirit of Sarah, causing Victoria to be sent back to 1795.

Episode 366    Victoria is startled to meet the 18th century Collins family members, who resemble those she knows in the 20th century.

Episode 368/9  Angélique arrives from Martinique.

Episode 370    Josette and Barnabas are reunited.

Episode 374    Angélique uses witchcraft to cause Josette to fall in love with Jeremiah Collins.

Episode 393    The Collins family leave the Old House and move into the new Collinwood mansion.

Episode 397    Barnabas Collins marries Angélique Bouchard.

Episode 400    Abigail Collins summons Reverend Trask to exorcise the Old House, causing him to declare Victoria Winters is the witch.

| | |
|---|---|
| Episode 405 | Angélique curses Barnabas, causing him to become a vampire. |
| Episode 414 | As a vampire, Barnabas attacks his first victim, Ruby Tate, on the Collinsport docks. |
| Episode 425 | Josette jumps from Widows' Hill to her death. |
| Episode 437 | Victoria Winters is sentenced to hang for witchcraft. |
| Episode 442 | Barnabas bricks up Trask in the Old House basement. |
| Episode 461 | Victoria returns to 1968. |
| Episode 466 | Barnabas and Victoria are hospitalized following a car crash. Barnabas is temporarily cured with the help of Dr. Eric Lang. |
| Episode 473 | Wearing a black wig, Angélique shows up at Collinwood as Cassandra Collins, the bride of Roger Collins. |
| Episode 477 | Cassandra initiates the Dream Curse, intended to return the vampire curse to Barnabas. |
| Episode 478 | Maggie is the first person to have the dream. |
| Episode 485 | Barnabas and Julia assist Dr. Lang in his efforts to create an artificial man. |
| Episode 490 | Adam comes to life. |
| Episode 499 | Cassandra ages and causes Sam Evans to go blind. |
| Episode 521 | Nicholas Blair arrives at Collinwood. |
| Episode 535 | Barnabas has the dream. |
| Episode 548 | Cassandra dies. |
| Episode 556 | Angélique returns as a vampire. |
| Episode 565 | Tom Jennings attacks Julia. |
| Episode 595 | Eve, a mate for Adam, is created. |
| Episode 606 | Angélique attacks Barnabas. |
| Episode 626 | Adam kills Eve. |
| Episode 633/4 | Nicholas is destroyed. |
| Episode 636 | Jeff Clark discovers he is Peter Bradford. |
| Episode 639 | David and Amy Jennings contact the ghost of Quentin Collins on an old disconnected telephone. |
| Episode 646 | The ghosts of Quentin Collins and Beth Chavez appear and possess David and Amy. |
| Episode 650 | Victoria and Jeff disappear into the past. |
| Episode 661 | Barnabas returns to 1796 to save Victoria. |
| Episode 672 | The werewolf attacks Carolyn Stoddard. |
| Episode 693 | Professor T. Eliot Stokes attempts to exorcise Collinwood. |
| Episode 694 | The family abandons Collinwood as the ghost of Quentin takes control. |
| Episode 700 | Using the I-Ching wands, Barnabas travels to the year 1897. |
| Episode 703 | Barnabas introduces himself at Collinwood as a cousin from England. |

| Episode 710 | Quentin Collins and Evan Hanley perform a black magic ceremony which causes Angélique to appear. |
| Episode 714 | Edith Collins' will reveals that Judith Collins is the head of Collinwood. |
| Episode 718 | Angélique confronts Barnabas. |
| Episode 720 | A crazed Jenny Collins stabs Quentin and leaves him to die. |
| Episode 721 | Angélique causes Quentin to rise as a zombie. |
| Episode 729 | Laura Collins arrives to reclaim her children Jamison and Nora from Edward Collins. |
| Episode 748 | Quentin accidentally kills Jenny, the sister of the gypsy Magda Rakosi. |
| Episode 750 | Magda places a werewolf curse on Quentin. |
| Episode 751 | Quentin transforms into the werewolf for the first time. |
| Episode 771 | Carl Collins brings music hall performer Pansy Faye to Collinsport. |
| Episode 778 | The hand of Count Petofi first appears. |
| Episode 786 | Charity Trask dreams of a romantic duet and dance with Quentin, singing *I Wanna Dance With You*. |
| Episode 793 | Victor Fenn-Gibbon, alias Count Petofi, arrives at Collinwood. |
| Episode 801/2 | Jamison Collins is possessed by the spirit of Petofi. |
| Episode 812 | Quentin meets Amanda Harris. |
| Episode 816 | Count Petofi imprisons Barnabas by chaining him in his coffin. |
| Episode 837 | Julia arrives in 1897 to save Barnabas. |
| Episode 844 | Barnabas meets Lady Kitty Hampshire, the true reincarnation of Josette. |
| Episode 845 | Possessed by Pansy, Charity Trask stakes Barnabas' doppelganger. |
| Episode 856 | Petofi's mind takes over Quentin's body. |
| Episode 885 | Barnabas follows Josette to 1796. |
| Episode 886 | Barnabas is captured by the Leviathans. |
| Episode 889 | Barnabas is returned to 1969. |
| Episode 891 | Barnabas gives the naga box to Philip and Megan Todd. |
| Episode 905 | Suffering from amnesia, Quentin appears in the present under the name of Grant Douglas. |
| Episode 913/4 | The Leviathan child Michael appears. |
| Episode 923 | Julia discovers that Angélique is back, married to Skyler Rumson. |
| Episode 934 | Amanda is crushed under a cavein. |
| Episode 935 | The Leviathan adult Jebez Hawkes appears. |
| Episode 950 | Jeb turns Barnabas back into a vampire. |
| Episode 953 | Nicholas Blair returns to assist the Leviathans. |
| Episode 969 | Visions of Parallel Time are seen in an abandoned room in the east wing of Collinwood. |

| Episode 980 | Barnabas flees to parallel time to avoid harming Maggie. |
| Episode 981 | Quentin arrives with his bride Maggie Evans. |
| Episode 982 | William H. Loomis chains Barnabas in his coffin. |
| Episode 988 | Cyrus Longworth turns into John Yaeger for the first time. |
| Episode 1001 | Alexis Stokes is murdered by her twin sister Angélique. |
| Episode 1036 | Julia passes into Parallel Time and kills her look-alike, Hoffman the housekeeper. |
| Episode 1056 | Roxanne Drew comes to life. |
| Episode 1061 | Barnabas and Julia leave Parallel Time and discover they have traveled forward to Collinwood in the year 1995, when the mansion is in ruins. |
| Episode 1062 | Barnabas and Julia encounter an insane Carolyn. |
| Episode 1063 | The ghost of Gerard Stiles appears for the first time. |
| Episode 1067 | The ghost of Daphne Harridge appears for the first time. |
| Episode 1070 | Barnabas and Julia arrive back in 1970. |
| Episode 1097 | David Collins and Hallie Stokes are possessed by the spirits of Tad Collins and Carrie Stokes. |
| Episode 1108 | Sebastian Shaw takes Maggie to Windcliff. |
| Episode 1109 | Gerard's ghost enlists a band of pirate zombies to destroy Collinwood. Julia escapes to 1840. |
| Episode 1112 | Barnabas is released from his coffin in 1840. |
| Episode 1130 | Leticia Faye is possessed by the head of Judah Zachery. |
| Episode 1131 | Angélique returns to Collinwood. |
| Episode 1132 | Daphne arrives to be governess at Collinwood. |
| Episode 1133 | Barnabas meets Roxanne Drew. |
| Episode 1165 | Quentin is placed on trial for witchcraft. |
| Episode 1179/80 | Joanna Mills appears in the courtroom. |
| Episode 1186 | Daphne sees a vision of Parallel Time in the abandoned east wing room at Collinwood. |
| Episode 1197 | Angélique saves Quentin and Desmond Collins. |
| Episode 1205 | Bramwell Collins interrupts the wedding ceremony of Morgan Collins and Catherine Harridge. |
| Episode 1212 | The family lottery is held. |
| Episode 1219 | Catherine informs Bramwell that she is pregnant with his child. |
| Episode 1222 | The spirit of James Forsythe possesses Morgan Collins. |
| Episode 1243 | Morgan locks Bramwell and Catherine in the cursed room at Collinwood. |
| Episode 1245 | The final show. |

## TV SERIES PRODUCTION CREDITS

JOE ADAMS Unit Manager/Production Supervisor
MICHAEL ALTIERI Video
ANTHONY AMODEO aka TONY AMODEO Audio
SYD ANDREWS Stage Manager
BIL BAIRD Bat
FRANK BAILEY Audio
ANDY BALINT Video
PATRICIA BANNON Associate Director
GLORIA BANTA Assistant to the Producer
ERNEST BAXTER Stage Manager
NICK BESINK Video
ROZ BIGELOW Lighting Director
PATRICIA BANNON Associate Director
GIRISH BHARGAVA Videotape Editor
ED BLAINEY Sound Effects
GARY BLOHM Unit Manager
NEIL BOBRICK Audio
MICHAEL BROCKMAN Unit Manager
LEE BURTON Video
JOE CALDWELL Writer
NICK CARBONARO Audio
ROBERT COBERT Music Composer
RANDY COHEN Videotape Editor
JOHN CONNOLLY Lighting Director
ROBERT COSTELLO Producer
DAN CURTIS Executive Producer/Director
JOHN DAPPER Scenic Design
ART DeCENZO Music Supervisor
BILL DEGENHARDT Technical Director
JOHN DeVOE Stage Manager
GEORGE DiCENZO Assistant to the Producer/Associate Producer
GARY DUDA Videotape Editor
DENNIS EGER Makeup
CLEM EGOLF Unit Manager

RALPH ELLIS Writer
LEE FAIRCHILD Stage Manager
BERNARD FAMBROUGH Sound Effects
MELISSA FOSTER Production Assistant/Assistant to the Producer
CHUCK GARDNER Videotape Editor
STUART GOODMAN Cameraman
FRANK GUILIANO Videotape Editor
SAM HALL Writer
IRENE HAMALAIN Hair Stylist
MEL HANDELSMAN Lighting Director
NANCY HARWICH Assistant to the Producer
LEONARD HIRSHFIELD Audio
ALAN HOLDEN Audio
MILT HONIG Graphic Arts
BILL ITKIN Lighting Director
PENBERRY JONES Director
DEET JONKER Technical Director
DENNIS KANE Director
HENRY KAPLAN Director
AL KASSEL Unit Manager
KAREN KAYSER Production Assistant
JACK KELLY Audio
HECTOR KICELIAN Video
TOM KING Stage Manager
RENE LABAT Videotape Editor
FRED LABIB Videotape Editor
LEE LANGSTON Video
JACK LeGOMS Hair Stylist
BOB LIVINGSTON Associate Director
MARVIN LONG Stage Manager
VINCENT LOSCALZO Makeup
J.J. LUPATKIN Technical Director
LOU MARCHAND Technical Director
MALCOLM MARMORSTEIN Writer
TOM McCUE Audio

*Sam Hall*     *Lela Swift*     *Robert Costello*

KEN McEWEN Associate Director/
   Assistant Director
MARY McKINLEY Costume Design
EVERETT MELOSH Lighting Director
EDWARD MELTON Stage Manager
MICHAEL MICHAELS Video
PETER MINER Producer
DICK MOLLER Video
PAT MORAN Production Assistant
BILL MORRIS Technical Director
ALEX MOSKOVIC Videotape Editor
RAMSE MOSTOLLER aka MOSTOLLER
   Costume Design
PETE MURPHY Videotape Editor
CHESTER NOWEL Videotape Editor
JOHN OLFF Stage Manager
SY PAGET Audio
DIANE PALIOTTA Assistant to the Producer
CHESTER PAWLAK Videotape Editor
MURDOCK PEMBERTON Stage Manager
RUDY PICIRILLO Video
PATRICK PLEVEN Unit Manager
HENRY PLIMACK Audio
ALAN POLLACK Associate Director
CARL POLLACK Videotape Editor
ED PONTORNO Video
PETE PRESCOTT Sound Effects
JUNE PULEO Wardrobe
ALAN PULTZ Associate Director
MICHAEL REAM aka MIKE REAM
   Assistant Director/Associate Director
FRED RIPPLE Audio
ERSKIN ROBERTS Videotape Editor
HARRIET ROHR Production
   Assistant/Assistant to the Producer
DICK ROSE Audio
DANNY ROSENSON Videotape Editor
TERRY ROSS Sound Effects
BERT ROTH Makeup

HAZEL ROY Costume Design
FRANK RUBIN Videotape Editor
GORDON RUSSELL Writer
INDRA SADOO Videotape Editor
MANFRED SCHORN Videotape Editor
JOHN SEDWICK Director
HOWARD SHARROTT Lighting Director
STANLEY SIMMONS Costume Design
ROSS SKIPPER Video
AL SMITH Technical Director
DICK SMITH Special Makeup
RON SPROAT Writer
MICHAEL STANISLAVSKY Associate
   Director
BOB STEINBACK Videotape Editor
CHARLES STEPHENSEN Videotape Editor
ALEX STEVENS Stunt Coordinator
JACK SULLIVAN (aka SEAN DHU
   SULLIVAN) Associate Director/Director
FRANCIS SWANN Writer
LELA SWIFT Director/Producer
ROY THOMPSON Video
DAVID THUESEN Audio
EDITH TILLES Hairdresser
SY TOMASHOFF Scenic Design/Associate
   Producer
STEVE VERNICK Technical Director
ART WALLACE Writer/Story Development
PAUL WATHEN Unit Manager
JOHN WEAVER Associate Director/Director
SYBIL WEINBERGER Music Supervisor
DICK WEISS Lighting Director
DIANA WENMAN Assistant to the Producer
GEORGE WHITAKER Technical Director
DAVID WHITE aka DAVE WHITE Video
JOHN WOODS cameraman
Fashions courtesy of Ohrbach's
Miss Scott's clothes courtesy of Junior
   Sophisticates

*Edith Tilles*

*Vincent Loscalzo*

*Diane Paliotta*

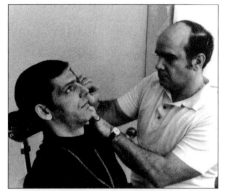

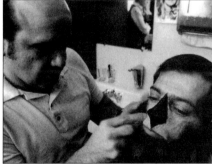

*Vincent Loscalzo transforms
Alex Stevens into the Werewolf.*

# Episode Tallies

## DIRECTORS

There were 9 different directors

Dan Curtis—21 episodes
Penberry Jones—5 episodes
Dennis Kane—5 episodes
Henry Kaplan—293 episodes
John Sedwick—254 episodes
Jack Sullivan—12 episodes
Sean Dhu Sullivan—49 episodes
Lela Swift—580 episodes
John Weaver—6 episodes

## WRITERS

There were 9 different writers

Joe Caldwell—63 episodes
Ralph Ellis—2 episodes
Sam Hall—316 episodes
Malcolm Marmorstein—80 episodes
Gordon Russell—366 episodes
Ron Sproat—214 episodes
Francis Swann—36 episodes
Art Wallace- 65 episodes
Violet Welles—84 episodes

## OPENING VOICE-OVERS

Fifty different actors spoke the following number of episode openings:

Humbert Allen Astredo—12
Nancy Barrett—116
Emory Bass—1
Joan Bennett—74
Chris Bernau—1
Clarice Blackburn—23
Don Briscoe—11
Vala Clifton—2
Mary Cooper—2
Don Crabtree—1
Terry Crawford—7
Joel Crothers—1
Thayer David—45
Roger Davis—9
Jane Draper—2
Betsy Durkin—1
Louis Edmonds—33
Elizabeth Eis—1
Jonathan Frid—12
Kay Frye—1
Grayson Hall—156
Colin Hamilton—1
John Harkins—4
David Henesy—3
Cavada Humphrey—2

Kate Jackson—13
John Karlen—24
Jerry Lacy—19
Paula Laurence—2
Peter Lombard—1
Ken McEwen—3
Diana Millay—3
Alexandra Moltke—387
Vince O'Brien—1
Lara Parker—66
Norman Parker—1
Dennis Patrick—2
Chris Pennock—12
Keith Prentice—2
Lisa Richards—5
Ed Riley—1
Kathryn Leigh Scott—75
David Selby—46
James Storm—12
Gail Strickland—1
Michael Stroka—6
Brian Sturdivant—1
Virginia Vestoff—10
Marie Wallace—9
Donna Wandrey—2

# SHADOWS FACTS

☩ In the beginning, each episode's opening voiceover is spoken by Alexandra Moltke, who starts by saying, "My name is Victoria Winters," although this line is omitted by mistake in episode 6. She speaks this line for the last time in episode 274. After this, the voiceover is spoken by various actresses, including Alexandra, and, later, actors, who do not identify their characters, for the remainder of the show's run.

☩ Alexandra Moltke left the show because she was going to have a baby. Her departure was abrupt; her last episode was 627, and in 630 Betsy Durkin was introduced as Victoria Winters. Carolyn Groves assumed the role for the character's final four appearances.

☩ Bob Lloyd is the ABC announcer who provides the closing voiceover beginning in episode 1: "Dark Shadows is a Dan Curtis production." The last day on which his voice is heard is September 27, 1967, at the end of episode 328. During a few subsequent episodes, the closing voiceover is made by the actress who speaks the opening voiceover and who also makes the mid-break announcement. The actresses who make these announcements are: Grayson Hall, for episodes 332 and 333 on October 3 and 4, Alexandra Moltke for episodes 334, 336 and 338 on October 5, 9, and 11, and Joan Bennett for episode 335 on October 6th.

☩ Bil Baird, noted puppeteer, supplied the bat that bit Barnabas Collins, leading to the curse of the vampire, in episode 405, repeated in episode 406. Other bats by Bil Baird appear in episodes 403, sent by Angélique Collins to spy on Barnabas, and in 330, repeated in 331, sent by Barnabas to attack David Collins.

# Ratings

## NATIONAL VIEWERSHIP

| Date | Rating | Share | Daily Homes | Weekly Viewers |
|------|--------|-------|-------------|----------------|
| July, 1966 | 4.3 | 17.8 | 2,640,000 | 9,000,000+ |
| June, 1967 | 5.0 | 19.6 | 2,750,000 | 10,000,000+ |
| June, 1968 | 7.5 | 28.8 | 4,200,000 | 16,000,000+ |
| 1968-1969* | 8.4 | 27 | 4,790,000 | 18,000,000+ |
| 1969-1970* | 7.3 | 23 | 4,230,000 | 16,000,000+ |
| 1970-1971* | 5.3 | 16 | 3,130,000 | 12,000,000+ |

Source: Nielsen Ratings       *Season Averages

A rating represents the percentage of homes with a television that are viewing the program. The share refers to the program's percentage of viewing homes with sets actually in use while the program is airing. For example, the July, 1966 figures indicate that 4.3% of all homes with television were watching *Dark Shadows* and that 17.8% of all homes watching television were viewing *Dark Shadows*.

The 1971 figures reflected lower ratings which partly resulted from lower clearances. Beginning in the fall of 1970, several ABC stations across the country had taken the show off due to falling viewership. Ironically, Nielsen ratings for March of 1971—the last full month that *Dark Shadows* was on the air—revealed that viewership of *Dark Shadows* had risen in its final weeks.

*Don Briscoe relaxes in the studio rehearsal hall.*

## TV-Q RANKINGS

The TV-Q Rankings rate programs and personalities for their recognizability and popularity. With a total Q-score of 37, *Dark Shadows* tied *Bewitched* for the number one spot for daytime television in the spring of 1968.

By achieving an average Q-score of 46 among young women and female teens, *Dark Shadows* topped all other daytime shows to rank number one in that demographic group.

### The Best Liked Daytime TV Series—March, 1968
Top Three Programs

| Total Audience | Q-Score | Females Age 12-34 | Q-Score |
|---|---|---|---|
| 1. *Dark Shadows* | 37 | 1. *Dark Shadows* | 46 |
| 2. *Bewitched* | 37 | 2. *Another World* | 41 |
| 3. *Another World* | 36 | 3. *Bewitched* | 40 |

Source: March, 1968 TV-Q

*Carl Collins (John Karlen) and Pansy Faye (Kay Frye).*

# Syndication

---

**S**HORTLY BEFORE *DARK SHADOWS* ENDED ITS ORIGINAL RUN ON ABC-TV, it was announced that the series would be seen in reruns on local stations. This was a landmark declaration, since no other daytime soap opera had ever been rebroadcast.

It was highly unusual for a former daytime program with such a large inventory of episodes (1,225 shows) to be offered for repeat showings. The large number of episodes would mean high residual payments for the actors, writers and directors. That factor, along with general resistance from television stations, kept the series from immediately rerunning as planned. The station managers weren't entirely convinced there would be a large enough audience to watch an extended daily serial which had just finished a widely viewed network run.

Around this time, the Federal Communications Commission forced the networks to sell off their domestic syndication companies, which further delayed the launch of *Dark Shadows* repeats in the United States. ABC Films, which owned the syndication rights for *Dark Shadows* and had been selling the series in foreign markets, was spun off into a new independent company entitled Worldvision Enterprises.

By 1975, Worldvision had mounted an aggressive campaign to place *Dark Shadows* reruns on stations across America. To maximize the series' chance of success, Worldvision chose to skip over the early 1966-67 shows and begin the syndication package with episode 210—the introduction of vampire Barnabas Collins.

Stations were still cautious about the unorthodox broadcasting of an old daily network soap opera, and initially only 130 episodes-running six months—were released into syndication. This cycle ended with episode 340, the day before Dr. Woodard's murder.

Out of the handful of stations who initially aired the reruns, WOKR-TV in Rochester, New York, was especially successful—rating number one with

*Dark Shadows* in the 4:00-4:30 afternoon time period. Partially as a result, Worldvision released another 130 episodes in 1976, making an entire year's worth of episodes available for rebroadcast. Lucky viewers were now able to see the 1795 flashback for the first time since 1967-68.

However, not enough cities had picked up the reruns to make it cost-effective to release additional episodes. For the next few years, the syndication package remained limited to the first 260 Barnabas episodes. Various stations would purchase the batch and then run out of episodes, unable to offer viewers the remaining years of the show. By the early 1980s, the syndication of *Dark Shadows* died down.

With the growth of new UHF independent stations throughout the United States, Worldvison decided to give the show another push. The 1981-82 relaunch was fueled in part by a group of NBC affiliates, including flagship station WNBC-TV in New York, who had purchased the repeats for airing beginning in the spring of 1982.

Unfortunately, in highly competetive markets such as New York, demands and expectations were intense. Where *Dark Shadows* was not the blockbuster that station managements expected, it was taken off the air, usually after six months or a year.

At this time, *Dark Shadows* reruns fared better on smaller independent stations which possessed more reasonable aspirations. As a sign of good faith, Worldvision began with releasing more episodes (beyond 260) for rebroadcast. But another setback occurred when one of the supporting stations, WWAC-TV in Atlantic City, went out of business in early 1983. At that time only 50 additional episodes had been issued for a second year of syndication, and the release of further episodes was stopped.

By the fall of 1983, additional stations had progressed to the point of demanding more episodes. Worldvision released an additional 210 shows to complete a second full year of syndication, making a total of 520 episodes available, including the first few weeks of the 1897 storyline.

In March, 1982, Public Broadcasting station WYES-TV in New Orleans had quietly become the first non-commercial station to air *Dark Shadows* reruns. The show proved to be an incredible success at fund-raising time and brought an expanded viewership to the station. As a result, the New Jersey Network system of four PBS stations covering virtually all of New Jersey and parts of New York, Pennsylvania, and Connecticut, picked up *Dark Shadows* for airing in the fall of 1983. Slotted in the early evening news hour, the show was extremely well received.

Meanwhile, several other stations reached another halt by the middle of 1984, when they were denied a third year of episodes to rerun. Once again, the sporadic nature of *Dark Shadows'* syndication and the difficulty in coordinating enough stations to finance the release of more shows seemed insurmountable. A major obstacle was the inability to synchronize stations to need the "new" episodes at the same time. If a station ran out of shows, they usually wanted additional ones immediately.

In the fall of 1985, New Jersey Network completed airing the available batch of 520 shows, and they wanted more. Aided by the support of the *Dark Shadows* Festival fan convention, NJN had achieved success with the show, and the loyal viewers were clamoring for the rest of the series. With the help of a few other stations who had already exhausted all of the available episodes, NJN was able to debut a third year of syndication, offering 260 more shows in reruns for the first time. This would enable devotees to view the remainder of the 1897 story through the beginning of 1970 Parallel Time.

Spurred by NJN's success, more PBS stations picked up *Dark Shadows* reruns. Even so, a management change at NJN brought about the unexpected termination of *Dark Shadows* in October, 1986, at the close of the third syndicated year. There was still nearly a full year of episodes remaining to be seen.

Over the next couple of years, prospects for releasing the final year into syndication wavered back and forth. Unfortunately, a renewed sense of traditionalism at PBS stations caused the series to gradually disappear from member stations, despite its years of popularity.

By 1990, *Dark Shadows* reruns had completed rerunning in the various markets and was no longer airing anywhere in the United States. The home video releases of the episodes had begun in late 1989 and appeared to be the only likely distribution method for the series—including the elusive final year and the first year before Barnabas.

Once more a new lease on life was granted in the form of an upstart national cable service, the Sci-Fi Channel. It was announced that *Dark Shadows* was the channel's first series purchase and that the entire run of 1,225 episodes would begin in 1990 or 1991. Due to the increased competition of the cable industry and other financial matters, Sci-Fi delayed its launch until September of 1992, after being purchased by the USA Network.

Eventually, Sci-Fi aired the full run of *Dark Shadows*, beginning with Victoria Winters' 1966 Episode 1 arrival and also including an abridged version of MPI's reconstruction of the infamous missing episode 1219. Sci-Fi aired two episodes back-to-back on a daily basis (later reducing the schedule to one episode on Fridays) and began reairing the series for a second time in March of 1995.

Although the entire series has been released on home video, the traditional broadcast on (cable) television, remains a vital form of exposure for *Dark Shadows*. For as long as it chooses to air the program, the Sci-Fi Channel possesses exclusive broadcast rights.

## BROADCAST SYNDICATION CYCLES

As noted in the syndication history section, Worldvision Enterprises began syndicating *Dark Shadows* reruns with Original Episode 210, the introduction of Barnabas Collins.

During its initial syndication from 1975-1990, the Worldvision package was comprised of six-month cycles, containing 130 episodes each. It is important to mention that these cycles were specifically structured for broadcast syndication sales, where individual stations would purchase the reruns in cycles. Worldvision eventually released six cycles, covering approximately the middle three years of the series.

After an episode was placed out of sequence in the reruns and six missing episodes were added to the syndication package, some of the cycles were revised, as detailed below.

Broadcast Syndication Cycle I
Original Episodes 210-340
(Worldvision Rerun Episodes 1-130)

Syndication Cycle II
Original Episodes 341-472
(Worldvision Rerun Episodes 131-260)

Syndication Cycle III
Original Episodes 473-603
(Worldvision Rerun Episodes 261-390)*

Syndication Cycle IV
Original Episodes 604-735
(Worldvision Rerun Episodes 391-519)**

Syndication Cycle V
Original Episodes 736-867
(Worldvision Rerun Episodes 520-645#

Syndication Cycle IV
Original Episodes 868-1001
(Worldvision Rerun Episodes 646-775##

---

*Cycle III originally included Original Episode 771 out of sequence as Worldvision Rerun 299. It was subsequently relocated to its proper sequence in Cycle V and renumbered as Episode 554A. As a result, there is no longer a show numbered Rerun 299. At the same time, missing Original Episode 509 was added to Cycle III and designated as Rerun 296A.

** Cycle IV originally included Original Episode 736 (Worldvision Rerun Episode 520), but that show was moved to Cycle V when missing Original Episode 683 was added to Cycle IV and designated as Rerun 467A.

# Cycle V originally included Original Episodes 868-873 (Worldvision Rerun Episodes 646-651), but those shows were moved to Cycle VI when the out of sequence Original Episode 771 was moved to Cycle V and designated as Rerun 554A, and when missing Original Episodes 797, 801/802, 805, and 813 were also added to Cycle V, designated as Reruns 579A, 582A, 585, and 592A respectively.

## Cycle VI originally included Original Episodes 1002-1007 (Worldvision Rerun Episodes 776-781), but those shows were removed after Original Episodes 868-873 were added to Cycle VI as described the the preceding paragraph.

## OUT OF SYNC SHADOWS

As mentioned above, Original Episode 771 was originally rerun out of sequence in syndication. A brief synopsis follows:

In 1897, Carl Collins returns from Atlantic City with Pansy Faye, a mentalist and music hall performer. In a trance, Pansy declares that Dirk Wilkins has been murdered. Later, Barnabas finds Pansy dead at the Old House.

## CABLE TV RERUNS VS BROADCAST SYNDICATION

When a program such as *Dark Shadows* is sold to a cable television channel for exclusive airings, it means that regular local broadcast channels or other cable channels cannot buy the program for the period of exclusivity. This is different from syndication, which involves selling a program to individual television outlets in different cities.

The sale of *Dark Shadows* to the Sci-Fi Channel cable outlet, which began airing the series in 1992, also meant that the final and first years of the show could be rerun for the first time, primarily because of lower residual payments to the actors, writers, and directors for cable usage.

Accordingly, the Sci-Fi Channel began *Dark Shadows* reruns with Original Episode 1 and repeated the entire series, through Original Episode 1245.

Should *Dark Shadows* return to syndication on regular local broadcast stations, the first and final years of shows remain unavailable for rerunning unless enough stations are willing to buy them simultaneously, allowing enough funds to cover the extensive broadcast residual costs to the actors, writers, and directors. However, the entire series remains available for reairing on cable channels indefinitely.

## KINESCOPED SHADOWS

Each episode of *Dark Shadows* was recorded and broadcast on the then network standard 2-inch videotape. In addition, through the fall of 1970, ABC-TV also made filmed kinescope copies of each episode. These kinescopes were shot in black-and-white on 16mm film. Even when *Dark Shadows* went to color, the kinescopes were still filmed only in black and white. (The networks rarely made color kinescopes.)

Kinescopes are simply copies of a program which are filmed off a television monitor. Kinescopes were conceived in the early days of television, before videotape was invented, as a method to preserve shows that were broadcast live. Although videotape became available in the late 1950s, the television networks continued to simultaneously make kinescopes of shows that were presented live or originated on videotape. Although vastly inferior in quality to video, kinescopes were still made in the mid-1960s because various stations across the country did not always telecast certain shows at the exact time that the network would transmit them. Since some stations did not yet have the expensive videotape equipment needed to record a program for a later playback, the network would provide filmed kinescope copies within days of the original broadcast.

By the fall of 1970, the kinescope process had become outdated, and ABC ceased making them for *Dark Shadows*.

Fortunately, the kinescope negatives for *Dark Shadows* were preserved along with the videotape masters. In the years since the episodes first aired on ABC, some of the videotape masters have been lost or damaged. This is why, when the series is shown in reruns and on home video, filmed kinescope prints are seen for several of the episodes. These episodes are now seen only in black and white, even after the series went into color.

The following is a list of *Dark Shadows* episodes which only exist in kinescope form:

Episodes 83, 120, 145, 149, 151, 193, 194, 211, 260, 296, 300, 318, 320, 323, 325, 335, 341, 344, 351, 352, 368/369, 437, 509, 683, 797, 813, 1006, 1017

Episodes 289 and 367 were previously rerun in kinescope form, but videotape masters were located in 1989 and have replaced the kinescope versions.

## MISSING SHADOWS

The fact that tapes and filmed kinescopes of all but one of the *Dark Shadows* episodes have survived is nothing short of a miracle. Very few tapes of other 1960s daytime dramas still exist. At the time, no one had any idea that there would be a future use for those shows. In more ways than one, *Dark Shadows* was a ground-breaking series.

When *Dark Shadows* was activated in syndication, it was discovered that videotapes of several of the shows were missing. Fortunately, filmed kinescope copies were usually found to replace the lost tapes. However, a few episodes proved elusive.

Episodes 509, 683, 797, 801/802, 805, 813 were skipped in the 1975-1990 syndication package. This was because the syndicator, Worldvision Enterprises, did not realize that kinescopes for these shows were available. One of the shows, Episode 805, had not been rerun because the master tape was ripped.

However, when *Dark Shadows* was licensed for home video release in 1989, extensive research was conducted to locate the missing shows.

Black and white kinescope negatives were found for Episodes 509, 683, 797, and 813. In addition, the color videotape master for Episode 801/802 was located, and the damaged color tape for Episode 805 was salvaged by inserting sepia-tinted kinescope footage for the brief segment that was damaged on the tape master.

It was during this search that the copies of two other syndicated episodes were upgraded for home video. A Spanish videotape copy was found of Episode 289, which had been rerun only in kinescope form. The English kinescope audio was merged with the Spanish video for a greatly enhanced picture.

Also, a color videotape master was found for Episode 367, which had previously been rerun in kinescope form.

Short descriptions of the formerly missing episodes follow:

### EPISODE 289
Outside the Old House, Dr. Julia Hoffman spies on Barnabas Collins and sneaks into the basement after sunrise. She discovers Barnabas in his coffin.

### EPISODE 367
In 1795, Victoria Winters is menaced by Abigail Collins, meets Jeremiah Collins and is interviewed by Joshua Collins to become the new governess.

### EPISODE 509
Sam Evans befriends Adam, but Adam runs away when Professor Stokes arrives at Sam's cottage. Stokes questions Victoria about her experiences in 1795.

### EPISODE 683
The ghost of Beth Chavez appears to Chris Jennings and leads him to discover a child's coffin which he and Barnabas Collins dig up.

### EPISODE 797
Quentin Collins, Barnabas, and Magda hold a seance to contact Julianka's spirit, hoping to find a way to remove the werewolf curse from Quentin.

### EPISODE 801/802
Victor Fenn-Gibbon admits that he is Count Petofi. Quentin learns that Tim Shaw has Petofi's severed hand. Jamison Collins is possessed by Petofi.

### EPISODE 805
Barnabas locks up the possessed Jamison in an Old House basement cell. Gregory Trask informs Evan Hanley of his plan to take control of the Collins family.

### EPISODE 813
Still possessed by Petofi, Jamison forces Nora Collins to give him the box she's been hiding which contains the magical severed hand of Petofi's.

# THE LOST EPISODE

The final year of *Dark Shadows*, 1970-71, had not been seen anywhere in over twenty years when MPI began issuing those episodes on home video in 1992-1993. While the videotapes were being duplicated for the MPI releases, it was learned that the master for Episode 1219 was missing. The episode had originally aired on February 25, 1971. Inside the storage case for that show was an unmarked reel of blank videotape from the ABC-TV library.

Although videotape masters for other *Dark Shadows* had been lost over the years, there had always been filmed kinescope copies to replace them. Unfortunately, this was not possible with Episode 1219, because this episode originated after ABC-TV had ceased making kinescopes in the fall of 1970.

Realizing that a lost episode would be traumatic for the fans, MPI decided to reconstruct Episode 1219 by using an audio recording and enlisting the services of *Dark Shadows* actress Lara Parker (Catherine Harridge).

A reasonably clear audio copy of the lost show was provided by longtime *Dark Shadows* fan Wendy "Josette" Kernaghan. The opening voice-over, originally read by Keith Prentice (Morgan Collins), was incomplete on the audio tape, so it was rerecorded by Lara Parker.

MPI added to the audio by editing together still-frame pictures of the characters from surrounding episodes. Each actor was depicted in the correct setting and with the correct wardrobe. In addition, Lara Parker summarized the episode with wrap-around host segments prior to each act.

Footage from the closing scene of Episode 1218 and footage from the opening scene of Episode 1220 was also utilized in the Episode 1219 reconstruction as seen on the original broadcast of Episode 1219.

An abridged version of the reconstructed lost episode has been shown on the Sci-Fi Channel, consisting only of Lara Parker's host segments. The complete audio of Episode 1219 and the full still-frame assembly is only available on MPI Home Video *Dark Shadows* Volume 195.

### A BRIEF SUMMARY FOR LOST EPISODE 1219 FOLLOWS.

Carrie Stokes admits to Daphne Harridge that she has seen a vision of Daphne's grave. Bramwell Collins announces that he and Daphne have been married. Carrie brings Morgan Collins an old letter addressed to James Forsythe. A supernatural occurance causes the lights to go out and the letter goes up in flames. Catherine Harridge secretly reveals to Bramwell that she is pregnant with his child.

*A publicity photograph of Humbert Allen Astredo, as Nicholas Blair, with an
experimental make-up beard never actually seen on the show.*

# The Episodes That Never Were

The following four preliminary scripts from 1968 were never produced. However, some of the material was utilized in actual produced episodes from this period. Note that Chris and Amy Jennings are referred to by their originally intended names of Bob and Molly.

### SUMMARY OF PRELIMINARY SCRIPT FOR EPISODE 628

**Cast:** Eve, Angélique, Jeff, Adam

**Sets:** Jeff's Room, Angélique's Crypt, Blair House

**Writer:** Gordon Russell

**Voiceover:** "The truth about a young man's past hangs like a shroud over the great house at Collinwood. What had promised to be a bright and happy future for two young people is now nothing. The strange woman in this latest tragedy believes she will now finish what she has started. What she does not know is that her own destruction is being planned by someone else."

**Teaser:** Angélique rises, uses the mirror and sees Eve getting ready to go out. Adam forbids her to leave Blair House. When this doesn't stop her, he threatens her.

**Act One:** Continuation. When Eve realizes Adam meant what he's saying, she changes strategy and cons him into believing that her love for him is finally beginning to show through. He is so happy about this that he agrees to let her go out for awhile. Angélique has watched it all and wears a smile of deep satisfaction. She couldn't have engineered the thing better herself.

**Act Two:** Eve arrives at Jeff's room. The mere sight of her angers him. She knows she's ended it between Jeff and Vicki and says he might as well become resigned to it himself. She becomes puzzled and angry when he says he should be grateful to her for showing him the truth and keeping Vicki from making the greatest mistake of her life.

Jeff gradually realizes that he is not in his own time, that he does not really exist in this time. He has no fear. Since he won't be here long, no rules need apply. He realize he is capable of killing. He begins to strangle Eve.

**Act Three:** Continuous action. There is little question but that Jeff has gone momentarily insane. He maintains the tight grip on Eve's throat. He is unmoved by the terror in her eyes. She has struggled as long as she could find the strength. Now her arms have fallen to her sides. Her life is slipping away fast. There is a terribly pathetic look on her face. Then tears comes to her eyes. And it is the sight of these that causes something to snap in Jeff. He feels a sudden surge of pity for her, and then a glint of recognition comes into his eyes and he realizes what it is he's doing. With a lightning swift movement, he pulls his hands away from her throat, and Eve gasps hungrily for the life that is still hers.

Adam is alone and for once has a look of contentment about him. He is startled and frightened when Angélique suddenly materializes in the room. Adam warns her she shouldn't be there. If Nicholas catches her she's dead. Angélique knows that Nicholas is occupied with Maggie. She wants to talk about Eve. Does Adam have any idea where Eve is at this moment? Adam tells her where he thinks Eve is, and Angélique jars him by saying where she really is. Adam doesn't believe her. Angélique says it will be easy enough to prove. She'll take him there and show him.

Jeff is still trying to get rid of Eve. He tells her there isn't a chance for the two of them, because he's leaving Collinsport for good. Eve begs him to take her with him. Jeff isn't in the least interested. We pan to the window of Jeff's room and see the faces of Angélique and Adam.

### SUMMARY OF PRELIMINARY SCRIPT FOR EPISODE 629
(Partially used in produced Episode 627)
**Cast:** Joe, Angélique, Adam, Julia, Bob Jennings, Nurse (U/5)
**Sets:** Joe's Hospital Room, Hospital Waiting Room, Limbo Woods,
Ext. Window Area of Jeff's Room
**Writer:** Gordon Russell

**Voiceover:** "The aura of tranquility that surrounds the great house at Collinwood this night is in contrast to what is happening not far away. On the outskirts of Collinsport, outside the window of a rooming house, a woman bent on liberating herself from a supernatural state has taken the first step of a dangerous and evil plan—a plan which could bring death to all who become involved in it."

**Teaser:** Adam tells Angélique she was right. He's in such a rage he's ready to go inside Jeff's room and kill him on the spot.

**Act One:** Continuation. Angélique talks him out of it, then proceeds on the next step of her strategy—to poison his mind against Nicholas. She tells Eve's history and why Nicholas chose her. She says Adam will never escape from Nicholas unless he sides with her. Adam is clearly confused and scared. He doesn't know what to do. To add to his dilemma he notices Angélique staring at his neck. She is aware that the lust is upon her, and she knows she can't at this point victimize Adam. She tells him to think over what she's said and meet her here in the woods later tonight.

Hospital room. Joe is in bed. A nurse comes in to collect an empty tray, then leaves. The door opens and a man walks in. Joe looks horror stricken, believing the man is Tom Jennings.

**Act Two:** The nurse comes running in in response to Joe's anguished cries. The man, Bob Jennings, is mystified by Joe's reaction. He and the nurse finally calm Joe. The man, of course, is Tom's brother, and he says he has come to Collinsport to investigate the circumstances of Tom's death. He questions Joe, who turns out not to be very cooperative. At one point Joe hears the fluttering of wings outside the window and becomes terrified. Bob looks out the window and assures him it was only a bird. Bob asks Joe about Molly, and Joe tells him she is in Windcliff Sanitarium. Julia enters the room, takes one look at Jennings and screams. Jennings is further mystified. Julia recovers and asks Jennings to wait outside while she examines Joe. Before she leaves, Joe asks her to open the window.

Waiting room. Jennings asks Julia why she screamed when she saw him. She can't tell him the real reason. She responds by questioning him— why he's here, where he come from, etc. As he answers her questions, she finds something strangely disturbing about him, something she's unable to put her finger on. Angélique materializes in Joe's room.

**Act Three:** Joe sees her. She warns him not to scream. He asks why him, why didn't she go to someone else. She tells him she needed him, not someone else. She zaps him.

Julia says goodbye to Jennings, goes into Joe's room, discovers fresh wounds on his neck.

Angélique and Adam meet again in the woods. He's made his decision and will go along with her. What must be done? First, says Angélique, Eve must be destroyed.

## SUMMARY OF PRELIMINARY SCRIPT FOR EPISODE 630
**Cast:** .Elizabeth Collins Stoddard, Angélique, Jeff Clark,
Nicholas, Adam, Eve
**Sets:** Limbo woods, Jeff's Room, Blair House, Eve's Room
**Writer:** Ron Sproat

**Voiceover:** "In the dense, dark forest, not far from the great estate of Collinwood, the eerie light of a watchful moon slices down among the trees. It reveals the figure of a beautiful but unearthly woman, to whom the night alone can give protection—and even life. She waits now for one whose mind she must win, so she may instruct him in the ways of evil. If she prevails, this lonely night must end in death!"

**Teaser:** Recap of #629. Angélique tells Adam that Eve must be destroyed.

**Act One:** Adam argues with Angélique, who tries to further shake his faith in both Eve and Nicholas. Adam is confused, noncommittal.

Adam returns to Blair House where Nicholas senses Adam is worried about something. Adam refuses to explain his nervousness to Nicholas. Nicholas then berates Eve for not keeping Adam happy.

**Act Two:** Liz comes to Jeff's room to return Vicki's engagement ring. She is cold at first but warms to him as she senses he still loves Vicki.

Nicholas receives a call from Maggie and agrees to drive her to Bangor. He instructs Adam to keep the house in order. Adam tells him that Eve has again left the house.

Eve comes to visit Jeff Clark and discovers he is planning to leave. He refuses to tell her where he is going. Not able to get rid of her, he leaves her in his room while he goes to the cannery to pick up some belongings. Eve discovers his bus schedule and finds out when Jeff will be leaving.

**Act Three:** Eve comes back to Blair House just after Nicholas has left. She too begins to pack. Adam tries to stop her. Enraged, she goes to Adam with a pair of scissors. Adam stops her in time and strangles her to death.

Jeff, returning to his room, discovers the corpse of Eve.

### Summary of Preliminary Script for Episode 631
(Partially used in produced episode 627)
**Cast:** Jeff, Eve, Angélique, Adam, Sheriff
**Sets:** Jeff's Room, Angélique's Crypt

**Writer:** Ron Sproat

**Voiceover:** "Rhe night covers Collinsport in a darkness of seeming peace. But beneath that cover of darkness, the night has brought terror. One who would escape this terror returns for what he believes will be the last time to his room in a small boarding house . . . He does not know that the only true escape—death—waits to make him her prisoner. Nor does he know that before this horrifying night will end, the elements themselves will clash . . . And the fire of the greatest evil of all will flare. "

**Teaser:** Jeff returns to his room and finds Eve there—dead!

**Act One:** Continuation. Jeff is panicked. He considers leaving as he had planned, but reconsiders and calls the sheriff.

Adam comes to Angélique's crypt. He tells her that he has killed Eve. Angélique is pleased at this but is horrified to hear that Adam, to get back at Jeff, has placed the corpse in his room. Angélique continues to poison Adam's mind against Nicholas. They can't kill him, she says, but they can ruin every plan he has.

**Act Two:** In a voiceover, Jeff considers what he can tell the sheriff. He finally decides he will have to tell as much of the truth as he can. The sheriff arrives, examines the body, and questions Jeff. Jeff's story succeeds only in making the sheriff more and more suspicious, and his questions come faster and faster. By the end, he is just about convinced Jeff is the murderer.

**Act Three:** Continuation. The sheriff informs Jeff that there will be more questions. He forbids Jeff to leave town. Jeff is to consider himself arraigned. The sheriff says he will take Jeff down to the station to book him. They leave.

In Angélique's crypt, Adam broods about his present and future loneliness. Angélique urges him to return to Blair House and act as if nothing had happened: leave things to her. Adam leaves. Angélique then incants, summoning her master, with the intention of getting him to get rid of Nicholas. At the end of her incantation, there is thunder and lightning, and flames burst forth from her coffin.

## INTERNATIONAL SHADOWS

When the original *Dark Shadows* daytime series was produced, network soap operas did not yet commonly air in Europe or other foreign counties. However, the series was eventually seen in the following areas outside of the United States—many of which aired the Spanish dubbed version.

The title of the series in Spanish, announced during the main title opening music, is *Sombres Tenebrosas*. With *Dark Shadows'* phenomenal success in Latin America, Jonathan Frid made two promotional tours to Mexico in the 1970s to promote the Spanish-dubbed reruns. He even lived in Mexico for a time in the mid-1970s.

| | | |
|---|---|---|
| Argentina | Eduador | Puerto Rico |
| Australia | El Salvador | Suriname |
| Barbados | Guatemala | Thailand |
| Brazil | Honduras | Trinidad |
| Chile | Jamaica | Tobago |
| Columbia | Mexico | Uruguay |
| Costa Rica | Nicaragua | Venezuela |
| Curacao | Panama | |
| Dominican Republic | Paraguay | |

# Shadows Over Britain

### by
### Stuart Manning

The road that brought *Dark Shadows* to British television proved to be a long and winding one, which in many ways brought the show full circle, some of its earliest music recordings having been made in London. Until 1995, Britain had never received the show, although it was submitted to the BBC in the 1970s for consideration. That did not stop it reaching its shores in a number of other forms.

Patchy imports of the Gold Key comic books notwithstanding, it fell to *House of Dark Shadows* to introduce would-be fans to the residents of Collinwood, as part of a double-bill with *The Hooded Executioner. Night of Dark Shadows* was apparently never seen in British cinemas, though both films would play on British tel-

evision repeatedly. The mid-1980s saw *House of Dark Shadows* released for the home video market, where it remained available for several years.

Such fragmented exposure aside, the first notable *Dark Shadows* 'invasion' was mounted by the forces of Paperback Library, who remaindered huge numbers of their *Dark Shadows* novels to British booksellers during the 1970s. Even today, many titles can still be found at British book-fairs for cheap prices. For the small, but dedicated legion of British readers that became fans through these books, it would be some two decades before they would see the actual show the stories were based upon.

The 1990s boom in the European cable and satellite industry seemed to hold the key to making *Dark Shadows* available to British viewers. BSB considered purchasing the original series, while the British Broadcasting Corporation bought the rights to the 1991 revival, though never screened it.

News in 1995 of the establishment of a European arm of the American Sci-Fi Channel offered hope. Initially available only to a minuscule number of cable viewers in Europe and South Africa, *Dark Shadows* debuted on Sci-Fi Channel Europe at 2:00 pm on November 2 1995, their first day of scheduled broadcast.

Two episodes were screened each weekday, whilst the revival series played on Saturday nights at 8:00 pm commencing from November 4. By coincidence, *Dark Shadows* was to receive its first British terrestrial broadcast only weeks later in the form of Episode 737, which formed part of a special 'Soap Weekend' on Channel 4, broadcast on December 3 1995.

As part of Sci-Fi's initial publicity campaign, Kathryn Leigh Scott was employed in a number of specially shot promotional films, produced for the channel by Kevin Davies. Edited into compact 30-second segments, these were broadcast prior to episodes along with other spots utilizing an existing interview with

Dan Curtis. The most elaborate of these was *Dark Shadows: The Early Years*, a three-minute mini-documentary composed of Curtis and Scott's interviews and clips from 1966 episodes. These played frequently until late 1997, whereupon Sci-Fi Europe ceased all onscreen promotion for the show.

The years that followed brought mixed fortunes for the growing number of British *Dark Shadows* fans. 1996 saw the establishment of the *Dark Shadows Journal*, the first overseas *Dark Shadows* fanzine, and Kathryn Leigh Scott made personal appearances to meet fans. Meanwhile, late-night satellite repeats made the show available to a wider audience, and the revival series enjoyed several repeat runs. March 8 1997 saw Sci-Fi Europe bring viewers the *Dark Shadows* Chain Reaction, a day of 10 stripped episodes selected from a fan-poll. Early plans for specially shot fan interviews and linking materials were ultimately abandoned, though a fan contact address was shown following certain episodes. The special received modest press coverage, though certainly more than most Sci-Fi Europe broadcasts at the time.

Conversely, at the same time as this upshot of activity, the ongoing broadcasts of the show had reached something of a crisis point, reduced to just one new episode a week. The summer of 1997 saw the show disappear from schedules altogether, returning the following winter to little fanfare, though now with an episode seen every weekday. Undoubtedly the show's audience had already suffered adversely from the inconsistency of such scheduling, and this would ultimately begin *Dark Shadows*' slide towards cancellation. Following a turbulent time during 1998, a drastic shake-up of Sci-Fi Europe's broadcast range took place, leaving many viewers unable to see episodes for months on end, with others unable to obtain the show at all. Following a complete overhaul of Sci-Fi Europe's image, their interest in sustaining *Dark Shad-ows* had seemingly evaporated. Without vital promotion, the show limped through to its final year, increasing to two weekday episodes during its last weeks. Very little about the final months of Sci-Fi Europe's broadcast remains noteworthy, though by coincidence Keith Prentice's *Dark Shadows* debut aired on September 27 1999, the seventh anniversary of his death.

The final episode of *Dark Shadows* aired on Sci-Fi Europe on November 3, 1999. The problems posed by an embryonic cable industry and a channel with ever changing programming policies had robbed many viewers of an opportunity to enjoy the show, Sci-Fi Europe having decided that it lacked the 'mainstream popularity' they desired. As of this writing, they have no plans to repeat *Dark Shadows*, though doubtless the Collins family would feel heartened to learn that their loyal branch of 'cousins from England,' patiently awaits its return.

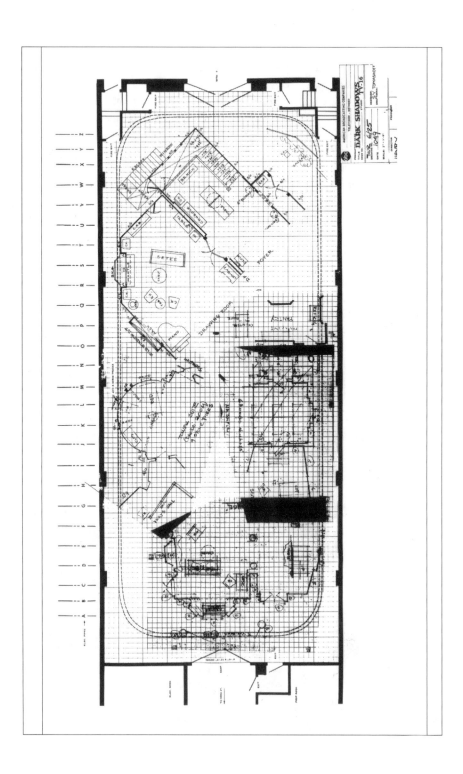

# Studio History

WHEN *Dark Shadows* DEBUTED IN JUNE OF 1966, THE SERIES WAS TAPED at ABC-TV's Studio 2 at 24 West 67th Street. In late August of 1966, the show moved to ABC Studio 16, a newly renovated structure at 433 West 53rd Street that had previously been a lumberyard. *Dark Shadows* would remain at this studio for the remainder of its run. After the series ended in 1971, PBS leased the studio from ABC through most of 1972. During this time, a variety of PBS shows were taped at Studo 16, including some episodes of *The Great American Dream Machine*, and a variety series entitled *Free Time*. The latter was particularly noteworthy for an installment starring John Lennon and Yoko Ono (*A World in the Grapefruit of Park*) on the very floor where Barnabas and company once roamed.

From 1972 to 1975, Studio 16 was home to various ABC network and local news and public service programs. In 1975, the ABC soap opera *Ryan's Hope* debuted in the studio, remaining there until the mid-1980s.

The studio was empty for a few years until it was sold and renovated as the Red Zone night club and restaurant in 1989. After that establishment closed, the studio was again vacant, but was turned back into a television studio in 1994 for the short-lived syndicated topical discussion program *Last Call*. In 1995, a new syndicated talk show featuring singer Carnie Wilson moved in, followed by the *Montel Williams Show*.

## DAILY STUDIO SCHEDULES
### STANDARD SCHEDULE IN 1966

| | |
|---|---|
| 7:00–11:00 a.m. | Lighting |
| 8:30–10:30 | Morning Rehearsal |
| 10:30–11:30 | Break/Make-Up |
| 11:00–12:00 | Engineering Set-Up |
| 11:30–2:00 | Camera Blocking & Run Through |
| 2:00–2:30 | Dress Rehearsal |
| 2:30–3:00 | Test Pattern |
| 3:00–3:30 | Episode Taping |
| 3:30–4:00 | Knockdown |
| 3:45–4:15 | Technical Meeting |
| 4:00–6:30 | Dry Rehearsal for Next Episode |
| 4:00–7:00 | Reset Studio |

### REVISED SCHEDULES

The schedule would vary slightly over the five years of production.

By 1967, *Morning Rehearsal* was from 8:00–10:00, with *Break* from 10:00-11:00, followed by *Camera Blocking, Run Through,* and *Dress Rehearsal* from 11:00–3:00.

By 1968, *Morning Rehearsal* was from 8:00–10:30, with Break from 10:30-11:30, followed by *Camera Blocking, Run Through,* and *Dress Rehearsal* from 11:30–3:15. Taping was from 3:15-3:45, usually followed by *Dry Rehearsal* for the next episode from 4:00–6:30 (later changed to 4:30–6:30).

In 1970, *Camera Blocking, Run Through,* and *Dress Rehearsal* were extended to 3:30, with Taping taking place from 3:30–4:00. The times for *Morning Rehearsal, Break,* and *Dry Rehearsal* remained unchanged.

*Morning Rehearsal*–The actors review and read through the script in the upstairs rehearsal hall, along with the director and production assistant. Initial blocking is also done in the rehearsal hall, informing the actors where they will stand in the studio for each scene they are to appear in that dat. The script is timed and dialogue may be deleted should the script run too long.

*Break*–Although this was the only time for the actors to eat lunch, albeit rather early in the day, many of the performers were in the make-up room during this time or they spent additional time rehearsing their lines privately or with other conscientious actors.

Camera Blocking–The process in which the director arranges the place-
ment of the actors on the sets for the various scenes to be taped that day.

Run Through–The entire day's show is rehearsed in sequence on the set,
with final alterations made.

Dress Rehearsal–A fully costumed performance of the day's episode,
performed as if it were the actual taped show.

Notes–Final comments given to the actors from the director and last
minute cuts or changes made in the script.

Taping–The actual performance of the episode which is recorded on
videotape for broadcast.

Dry Rehearsal–The time when the actors sit down with the director for
a rough reading of the next day's episode.

*Studio Moments: John Karlen and
Grayson Hall, Grayson and Jonathan Frid
(in character as Magda and Barnabas)
and Michael Stroka greet fans outside;
Producer's assistant Harriet Rohr and
Joel Crothers; Diana Millay.*

✜ In 1966, prior to going on the air and moving in to its ABC-TV studio, the first rehearsal hall for *Dark Shadows* was the Terrace Room of the Empire Hotel, 63rd Street & Broadway in New York. When the show began, Dan Curtis Productions was located in the Hotel Buckingham, 57th Street & 6th Avenue, New York. Curtis' office later moved to Madison Avenue.

✜ *Dark Shadows* utilized more sets than the regular daytime dramas. In a given year, the series would use approximately 100 sets compared to around 30 for an average soap opera.

✜ The format of each *Dark Shadows* episode includes a teaser (the beginning portion of the show which contains the opening voice-over), the main title (the portion with the theme music), following by either three or four acts, and the closing credits. When the show began in 1966, it contained three acts plus a brief "tag" segment at the end. The tag was dropped after Episode 34. Starting with Episode 589 the series changed to three acts, and with Episode 1051, the series returned to four acts. Also, starting with that episode, the first act aired immediately after the main title, with no commercial break between the two segments. This final format was retained for the remainder of the series.

✜ Over a period of time, teasers which repeat the end of the previous show become common, but they were rare in the show's first months. The very first repeat teaser, actually a rerun, begins episode 51, in which Carolyn Stoddard watches Victoria Winters scream as she looks over the crest of Widows' Hill to see a body face down on the rocks below.

*Victoria Winters' bedroom.*

*Morning rehearsal in the studio.*

✠ Not including commercial time, each episode of *Dark Shadows* runs approximately 21-22 minutes.

✠ *Dark Shadows* episodes were not always taped in sequence. The production schedule would sometimes require that episodes utilizing certain sets or special effects be taped back-to-back. On occasion, shows might also be taped out of order to accommodate a particular actor's schedule.

✠ ABC-TV recorded each episode of *Dark Shadows* on videotape by sending the video and audio signal over phone wires from the *Dark Shadows* studio to ABC's tape machines a few blocks away.

✠ The sound effect of a squeaking bat on *Dark Shadows* was made by rubbing cork on the side of a glass bottle. The show also had a sound effects library of over 3,000 recordings.

✠ On the technical page on several scripts, the Parallel Time Room is called the Time Warp Room.

✠ Episode 1182 is unique in that the cast consists of only four actors who are all shown together in one scene.

*Right: Michael Stroka and director Henry Kaplan;*
*Below: Lighting director Mel Handelsman.*

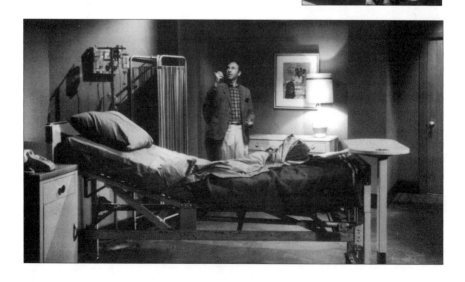

*David Henesy rehearses.*

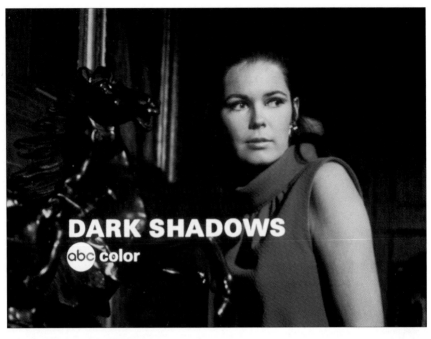

*Victoria Winters (Alexandra Moltke); The Old House.*

*Barnabas Collins (Jonathan Frid).*

*Collinwood.*

*Marie Wallace played Eve.*

*1897: Barnabas; Ct. Petofi (Thayer David) and Evan Hanley (Humbert Allen Astredo); Aristede (Michael Stroka); Edward Collins (Louis Edmonds).*

*1897: Quentin Collins (David Selby) and Edward.*

*1897: Angélique (Lara Parker).*

*Jeb Hawkes (Chris Pennock); Sabrina Stuart (Lisa Richards) and Bruno (Michael Stroka).*

*1970 Parallel Time: Roxanne Drew (Donna Wandrey) and Barnabas Collins.*

*1840: Leticia Faye (Nancy Barrett) and Dr. Julia Hoffman (Grayson Hall); rehearsal shots of David Selby, Kate Jackson and James Storm.*

*1841 Parallel Time: Flora Collins (Joan Bennett) and Catherine Harridge (Lara Parker); Melanie Collins (Nancy Barrett); Bramwell Collins (Jonathan Frid) and Daphne Harridge (Kate Jackson); 1840: Samantha Drew Collins (Virginia Vestoff).*

House of Dark Shadows: *Barnabas Collins (Jonathan Frid)
and Maggie Evans (Kathryn Leigh Scott).*

House of Dark Shadows: *Barnabas ages and attacks Maggie.*

Night of Dark Shadows: *Angélique (Lara Parker); Tracy Collins (Kate Jackson); Carlotta Drake (Grayson Hall).*

Night of Dark Shadows: *Promotional photograph session with Kate Jackson, Grayson Hall, Lara Parker, James Storm, John Karlen, Nancy Barrett and David Selby.*

## GOING TO COLOR

*Dark Shadows* was first televised in black and white. In the summer of 1967, after it had been on the air for more than a year, the change to color was made. For some time, large trucks with remote broadcast color equipment sat at the curb outside the studio, while inside the final black and white episodes were being produced. The last program produced in black and white was Episode 293, taped on Friday, July 21, 1967. From Monday, July 24, to Friday, July 28, the studio was closed so that the switch to color could be accomplished.

The first episode taped in color was Episode 294, which begins with Maggie's sudden reappearance at the Blue Whale. The show was taped on Monday, July 31, 1967, and shown on Friday, August 11, 1967. However, on that day it was not telecast in color, but in black & white.

On Tuesday, August 1, Episode 295, the first show originally televised in color, was taped. At the beginning of this show, an announcement stated, "Good news, this program, *Dark Shadows*, is now being presented in color."

To summarize, episode 294 was originally shown in black and white, and Episode 295 was originally shown in color. But when it came time for the reappearance of *Dark Shadows* in syndication, this was not the case. For the first time, Episode 294 was televised in color, as originally made, and Episode 295 was shown in black and white, because the original color tape had been lost and only a black and white kinescope was available. For this reason, the announcement that the program is presented in color was heard in reruns over an episode shown in black and white.

## TECHNICAL SHADOWS

✣ The actors were required to memorize their lines for each show. However, if someone forgot lines during an episode taping, the actor could look at the TelePrompter, a device which displays the lines of character dialogue onto a screen connected to the front of the camera. The type of TelePrompter used on *Dark Shadows* utilized a paper roll which contained the entire dialogue for each episode typed in extra-large print for easy reading.

# Shadows Sources

The following literary works inspired several *Dark Shadows* storyline:

Charlotte Bronte's *Jane Eyre* (Victoria Winters, 1966; Jenny Collins, Rachel Drummond, 1897)

Arthur Miller's *The Crucible* (Trask, Abigail & Victoria, *1795*)

Edgar Allan Poes' *The Cask Of Amontillado* (Barnabas & Trask, 1795)

Author Unknown *The Dream Deceivers* (The Dream Curse, 1968)

Mary Shelly's *Frankenstein* (Adam, 1968)

Edgar Allan Poe's *The Premature Burial* (Elizabeth, 1968)

Henry James' *The Turn of The Screw* (The Ghosts of Quentin & Beth, 1968-69; The Ghosts of Gerard & Daphne, 1970)

Edgar Allan Poe's *The Tell-Tale Heart* (Quentin & Edith, 1897)

Charles Dickens' *Nicholas Nickleby*; Dotheboys Hall (Trask's Worthington Hall, 1897)

Edgar Allan Poe's *The Pit & The Pendulum* (Aristede & Quentin, 1897)

Guy de Maupassant's *The Monkey's Paw* (Count Petofi's hand, 1897)

Oscar Wilde's *The Picture of Dorian Gray* (Quentin's Portrait, 1897)

H.P. Lovecraft's *The Cthulhu Mythos* (Leviathans, 1969-70)

Greek Mythology: *Orpheus In The Underworld* (Quentin & Amanda, 1969-70)

Daphne DuMaurier's *Rebecca* (1970PT & *Night of Dark Shadows*)

Robert Louis Stevenson's *The Strange Case of Dr. Jekyll & Mr. Hyde* (Cyrus Longworth/John Yaeger, 1970PT)

Emily Bronte's *Wuthering Heights* (1841 PT)

Shirley Jackson's *The Lottery* (1841 PT)

# The Writers of Dark Shadows

**JOE CALDWELL** Has written plays, including *The Cockeyed Kite*, and novels, including *Under The Dog Star*. He's also wrote for the daytime soap opera *Love of Life* and the syndicated serial *Strange Paradise*.

**SAM HALL** Has written for the daytime soap operas *One Life To Live*, *Another World* and *Santa Barbara*. For primetime television, he has written for *The U.S. Steel Hour*, and the 1991 *Dark Shadows* revival series.

**MALCOLM MARMORSTEIN** Has written for other daytime soaps and the nightime serial *Peyton Place*. Has also written stage plays and films, including *Escape to Witch Mountain*.

**GORDON RUSSELL** Has written for the daytime soap operas *One Life to Live* and *A Time For Us*. He was originally a stage actor appearing in summer stock productions and wrote a play, *Art Forgers*, performed in London.

**RON SPROAT** Has written for the daytime soap operas *Capital*, *Love of Life*, and *Never Too Young*, in addition to the syndicated serial *Strange Paradise*. He's also written plays, including *Ravenswood*, a *Dark Shadows* parody.

**FRANCIS SWANN** Has written mystery novels in addition to being a contract writer for Warner Brothers in the 1940s, when he wrote screenplays for such films as *The Time The Place* and *The Girl and Two Guys From Milwaukee*.

**ART WALLACE** Has written for the daytime soap opera *All My Children*. He also wrote two episodes of the original *Star Trek* and an episode of *The Goodyear Playhouse* which inspired some of the characters he created for *Dark Shadows*.

**VIOLET WELLES** Has written as a ghost writer with Gordon Russell on several projects, but has spent most of her career as a theatrical press agent.

# Shadows Influences

The following were all influenced by *Dark Shadows*:

✛ Anne Rice's famous novel and film *Interview With the Vampire*, was preceded several years by a strikingly similar subplot on *Dark Shadows*. During the 1970 Parallel Time story, writer William H. Loomis entraps vampire Barnabas Collins so that Loomis may interview Barnabas for a book he's writing entitled *The Life and Death of Barnabas Collins*.

✛ *Dark Shadows* writer Ron Sproat's *Ravenswood*, a theatrical play with musical numbers set behind the scenes at a daytime soap opera which features a vampire. The play was first presented in Cincinatti in 1988.

✛ Producer Aaron Spelling's 1986 television film *Dark Mansions* was a pilot for a weekly prime-time soap opera which had more than a few similarities to *Dark Shadows*. The supernatural story centered on a wealthy shipbuilding family in Seattle. Veteram film actress Joan Fontaine starred as the matriarch and an "old house" was located on the family's estate. The family's main house was, ironically, the same mansion used for Collinwood in the 1991 *Dark Shadows* revival.

✛ The 1969-70 syndicated soap opera *Strange Paradise*. Made in Canada, this program ran for 195 episodes. Three *Dark Shadows* alumni—producer Robert Costello and writers Joe Caldwell and Ron Sproat—worked on this show, "a supernatural horror story of possession, witchcraft and voodoo that makes a prison of the castle and captives of all who reside on a mysterious island."

✛ Group W's proposed 1987 syndicated soap opera, *Salem's Children*. Jonathan Frid was even rumored to have been offered a part, but the program never sold despite a completed half-hour pilot, taped in Canada. The story was set on Salem Island, off the coast of Massachusetts. Promotional materials promised "contemporary drama in Gothic style replete with strange phenomena . . . time travel . . . an enduring conflict of good vs. evil . . . strange forces . . . and dark secrets."

✛ John Lutz's novel *Shadowtown* (1988; Mysterious Press) is a mystery centering around a murder on the set of a soap opera entitled *Shadowtown*. The only witness claims that the murderer is a vampire.

✛ *Dead of Night*, a Dan Curtis pilot for a proposed weekly primetime series about the supernatural, was commissioned by ABC-TV due to the success of *Dark Shadows* in the daytime. With the help of several *Dark Shadows* personnel, including writer

Sam Hall and director Lela Swift, the program was videotaped at NBC-TV studios in Brooklyn, New York, in the fall of 1968.

*Dead of Night* starred Kerwin Matthews as a psychic investigator and Marj Dusay as Angela Martin, who inherits a haunted mansion, complete with a mysterious caretaker—portrayed by *Dark Shadows*' Thayer David, reminiscent of his portrayal of Matthew Morgan. Louis Edmonds was also seen as the ghost of Commodore Nicholas Blaise. The pilot, titled *A Darkness at Blaisedon*, was the only episode produced and aired on August 26, 1969.

✛ Dan Curtis' TV production of Bram Stoker's *Dracula*, which aired on CBS-TV in 1974, borrowed a theme that had been so integral with Barnabas and Josette in *Dark Shadows*. In Curtis' *Dracula*, Lucy Westenra is identical to the vampire's lost-love. Another Josette connection in this critically accalimed version is the use of a music box. Director Francis Ford Coppola would later "borrow" these elements in his 1992 theatrical film, *Bram Stoker's Dracula*.

✛ Many network daytime soap operas, such as: *As the World Turns*, showcased a ghost story in a castle, revolving around a portrait and a family curse. *One Life to Live* offered a time travel story which sent a major character back to the nineteenth century and several actors played dual roles in the past and present. *Days of Our Lives* included a story involving Satanic possession.

*Above: Marj Dusay, Kerwin Mathews, Thayer David and Cal Bellini in* Dead of Night *(1969); Upper right: Jack Palance as* Dracula *(1974).*

1991 Dark Shadows cast, clockwise from top left: Barbara Blackburn, Roy Thinnes, Michael T. Weiss, Barbara Steele, Ely Pouget, Joanna Going, Joseph Gordon-Levitt, Veronica Lauren, Jim Fyfe, Jean Simmons and Ben Cross.

# Shadow Spin-offs

### Theatrical Motion Pictures

Dark Shadows was the first daytime series to spawn a pair of theatrical films—House of Dark Shadows in 1970, and Night of Dark Shadows in 1971. Both movies were released by MGM.

### Newspaper Comic Strip

From the spring of 1971 until the spring of 1972, an original serialization of Dark Shadows was produced by Newspaper Enterprise Association, appearing in daily and Sunday newspapers across the United States. This newspaper comic was not related to the Gold Key/Whitman Dark Shadows comic books.

### Off-Off-Broadway Play

In September and October of 1988, Dance Theater Workshop presented Dark Shadows on stage at the VIA Theatre in New York City, adapting the 1795 storyline into two acts.

### Primetime Revival

From January through March of 1991, a new weekly, hour-long version of Dark Shadows aired on NBC-TV. The revival featured an entirely new cast and offered many recreated portions of the House of Dark Shadows film along with the early Barnabas and 1795 storylines from the original ABC-TV daytime series. All twelve episodes were subsequently released on MPI Home Video, with additional footage being added to the first and last shows. The program has also been reaired several times on the national Sci-Fi Channel cable outlet. Pomegranate Press published Dark Shadows Resurrected, a book about the 1991 series.

## STAGE MUSICAL

In early 2000, Dan Curtis announced plans to collaborate with Tony award-winning writer and composer Rupert Holmes and composer Robert Cobert on a Dark Shadows stage musical, with an eye on Broadway. As this book goes to press, the trio have just begun their work and there is not yet a guarantee that the show will actually be produced.

*Jonathan Frid, Robert Costello, Grayson Hall, Roger Davis, WEST-AM's
Ron Barry, Robert Rodan and Humbert Allen Astredo.*

## 𝔖𝔥𝔞𝔡𝔬𝔴𝔰 𝔖𝔞𝔱𝔦𝔯𝔢𝔰

SPOOF *Magazine*, published by Marvel Comics, includes a six-page take-off entitled *Darn Shadows*, as well as a spoof of *The Mod Squad* television series. (October 1970)

*Dumb Shadows Radio Drama*–Easton, Pennsylvania D.J. Ron Barry produced a series of short parodies of *Dark Shadows* heard on his daily WEST-AM radio program. (1968-69)

*Comedy Tonight* CBS-TV summer program with ensemble member Jerry Lacy (Reverend Trask from *Dark Shadows*) appears as Count Drago and bites Tonya the witch, played by Madeline Kahn, in a vignette called *Strangest Shadows*, part of a satire on TV soap operas. (August 9, 1970)

# Bloopers

Like other daytime dramas of its period, *Dark Shadows* was shot "live" on videotape, usually without stopping the cameras. With a few exceptions, each day the entire episode would be videotaped in proper sequence and in real time—just like a stage show in a theater. As a result, many mistakes were telecast since modern videotape editing was not commonly available.

This is a partial list of bloopers, containing a few of the dozens of mishaps which occured during the run of *Dark Shadows*. These bloopers were all part of the episodes as broadcast, and most can be seen collected together on the MPI Home Video release *Dark Shadows* Bloopers.

### EPISODE 242
While talking to Dr. Woodard in 1967, Burke Devlin calls the microscope a "microphone."

### EPISODE 252
While Carolyn and Buzz embrace in the foyer below, Elizabeth is unable to open the door on the landing.

### EPISODE 276
During a Collinwood drawing room scene in 1966, a camera loses its balance, causing it to tilt to the ceiling and revealing stage lights above the actors.

### EPISODE 291
In 1967, Barnabas is tormented by a pesky fly in the drawing room of the Old House while Willie and Julia watch.

### EPISODE 343
While Julia works in her laboratory at the Old House, loud coughing noises are heard from off camera.

### EPISODE 411
When Barnabas confronts Angélique in the secret room of the mausoleum in 1795, a crew member can be seen in one corner.

### EPISODE 448
In 1795, Nathan Forbes becomes entangled with his jacket as he enters Collinwood.

### EPISODE 451

In 1795, when Bathia Mapes attempts to exorcise Barnabas, the actress forgets her lines, and producer Robert Costello can be heard supplying her lines to her off-camera.

### EPISODE 477

In 1968, while attempting to hypnotize Tony Peterson, the flame in Cassandra's cigarette lighter goes out, forcing her to restart it.

### EPISODE 486

In 1968, as he is dying, Doctor Lang dictates into his reel to reel tape recorder—even after the actor mistakenly turns off the machine.

### EPISODE 495

Adam knocks over a fake bush when David finds him in the woods in 1968.

### EPISODE 522

In 1968, Willie thinks aloud and talks to himself as he bricks up the wall where Trask broke free. Simultaneously, a crew member accidentally walks on screen.

### EPISODE 585

In 1968, while aiming a rifle at Adam, Barnabas cannot initially remember Julia's name, instead calling her "Vicki" and "Maggie."

### EPISODE 635

In 1968, while Adam restrains Victoria in the old house basement, Barnabas is seen picking his nose through the window of the basement door.

### EPISODE 703

During the closing credits, Jonathan Frid accidentally walks on screen carrying his wardrobe across the Collinwood foyer.

### EPISODE 779

In the cemetery in 1897, Angélique's dress tilts an apparently styrofoam tombstone.

### EPISODE 852

In 1897, Lady Kitty Hampshire is repeatedly bothered by a fly while resting in her bed.

### EPISODE 863

When Pansy visits Charles Delaware Tate at his studio in 1897, the window shade crashes to the floor after she enters.

### EPISODE 915

In 1969, Barnabas struggles to put out persistent candle flames in the Old House drawing room.

### EPISODE 935

When Sheriff Davenport visits Jeb at the Collinsport Antique Shop in 1970, the bell falls off the top of the door.

### EPISODE 964

In 1970, Quentin pulls a sword off the wall in the Collinwood drawing room and the crashing sound of breaking glass is immediately heard—making it apparent that the container holding the sword has fallen off the wall and knocked over the table lamp.

### EPISODE 1010

In 1970 Parallel Time, a nervous John Yaeger has difficulty in rehanging a painting over a wall safe in Cyrus Longworth's laboratory.

### EPISODE 1028

While menacing Sabrina Stuart in 1970 Parallel Time, John Yaeger attempts to reassemble his cane when it falls apart.

### EPISODE 1064

In 1995, a supposedly dead Mrs. Johnson is seen blinking her eyes as she lies against a tree.

### EPISODE 1190

When Gabriel abducts Daphne in 1840, he gags her with a handkerchief, but fails to properly tie it, forcing Kate Jackson to bite into the handkerchief to keep it from falling off.

*Kate Jackson, Michael Stroka and Chris Pennock visit a Tiger Beat magazine writer (1971).*

# Outside the Shadows

Many of the *Dark Shadows* actors have appeared in other films and television programs with supernatural and horror themes. Here is a list of some prominent examples.

**JOHN BEAL**   *The Vampire* aka *Mark of The Vampire* (1957 Film); *Amityville 3-D* aka *Amityville:The Demon* (1983 Film)

**JOAN BENNETT**   *The Eyes of Charles Sand* (1972 TV Movie); *Suspiria* (1977 Film); *This House Possessed* (1981 TV Movie)

**CHRIS BERNAU**   *The Passion of Dracula* (1980 TV Special)

**CLARICE BLACKBURN**   *Pretty Poison* (1968 Film)

**BARBARA CASON** *Exorcist II: The Heretic* (1977 Film)

**KATHY CODY** *Charley & the Angel* (1973 Film)

**THAYER DAVID** *Dead of Night* aka *A Darkness at Blaisedon* (1969 TV Pilot)

**ROGER DAVIS**   *The Twilight Zone* (1964 TV Episode); *The Sixth Sense* (1972 TV Episode); *Killer Bees* (1974 TV Movie); *Ruby* (1977 Film);

**LOUIS EDMONDS**   *Dead of Night* aka *A Darkness at Blaisedon* (1969 TV Pilot)

**HUGH FRANKLIN**   *Curse of the Living Corpse* (1964 Film)

**JONATHAN FRID**   *The Devil's Daughter* (1972 TV Movie); *Seizure* aka *Queen of Evil* (1974 Film)

**ROBERT GERRINGER**   *The Exorcist* (1973 Film); *The Sentinel* (1977 Film)

**GRAYSON HALL**   *Gargoyles* (1972 TV Movie); *Night Gallery* (1970 TV Episode); *The Two Deaths of Sean Doolitle* (1975 TV Special)

**JOHN HARKINS**   *Amityville 3-D* (1983 Film)

**BARNARD HUGHES**   *The Lost Boys* (1987 Film)

**KATE JACKSON**   *Satan's School for Girls* (1973 TV Movie); *Killer Bees* (1974 TV Movie); *Death Scream* (1975 TV Movie); *Death at Love House* (1976 TV Movie); *Topper* (1980 TV Movie), *Satan's School for Girls* (2000 TV Movie, remake)

*Joan Bennett in* Suspiria; *Lara Parker with Peter Fonda in* Race With the Devil; *Roger Davis and Kate Jackson in* Killer Bees; *David Selby in* The Norming of Jack 243; *John Karlen with Shane Briant in* The Picture of Dorian Gray.

**JOHN KARLEN** *Daughters of Darkness* (1971 Film); *The Sixth Sense* (1972 TV Episode); *Frankenstein* (1973 TV Special); *The Picture of Dorian Gray* (1974 TV Special); *The Invasion of Carol Enders* (1974 TV Special); *Trilogy of Terror* (1975 TV Movie)

**JERRY LACY** *Bloodbath* (1974 Film)

**JOHN LASELL** *Twilight Zone* (1961 TV Episode); *One Step Beyond* (1961 TV Episode); *Night Gallery* (1972 TV Episdoe)

**KENNETH McMILLAN** *Salem's Lot* (1979 TV Movie)

**GEORGE MITCHELL** *The Twilight Zone* (1960 & 1963 TV Episodes)

**LARA PARKER** *The Night Stalker* (1975 TV Episode); *Race With the Devil* (1975 Film)

**DENNIS PATRICK** *One Step Beyond* (1960 TV Episode); *Dear, Dead Delilah* (1972 Film)

**CHRISTOPHER PENNOCK** *Tucker's Witch* (1983 TV Episode)

**ADDISON POWELL** *The Reincarnation of Peter Proud* (1975 Film); Doctor *Franken* (1980 TV Movie/Pilot)

**LOVELADY POWELL** *The Possession of Joel Delaney* (1972 Film)

**KATHRYN LEIGH SCOTT** *The Turn of the Screw* (1974 TV Special)
*Witches' Brew* (1980 Film); *Hammer House of Horror: Visitor From The Grave* (1982); *Shadow Chasers* (1986 TV Episode)

**DAVID SELBY** *The Norming of Jack 243* (1975 TV Special); *Doctor Franken* (1980 TV Movie/Pilot); *Grave Secrets: The Legacy of Hilltop Drive* (1992 TV Movie)

**ALEX STEVENS** *Silent Night, Bloody Night* (1973 Film)

**JAMES STORM** *The Invasion of Carol Enders* (1974 TV Special); *Scream of the Wolf* (1974 TV Movie); *Trilogy of Terror* (1975 TV Movie); *Curse of The Black Widow* (1977 TV Movie)

**MICHAEL STROKA** *Next Step Beyond* (1978 TV Episode)

**ABE VIGODA** *Tales From the Darkside* (1986 TV Episode)

**ELIZABETH WILSON** *The Addams Family* (1991 Film)

# 𝔇ark 𝔖hadows 𝔐usic

✝ With just a few isolated exceptions, all of the music heard on *Dark Shadows* was composed by Robert Cobert.

✝ Cobert has scored nearly every Dan Curtis Production since *Dark Shadows*, including *War and Remembrance*, for which he received an Emmy nomination. Some of Cobert's other daytime credits include, *The Doctors*, *The Young Marrieds*, and *The $20,000 Pyramid*.

✝ Robert Cobert composed and arranged approximately 330 music recordings, known as cues, available for use on *Dark Shadows*. This included different versions of some of the compositions. (For example, several piano recordings, using different, styles, were made of *Ode to Angélique*. A harpsicord version was also recorded but was never actually heard on the show.)

✝ Although the actors could not hear the music, the recordings heard on each episode were actually played in the studio at the same time as the show was being videotaped. When the series began, the music cues were played from record discs. Later, individual tape cartridges for each selection were utilized.

✝ The original *Josette's Music Box* melody heard on the series during the early Barnabas storyline was written by Canadian composer Robert Farnon. Cobert's version was used starting a few months later when Josette's music box was first seen in the 1795 storyline.

✝ The musical score of *Dark Shadows* played an integral part in creating the many moods expressed on the series. The popularity of the show's music carried over the Billboard record charts in the summer and fall of 1969 when *The Original Music from Dark Shadows* soundtrack album reached #18. It remains one of the top ten best-selling television soundtrack albums of all time.

✝ In 1969, *Quentin's Theme* from by the Charles Randolph Grean Sound reached #13 on the *Billboard Hot 100* singles chart and #3 on the *Billboard Easy Listening* chart. The Charles Randolph Grean album *Quentin's Theme* reached #23 on the *Billboard Top Album* chart. The song was subsequently recorded by over two dozen artists, including Henry Mancini and Lawrence Welk.

✝ Despite the success of the *Dark Shadows* soundtrack album and the Charles Randolph Grean Sound release of *Quentin's Theme*, the soundtrack single of *Shadows of the Night* by David Selby, backed with *I'll Be With You Always* by Jonathan Frid, only reached #125 on *Billboard's Bubbling Under the Hot 100* chart.

✝ *Quentin's Theme* earned Cobert a Grammy Award nomination by the National Academy of Recording Arts and Sciences for Best Instrumental Theme, 1969.

✝ Jonathan Frid and David Selby recorded their dramatic recitations for the *Original Music From Dark Shadows* soundtrack album in May of 1969 at Regent Sound Studios in New York City.

✝ In 1970, it was announced that a second *Dark Shadows* television soundtrack album might be issued by Mercury Records (the parent company of Philips Records). However, a second album, entitled *Original Music from Dark Shadows Volume 2*, wasn't issued until 1986 by the independent Media Sound label, formed by *Dark Shadows* composer Robert Cobert. The label subsequently issued *Original Music from Dark Shadows Volume 3* in 1987 and *Original Music from Dark Shadows Volume 4* in 1988. All four albums were reissued by MPI Home Video on compact disc and audio cassette in 1992.

✝ Varese Sarabande reissued the *Original Music from Dark Shadows* album as a "Deluxe Edition" compact disc in 1999, featuring the original album with over 40 minutes of bonus radio interviews from 1968 (Jonathan Frid, Grayson Hall, Roger Davis, Humbert Allen Astredo, Robert Rodan, Don Briscoe) and 1969 (David Selby) from with WEST-AM, Easton, PA with deejay Ron Barry.

✝ The *Dark Shadows* theme as heard on the main title opening sequence for each episode is an arrangement featuring an alto flute, a double bass, vibes, a harp, and a theramin.

✝ The complete closing credit music contained an extra stanza with a high pitch. In addition, during 1966 episode 45 featured the closing music with a slightly different sounding reverb echo like the version heard on the early 1966 ABC-TV promos for the series.

✝ Episode 625 is unique in that thunder is heard during the closing theme music.

✝ Robert Cobert began composing music for *Dark Shadows* on April 20, 1966. The early recording sessions for the series were held in London, England.

✝ The black-and-white episodes featured sound effects of waves crashing and wind howling during the opening *Dark Shadows* theme.

✝ Although Bob Cobert composed three different songs for use in the Blue Whale, in the first year of the series there were a few recordings, supposedly playing on the jukebox, which were not Cobert's songs. These were all instrumental recordings, including popular songs such as *Willow Weep For Me* and *I'll Be There*.

✝ The character of Adam repeatedly listened to a reel-to-reel tape containing classical music, along with Dr. Lang's message to Julia Hoffman. The classical piece was Mozart's *Serenade No. 13 in G, K. 525* ("Eine kleine Nachtmusik").

✠ In Episode 501, when Adam abducts Carolyn from Collinwood in 1968, the song heard playing on the portable radio is the *Theme From A Man and A Woman* from the film of the same name. The tune was also heard in the Blue Whale in episode 307.

✠ In Episode 841, Hungarian folk music is heard while Count Petofi is in an I Ching trance in the abandoned mill in 1897.

✠ In Episode 866, Quentin Collins, while possessed by Count Petofi, plays Mozart's *Fantasy and Fugue in F Minor* on his grammophone.

✠ All of the original *Dark Shadows* series music compositions were mixed to single track monaural sound. Accordingly, none of the soundtrack albums are in true stereo. However, the selections on the first album, the *15*, are heard in artificially-created strereo—an electronic process which enhances the treble in one channel and enhances the bass in the other channel. However, the overlaying dramatic recitations by Jonathan Frid and David Selby are heard in true stereo. In addition, stereo effects were added to a few tracks, exclusively for the album. This includes a tamborine on *Back At The Blue Whale* that was not heard on the song when it was used on the television show.

✠ The vocal version of *Quentin's Theme* is called *Shadows of the Night*. In addition to being recited by David Selby, the song was recorded by Andy Williams, Claudine Longet, The Ray Conniff Singers, Robin Grean, and The Midas Touch.

✠ While many of the traditional soap operas still used organ music in the 1960s, *Dark Shadows* featured orchestra music. Some of the recordings featured as many as 35 musicians.

✠ *Quentin's Theme* was first heard in Dan Curtis' 1968 TV drama *The Strange Case of Dr. Jekyll and Mr. Hyde*. Cobert later rerecorded the tune for *Dark Shadows*, as he did with many of his other *Jekyll & Hyde* compositions. *I'm Gonna Dance For* (aka *I Wanna Dance With You*) also originated in *Jekyll & Hyde*.

✠ While the original series was on the air, Cherry Lane issued sheet music for *Quentin's Theme*, and Criterion issued sheet music for the vocal version, *Shadows of the Night*, as well as *Ode to Angélique*. A player piano roll of *Quentin's Theme* was also available. In 1995, the first-ever *Dark Shadows Music Book* was issued by Pomegranate Press, including the aforementioned titles as well as the *Dark Shadows Theme*, *I Wanna Dance With You*, *The Playroom Theme*, and others.

✠ While appearing as a guest on *Joan River's Late Show* on FOX-TV in January of 1987, David recited *Shadows of the Night* acapella. He did the same thing again on Pat Sajack's CBS-TV talk show in October of 1989. On that show, Pat mentioned the home video release of *Dark Shadows* and showed a video clip of David as Quentin.

✠ Cobert also scored the two films, *House of Dark Shadows* and *Night of Dark Shadows*. The former was largely comprised of Cobert's original recordings from *The Strange Case of Dr. Jekyll & Mr. Hyde*, along with tracks from the *Dark Shadows* daytime series. *Night of Dark Shadows* featured several new recordings along with tracks from the daytime series.

✠ Rhino Records/Turner Classic Movies issued the first-ever soundtrack album for the MGM films *House of Dark Shadows* & *Night of Dark Shadows* on a single compact disc in 1996.

✠ Over the years, *Dark Shadows* music has been licensed for use on various television and radio programs and promotions, particularly around Halloween. The popular NBC-TV program *Saturday Night Live* has even used original *Dark Shadows* recordings in skits.

✠ Cobert recycled many of the *Dark Shadows* music recordings in later Dan Curtis productions such as *Turn of the Screw*, *Frankenstein*, *The Picture of Dorian Gray*, *The Invasion of Carol Enders*, *Nightmare at 43 Hillcrest*, *Come Die With Me*, and *Shadow of Fear*.

Dark Shadows *music composer Robert Cobert.*

✝ Cobert scored the entire 1991 *Dark Shadows* revival series, which included rerecordings of several music cues from the original series as well as new compositions. Some of the music is heard on the Varese Sarabande compact disc release by Cobert entitled *The Night Stalker & Other Classic Thrillers*, issued in 2000.

✝ The music video *I Barnabas* was created by engineer Alan Matlick at WNYC-TV in New York. The video originally aired a few times on the station in 1988, following reruns of the series. The video was later included on the MPI video release *Dark Shadows Music Videos*.

✝ The 1988 album *Lullaby*, by the group Book of Love, includes a song called *Witchcraft*, which contains the lyrics "Angélique takes Barnabas from Josette."

## JOSETTE'S MUSIC BOX

Near the end of episode 236, in 1967, Barnabas Collins takes Maggie Evans to Josette's room for the first time. He has kidnapped her with the intention of turning her into Josette Collins, his lost love of long ago, but Maggie has been unresponsive. Barnabas speaks of their romance in glowing terms, then presents her with Josette's wedding gown, which is as perfectly preserved as if it were new.

Barnabas then takes the antique music box from the table and holds it out to Maggie, describing it to her: "I brought this with me from the orient, and I intended to give it to you on a very special day. That day has come. This gift has crossed the seas as I have crossed the centuries. All for your sake. Listen." (He opens the box. A delicate and lovely tune tinkles away. Maggie seems to respond slightly.) "Do you hear it? This is your music. Listen to it and all the past will fade away to nothing—not even a memory. Listen—and you will forget what you have been and yearn only for what you are now. Listen—and all the fear and loneliness and unhappiness will disappear—forever. Listen—listen—" Barnabas holds out the music box. Maggie seems to be listening.

After Maggie escapes from Barnabas, he admits the failure of his attempt to turn her into Josette. He then gives the music box to Victoria Winters, who is more receptive to its music.

In 1795, the music box does not appear until after the wedding of Barnabas and Angélique. Josette duPrés Collins never sees the music box before her death at Widows' Hill.

In Episode 711 set in 1897, Barnabas presents the music box to Rachel Drummond and tells her about Josette. Meanwhile Angélique casts a spell. Rachel chokes, then collapses. Under the spell, she speaks as Josette, and Barnabas realizes Angélique has caused Rachel's collapse.

# The MGM Dark Shadows Movies

## HOUSE OF DARK SHADOWS

### Credits

JONATHAN FRID Barnabas Collins
GRAYSON HALL Dr. Julia Hoffman
KATHRYN LEIGH SCOTT Maggie Evans
ROGER DAVIS Jeff Clark
NANCY BARRETT Carolyn Stoddard
JOHN KARLEN Willie Loomis
THAYER DAVID Professor T.E. Stokes
LOUIS EDMONDS Roger Collins
DONALD BRISCOE Todd Jennings
DAVID HENESY David Collins
DENNIS PATRICK Sheriff George Patterson
LISA RICHARDS Daphne Budd
JERRY LACY Minister
BARBARA CASON Mrs. Johnson
PAUL MICHAEL Old Man
HUMBERT ALLEN ASTREDO Dr. Forbes
TERRY CRAWFORD Todd's Nurse
MICHAEL STROKA Pallbearer
JOAN BENNETT Elizabeth Collins Stoddard

MGM PRESENTS A DAN CURTIS
PRODUCTION

Producer/Director: Dan Curtis
Screenplay: Sam Hall and Gordon Russell
Associate Producer/Production Designer :
    Trevor Williams
Production Supervisor: Hal Schaffel
Assistant to Producer: George DiCenzo
Production Secretary: Diane Katz
1st Assistant Director: Bill Gerrity
2nd Assistant Director: Peter Bogart
Script Supervisor: Maggie James
DGA Trainee: Dwight Williams
Auditor: Bud Brown
Office Assistant: Sylvia Schaffel

Director of Photography: Arthur Ornitz
Camera Operator: Dick Mingalone
1st Assistant Cameraman: Felix Tromboli
2nd Assistant Cameraman: Jamie Jacobson
Still Photographer: Charles Moore
Additional Stills: Ben Martin
Sound Mixer: Bob Fine
Sound: Chris Newman and Jack C. Jacobsen
Boom Man: Pat Suraci
Recorder: Les Lazarowitz
Assistant Art Director: Otis Riggs
Casting Director: Linda Otto
Gaffer: Willie Meyerhoff
Best Boy: Sal Martorano
Dolly Grip: Mike Mahony
Best Boy: Edward Larkin
Construction Grip: Joe Williams
Grip: Thomas Gilligan
Scenic Artists: Gene Powell
andWilliam Chaiken
Outside Props: Ben Rutter
Set Dresser: Ken Fitzpatrick
Standby Props: Conrad Brink and Clint Marshall
Head Carpenter: Gilbert Gertsen and Richard Allen
Makeup Artist: Robert Layden
Special Make-up: Dick Smith
Hair Stylist: Verne Caruso
Costume Designer: Ramse Mostoller
Men's Wardrobe: Jim Hagerman
Ladies' Supervisor: Florence Foy
Stunt Coordinator: Alex Stevens
Unit Publicist: Baird Searles
Editors: Sid Katz and Arline Garson
Teamster Captain: James Fanning
Titles designed by: F. Hillsberg Inc.
Metrocolor 96 minutes. Released: September, 1970.
Filmed in Tarrytown, NY: The Lyndhurst Estate (Collinwood), The Sleepy Hollow
   Cemetery (Eagle Hill Cemetery), The Schoales Estate aka Beechwood (The
   Old House); Norwalk, CT: The Lockwood-Mathews Museum Mansion
   (Abandoned Monastery); Westport, CT; The Three Bear' Inn
   (The Collinsport Inn).

## NIGHT OF DARK SHADOWS

### Credits

DAVID SELBY Quentin Collins/Charles Collins
GRAYSON HALL Carlotta Drake
JOHN KARLEN Alex Jenkins
NANCY BARRETT Claire Jenkins
LARA PARKER Angélique
KATE JACKSON Tracy Collins
JAMES STORM Gerard Stiles
DIANA MILLAY Laura Collins
CHRISTOPHER PENNOCK Gabriel Collins
THAYER DAVID Reverend Strack
MONICA RICH Sarah Castle
CLARICE BLACKBURN Mrs. Castle
ART HAGGERTY Henchman
ALEX STEVENS Hangman

MGM PRESENTS A DAN CURTIS PRODUCTION
Producer/Director: Dan Curtis
Screenplay: Sam Hall
Story: Sam Hall & Dan Curtis
Associate Producer/Production Manager: George Goodman
Assistant to Producer: Bob Singer
Associate Producer/Art Director: Trevor Williams
Director of Photography: Richard Shore
Camera Operator: Ronald Lautore
First Assistant Cameraman: Bill Horgan
Second Assistant Cameraman: Emmanuel Metaxas
First Assistant Director: Stanley Panesoff
Second Assistant Director: Allan Wertheim
DGA Trainee: Mike Haley
Script Supervisor: Norma Goodman
Sound Boom: John Bolz

Sound Mixer: John Gleason
Sound Recordist: Ed Abele
Sound: Al Gramaglia
Gaffer and additional lighting: Lou Gerolomi
Best Boy: Charles Meere
Electrician: Salty Meyerhoff
Key Grip: Jack Volpe
Dolly Grip: Tom Volpe
Outside Prop Man: Ronald Ottesen
Standby Prop Man: Dick Tice
Set Dresser: Robert Wilson
Local Helper: Robert Neilson
Local Helper: W. Siegel
Local Helper: W. Maloney
Local Helper: P. Dente
Chief Construction Grip: Joseph Bauman
Construction Grip: Jack Kanaplue
Chief Carpenter: Gilbert Gertsen
Carpenter: Richard T. Allen
Scenic Artist (Chargeman): John Hughes
Scenic Artist: Joseph Novak
Scenic Artist: Murray P. Stern
Costume Designer: Domingo Rodriguez
Wardrobe: Yvonne David

Make-up: Reginald Tackley
Hair Stylist: Edith Tilles
Production Secretary: Helene Spinner
Production Assistants: Dennis Murphy / Carl Serbell / William Schwartz
Still Photographer: Charles Moore
Additional Still Photography: Lilo Raymond
Transportation Captain: James Fanning
Stunt Coordinator: Alex Stevens
Dog Handler/Trainer: Art Haggerty
Assistant Dog Handler: Eric Martinez
Publicist: Baird Searles
Casting: Lindo Otto
Extra Casting: Sylvia Fay
Location Auditor: Charles Ogle
Editor: Charles Goldsmith
Assistant Editor: Aviva Slesin
Lyndhurst Location Administrator:
Gerald L. Fiedler

Technical Advisor: Hans Holzer
Metrocolor 93 minutes. Released: September 1971
Filmed in its entirety on the Lyndhurst Estate in Tarrytown, NY.

*James Storm as Gerard Stiles in* Night of Dark Shadows.

# Shedding Light on Night of Dark Shadows

## by Darren Gross

N AUGUST 1999 IT WAS MY SUPREME PLEASURE TO UNCOVER DAN Curtis' legendary, lost director's cut of the 1971 feature film *Night of Dark Shadows*. I'd been passionately crusading for this film's restoration for several years and being an instrumental part of its discovery was an almost indescribable thrill. Most of *Dark Shadows*' die-hard devotées are aware that the film's original cut was chopped down from 129 to 97 minutes in an unreasonable and incredibly short period of time (stories vary as to whether the recutting period lasted two days or just under twenty-four hours, but the latter is most likely) and then released to a frequently baffled public. While the film did have its admirers (primarily due to its wonderfuly atmospheric photography and the Gothic location of the Lyndhurst Estate in Tarrytown, NY), many viewers were surprised at *Night of Dark Shadows'* seemingly slapdash story construction and character development.

At the time of the motion picture's release in September of 1971, many fans were aware that several important scenes were missing (MGM's original package of publicity photographs for the press included several shots of deleted scenes, and the magazine *Famous Monsters of Filmland* featured a synopsis which was based on the script, not on the final cut.[1]) However, the audience was not aware of how severely the film had been recut or the reasons why. In the years since its premiere, unauthorized copies of the script (most of which were made from an earlier draft and are missing some rewritten dialogue and a few crucial scenes) were distributed amongst fans and revealed a much more lucid and involving story.

I felt that there was a supportive, albeit modest fan following for the film that had been growing steadily through the years. It was my goal to give *Night of Dark Shadows* and the story of its studio-imposed recutting some greater exposure in order to increase appreciation for the finished product and Dan Curtis' accomplishments. Towards that goal, I wrote a 1996 article on *Night of Dark Shadows* which was published in *Video Watchdog* magazine (issue # 40), detailing exactly what had been cut from the film, approximately how long the scenes lasted and where the film had been restructured. In 1998, on the strength of the earlier article I was asked by Jim Pierson to contribute two chapters to the *Dark Shadows Movie Book*. This assignment granted me full access to Dan Curtis' notes and his final director's scripts. I also conducted around a dozen interviews with production personnel in order to accurately relate the detailed stories of the making of both *Night of Dark Shadows* and its 1970 predecessor, *House of Dark Shadows*.

At the time of the publication of Pomegranate Press' *Dark Shadows Movie Book*, the most current information on the state of *Night of Dark Shadows* was that the footage cut from the film was eventually discarded and would apparently never see the light of day again. When MGM/UA announced that the two *Dark Shadows* films were to be released on video in 1990, the company was reportedly overwhelmed with letters from *Dark Shadows* fans who requested that the uncut versions of both films be issued on video. (*House of Dark Shadows* had been trimmed of several crucial (and now infamous scenes) but those sequences were cut by Dan Curtis, not by MGM. The existing print is for all intents and purposes Curtis' final cut.)

I'd been told by Dan Curtis Productions that MGM/UA searched for the missing footage to both films but their efforts turned up nothing. The released video and laserdiscs were gorgeously presented but frustrating to fans who were hoping for much more. (Especially frustrating was the soundtrack for the video release of *Night of Dark Shadows*, which featured a terribly undermixed sound effects track. Dan Curtis' involving sound effects (rain, footsteps, wind etc.), which strongly contributed to the film's presence and involved the viewer in the story, were almost completely inaudible.[2]) Any hopes for a restored version of either film were quashed.

However, over the insuing years, a rumor spread that a slightly longer print of *Night of Dark Shadows* existed and occasionally reappeared in revival movie theaters. At first, this seemed like groundless hearsay [3] but the clarity

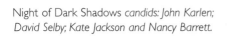

Night of Dark Shadows *candids: John Karlen;*
*David Selby; Kate Jackson and Nancy Barrett.*

and detail of one fan's account convinced me that the claim was genuine. In 1999, I made the acquaintance of Michael Miozza, who produced indesputable evidence that a longer print was indeed circulated as far back as 1971.[4] That year, Miozza had seen *Night of Dark Shadows* several times and had made an audio recording of the film at a drive-in theater. He provided me with a copy of the audio that proved once and for all that a 97 minute print was indeed distributed.

I contacted Dan Curtis Productions in order to inform them of the discovery and received authorization to continue my efforts to recover the missing footage. MGM's pre-1986 library, including the pair of *Dark Shadows* movies, had since been sold to Turner Entertainment Company and was now owned by the new conglomerate of Turner. and Warner Brothers. After literally dozens of letters of introduction and hundreds of persistent phone calls, I made several contacts at Turner/Warners. I contacted several 35mm and 16mm rental houses to ascertain whether they had longer prints of either of the films. I also examined Warners' sole 35mm rental print for *Night of Dark Shadows*. Though one 16mm print was listed as 97 mins, I had it measured and the Warners print and found they were both the standard 93.5 min version.

Following months of negotiating with Warners and the archive, I was able to gain authorization to examine the original negative for the film. As most video transfers are made from various intermediate 35mm prints, I figured the original negative probably hadn't been touched since 1971 and might yield the 97 minute version. The only condition Warners stipulated was that (understandably) negative film materials were not to be handled, because they were fragile and irreplaceable. In order to inspect the negative, a union editor would be required to do the examination. Though initially deflated by this hurdle, I mentioned this to a film-editor-friend, Glenn Erickson (responsible for restoring *Kiss Me Deadly*), who was between assignments and willing to examine the material.

At Warners' Burbank studio, we examined the negative under fairly close scrutiny. Unfortunately, it was the 93.5 min version and the archive records indicated there were no longer versions currently being held. I then asked the clerk to search the inventory database to double-check and see if anything further could be located, eventually yielding a computerized printout of the various materials on deposit for both films.

The form was almost all in code and listed over one hundred items for both *Night of Dark Shadows* and *House of Dark Shadows*. Every item in the archive was given an abbreviation and code number and provided very little detail of the materials. After combing through it a few times I came to the same conclusion that every one else at the archive had: the 97 min version of the film apparently no longer existed.[5] There was one item, though that pre-sented an anomaly and it haunted me: every print listed in the records ran 12 reels. Buried down the list were 45 cans labeled "Night of Dark Shadows 1-15". I discussed the item with the Turner/Warners archivists and they offered little light on the mystery. It became an obsession as I began to think, "If the short

version runs 12 reels, if there is a 15 reel version, it could be the original 'lost' cut!" I further deducted that since three reels roughly translates to around 30 mins, if it is the longer print the running time would match the time of the missing material (as I chronicled in the *Dark Shadows Movie Book*).

I was determined to examine the footage, except there was one prob-lem: the cans of material (divided into around 45 cans) were in the studio's safety vault, deep in a salt mine in Kansas City. I contacted the video depart-ment and tried to get them to foot the bill to have the material shipped, but as the film was considered a secondary title, they were uninterested in spend-ing any money to evaluate the elements, especially since the contents of the mysterious 15 reels of film were unknown. I finally convinced the head of the TV department of the importance of the discovery and the value of the long version if it was uncovered. I was informed it would take a few weeks for the materials to arrive, and waited anxiously.

When the materials finally arrived, Glenn Erickson again generously made himself available for two hours one morning. We examined the cans of film and found the contents pristine and unscratched, as though untouched since 1971. As the element was probably one-of-a-kind, running it through a projector was not an option. We resigned ourselves to gently rolling through the footage on a rewind bench. I had intended to slowly roll through each reel of the picture, stopping occasionally and looking for miss-ing scenes or shots. But knowing we had a time crunch, I grabbed reel 14 (figuring it should be close to the famous deleted séance sequence). Glenn rolled it slowly forward and stopped at the first few shots which revealed Quentin (David Selby) and Tracy (Kate Jackson) exploring the basement. In the recut version, Tracy is attacked by Angélique's ghost in the basement, Alex confronts Carlotta who jumps to her death from the tower, then Quentin forces the basement door open and cradles Tracy. Carlotta's jump from the tower isn't supposed to occur until about ten minutes later after the séance sequence. In the original version, Alex is supposed to enter the basement running and he helps Quentin pry the door open. As they open the door, light from their candelabra banishes Angélique's ghost away and saves Tracy. Claire then enters as Tracy regains consciousness. Alex and Claire had been edited out of the scene in the recut version.

Glenn rolled through the basement sequence slowly as I examined each shot over the light board on the table. Suddenly I let out a gasp, made a quiet whoop and whispered in a conspiratorial stage whisper to Glenn, "This is it, we found it. This is the uncut version!" Right in front of my eyes, in beautiful 35mm, Alex (John Karlen) appeared in the basement scene and ran to help Quentin. With only around 90 minutes left in our viewing session I had Glenn measure all fifteen reels so a 100% accurate running time could be calculated. As we measured reel 14, I requested that Glenn stop a few times so that I could review shots from the séance. Being able to finally see all the shots from this legendary sequence was such a thrilling revelation I had to stifle any yelps of joy. We finished measuring the film just in time to restock the materials and say our thanks and goodbyes to the archive personnel.

Since I wasn't going to be handling negative print materials anymore and had proven myself to be professional, I was allowed to make several return trips to the archive to examine the trailers for extra footage and to listen to all available audio materials to see if we had a complete soundtrack. It was devastating to discover that while a complete 129 minute version exists on film, only approximately 100 minutes of soundtrack (audio) survives. The longest remaining audio material is the original soundtrack which had been physically cut and spliced in order to create the shorter 97 minute soundtrack. This had been the actual track cut during Dan Curtis' legendary frantic re-edit session. Unfortunately, nearly all of the sound material that was trimmed was eventually disposed of and destroyed. [6]

During the last few months, attempts have been made to get the restoration off the ground. A budget has been created and studio locations and facilities have been chosen. The cast required to re-record dialogue have all responded with excitement and enthusiasm. The late Grayson Hall will need to be redubbed by a very good imitator. All that's needed is the official go-ahead. With hard work and a bit of luck, Dan Curtis' 129 minute version of *Night of Dark Shadows* may finally be unveiled.

---

1    This is not an unusual occurrence. Once a film has finished principal photography, all of the still photography negatives and material are delivered to the publicity department who spend several weeks selecting photos for the presskit and creating an advertising campaign. Copies of several reels of the unfinished motion picture film are given to the trailer department who spend several weeks editing various shots together to create the movie trailers (previews of coming attractions) and tv spots. While those departments are working on those materials, the director and editor are editing the picture into its final form. As most of the trailers and promotional material are distributed before the final cut of the picture, they usually contain shots of scenes ultimately deleted from the final cut.

2    Surprisingly, this is not an unusual or rare occurrence. A recent DVD release of *2001: A Space Odyssey* accidentally deleted lines of dialogue.

3    Oddball rumors occasionally circulate among fans which have no basis in reality. The most outrageous are claims to have seen the "Nancy Hodiak" scene from *House of Dark Shadows* during the film's original release back in 1970 even though the scene was never shot.

4    When *Variety* and *Hollywood Reporter* reviewed the film in August 1971, they listed the film's running time as 97 minutes. Copies of reviews from regional magazines and newspapers several weeks later report the film as 94 minutes. What most likely happened was this: several prints were probably made of the final 97 minute cut for press screening and internal studio purposes. After it was screened for the Hollywood trade papers, studio head James Aubrey must have went back into the cutting room with it and ordered the other trims. All of the material trimmed from the 97-minute version is either violence or sexually oriented scenes, so Aubrey probably cut it in an effort to tone it down for the *Dark Shadows'* younger fan base. The MPAA's records show that the film they rated GP back in 1971 was never given a stronger rating(Such as an R), so the cuts must have been made after the rating was granted. Somehow several 97-minute prints were accidentally distributed to theaters. After the film finished its run the returned and battered prints were most likely destroyed which is standard studio practice. This explains why the running time for the film is 97 minutes in most reference books, including *Leonard Maltin's Movie and Video Guide*. The current video release and available rental prints run 93.5 minutes, shorn of roughly 3-3.5 minutes of material.

5    At least as far as the MGM/Warner archive is concerned. 35mm prints of the 97-minute cut may be in the possession of private collectors who somehow obtained an original release print.

6    Because the film was trimmed so hastily, the audio for a few cut scenes was accidentally left intact on the original element so there are around three cut scenes with complete audio.

## DARK SHADOWS MOVIES FOREIGN TITLES

Both films were dubbed into foreign languages and released world-wide. They were mostly likely subtitled in Japan, Holland and Scandanavian countries whose audiences are more accepting of subtitled films

### House of Dark Shadows

| Country | Foreign Release Title | English Translation |
|---------|----------------------|---------------------|
| Italy | La Casa dei Vampiri | The House of the Vampire |
| Germany | Schloss der Vampire | Castle of the Vampire |
| Mexico | Sombras en la Obscuridad | Shadows in the Darkness |
| France | La Fiancée du Vampire | The Fiancée of the Vampire |
| Japan | | Lips of Blood |
| Belgium | La Broid de Noir | The Bride of Night |

### Night of Dark Shadows

| Country | Foreign Release Title | English Translation |
|---------|----------------------|---------------------|
| Italy | La Casa della Ombre Malladette | The House of the Cursed Shadows |
| Spain | La Maldacion de Sinestra | The Sinister House |

## FILM PROMOTIONS

To promote *House of Dark Shadows*, Jonathan Frid, Kathryn Leigh Scott and Nancy Barrett participated in separate press tours. These trips consisted of newspaper, television, and radio interviews. Jonathan went to Philadelphia (August 16-18), Indianapolis (August 18-19) and Chicago (August 19-20). Kathryn went to Boston (August 17), Detroit (August 17-18), Cincinnati (August 18-19), St. Louis (August 19-20). Nancy went to Charlotte (August 16-17), Atlanta (August 17-18), New Orleans (August 18-19), Dallas (August 19-20), and Washington, D.C. (August 20-21).

MGM sponsored a nationwide "Miss American Vampire Contest" to promote *House of Dark Shadows*. Regional winners from ten cities received an all-expenses paid trip to New York for the national finals. Contestants were required to appear in appropriately ghoulish costumes and makeup, and be between the ages of 18 and 25. Jonathan Frid and Nancy Barrett presented the national award at a ceremony at the Palisades Amusement Park in New Jersey. The winner of the contest was Christine Domaniecki. As a prize, she received a non-speaking role in episode 1126 of *Dark Shadows*, portraying a barmaid in the 1840 storyline.

To promote *Night of Dark Shadows*, Grayson Hall and her husband Sam Hall, the writer of the film, went on a press tour.

## The Lyndhurst Estate

The Lyndhurst mansion and estate, at the edge of the Hudson River in Tarrytown, New York, was used as Collinwood in the movies *House of Dark Shadows* and *Night of Dark Shadows*.

Seaview Terrace, the Newport, Rhode Island location that was used for the exteriors of Collinwood in the daytime television series, could not be utilized in the films because Seaview's interior had been converted into classrooms and dormitories for a girl's school.

Tarrytown was also a more convenient location for the New York based *Dark Shadows* personnel, requiring approximately one hour of travel time compared to three hours travel to Newport.

The Lyndhurst mansion represents the culmination of Gothic Revival architecture in America. It was designed in 1838 by Alexander Jackson Davis, one of America's most influencial architects. Originally called Paulding Manor, the house was built for William Paulding, a general in the War of 1812 and a mayor of New York.

The house was built as a country villa and later expanded to a Gothic mansion in 1864 for second owner, New York merchant George Merritt, who renamed the estate Lyndhurst. In 1880, the estate was purchased as a summer home for railroad magnate Jay Gould. His daughter Anna left the property to the National Trust for Historic Preservation when she passed away in 1961.

Among the additions made at Lyndhurst by the Merritts and Goulds was a coach house and carriage complex, a massive greenhouse, kennels, a bowling and recreation building, an indoor swimming pool, and a playhouse for the children named Rose Cottage.

The National Trust for Historic Preservations maintains the property through charitable donations. The estate is open to the public for tours during the spring, summer and fall.

## Film Trivia

Both films were shot in 35mm in a 1:1:85 theatrical aspect ratio. Dan Curtis has preferred this throughout his career, never shooting a film using wide-screen processes.

To produce the two MGM films, Dan Curtis set up a separate production entity called Collinwood Productions.

Both films were releasedwith an MPAA rating certificate of GP (surprisingly, considering the horror and violence), the equivalent of today's GP rating.

Paperback Library issued a softcover adaptation of *House of Dark Shadows* by Dan "Marilyn" Ross, but no novelization of *Night of Dark Shadows* was ever issued.

House of Dark Shadows *movie posters
from Spain and France.*

*Barnabas and Julia.*

*Roger Davis as Jeff Clark.*

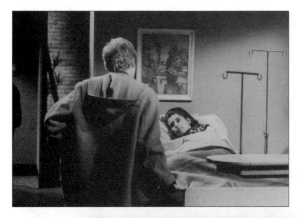

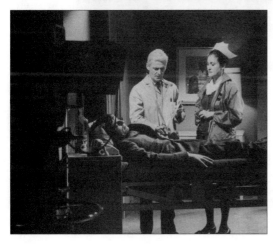

*The Collinsport Hospital:*
*Jeff and Vicki; Barnabas;*
*Dr. Eric Lang (Addison Powell)*
*and a nurse (Katherine Balfour).*

*Betsy Durkin (above with Roger Davis) replaced Alexandra Moltke
(below with Jonathan Frid) as Victoria Winters.*

*Angélique (Lara Parker), young and old, with Nicholas Blair (Humbert Allen Astredo).*

Miss Polish America Bobbi Ann Woronko—
appearing as a nurse—receives instructions from
director Lela Swift, relaxes with Roger Davis and
Don Briscoe, and watches Kathryn Leigh Scott and
Humbert Allen Astredo. Opposite page: Bobbi
with Robert Rodan as Adam.

*1897: Aristede (Michael Stroka); Jamison Collins (David Henesy);*
*Beth Chavez (Terry Crawford); Kitty Hampshire (Kathryn Leigh Scott).*

1897: Judith Collins (Joan Bennett) and Barnabas Collins (Jonathan Frid) discuss Quentin Collins' (David Selby) condition as a zombie.

*Donna Wandrey, Lisa Richards and Denise Nickerson.*

Preparing for the show, clockwise from top left: Denise Nickerson, Chris Pennock, hairdresser Edith Tilles with Grayson Hall and Lara Parker.

*Rehearsing: Nancy Barrett; David Selby;
David and Camila Ashland; James Storm
and Kate Jackson.*

*1840: Leticia Faye (Nancy Barrett).*

House of Dark Shadows: *Professor Stokes (Thayer David) and Dr. Hoffman (Grayson Hall);*
*Roger Collins (Louis Edmonds), Stokes, Jeff Clark (Roger Davis) and*
*Sheriff Patterson (Dennis Patrick).*

House of Dark Shadows: *David Collins
(David Henesy); Carolyn Stoddard
(Nancy Barrett) and Todd Blake (Don Briscoe);
Roger Collins (Louis Edmonds).*

House of Dark Shadows: *Barnabas (Jonathan Frid) and Maggie Evans (Kathryn Leigh Scott); Roger Davis with director Dan Curtis and cinematographer Arthur Ornitz.*

Night of Dark Shadows: *Nancy Barrett and Chris Pennock taking photo breaks; Deleted scene with David Selby as Quentin and Kate Jackson as Tracy.*

# Dark Shadows on Home Video

IN OCTOBER OF 1989, MPI HOME VIDEO BEGAN ISSUING THE ENTIRE run of the original *Dark Shadows* on video cassette. By June of 1995, all 1,225 episodes were released on a total of 254 tapes. Several compilations and special programs have also been issued by MPI.

*Dark Shadows Volumes 1-8* (MP 5001-MP 5008) feature a specially edited version of the early Barnabas storyline, spanning episodes 210-270. Many non-Barnabas scenes are deleted from these volumes and Episodes 213, 228 and 244 (which exclude Barnabas) are ommited entirely.

Volumes 9-199 (MP 5009-5199) feature five complete, unedited episodes per volume. Volume 200 (MP 5200) includes the final four shows, Episodes 1242-1245, plus special bonus material.

The pre-Barnabas shows, Episodes 1-209, are included on the MPI *Dark Shadows Collector's Series* releases. These 54 Volumes (MP 5201-5254) also include complete versions of the early Barnabas storyline Episodes 210-270.

## MPI Dark Shadows Episode Volumes

Volume 1–The Resurrection of Barnabas Collins–a 15 minute recap of Episodes 1-209, followed by edited versions of Episodes 210-220.
Volume 2–Edited versions of Episodes 221-229.
Volume 3–Edited versions of Episodes 230-236.
Volume 4–Edited versions of Episodes 236-241.
Volume 5–Edited versions of Episodes 242-250.
Volume 6–Edited versions of Episodes 251-255.
Volume 7–Edited versions of Episodes 256-261.
Volume 8–Edited versions of Episodes 262-270.
Volume 9–Episodes 271-275
Volume 10–Episodes 276-280
Volume 11–Episodes 281-285
Volume 12–Episodes 286-290
Volume 13–Episodes 291-295
Volume 14–Episodes 296-300
Volume 15–Episodes 301-305
Volume 16–Episodes 306-310
Volume 17–Episodes 311-315
Volume 18–Episodes 316-320
Volume 19–Episodes 321-325

Volume 20–Episodes 326-330
Volume 21–Episodes 330-335
Volume 22–Episodes 336-340
Volume 23–Episodes 341-345
Volume 24–Episodes 346-350
Volume 25–Episodes 351-355
Volume 26–Episodes 356-360
Volume 27–Episodes 361-365
Volume 28–Episodes 366-371*
Volume 29–Episodes 372-376
Volume 30–Episodes 377-381
Volume 31–Episodes 382-386
Volume 32–Episodes 387-392*
Volume 33–Episodes 393-397
Volume 34–Episodes 398-402
Volume 35–Episodes 403-407
Volume 36–Episodes 408-412
Volume 37–Episodes 413-417
Volume 38–Episodes 418-422
Volume 39–Episodes 423-427
Volume 40–Episodes 428-432
Volume 41–Episodes 433-437
Volume 42–Episodes 438-442
Volume 43–Episodes 443-447
Volume 44–Episodes 448-452
Volume 45–Episodes 453-457
Volume 46–Episodes 458-462
Volume 47–Episodes 463-467
Volume 48–Episodes 468-472
Volume 49–Episodes 473-477
Volume 50–Episodes 478-482
Volume 51–Episodes 483-487
Volume 52–Episodes 488-492
Volume 53–Episodes 493-497
Volume 54–Episodes 498-502
Volume 55–Episodes 503-507
Volume 56–Episodes 508-512
Volume 57–Episodes 513-517
Volume 58–Episodes 518-522
Volume 59–Episodes 523-527
Volume 60–Episodes 528-532/533*
Volume 61–Episodes 534-538
Volume 62–Episodes 539-543
Volume 63–Episodes 544-548
Volume 64–Episodes 549-553
Volume 65–Episodes 554-558
Volume 66–Episodes 559-563

Volume 67–Episodes 564-568
Volume 68–Episodes 569-573
Volume 69–Episodes 574-578
Volume 70–Episodes 579-583
Volume 71–Episodes 584-588
Volume 72–Episodes 589-593
Volume 73–Episodes 594-598
Volume 74–Episodes 599-603
Volume 75–Episodes 604-608
Volume 76–Episodes 609-613
Volume 77–Episodes 614-618
Volume 78–Episodes 619-623
Volume 79–Episodes 624-628
Volume 80–Episodes 629-633/634*
Volume 81–Episodes 635-639
Volume 82–Episodes 640-644
Volume 83–Episodes 645-649
Volume 84–Episodes 650-655*
Volume 85–Episodes 656-660
Volume 86–Episodes 661-665
Volume 87–Episodes 666-670
Volume 88–Episodes 671-675
Volume 89–Episodes 676-680
Volume 90–Episodes 681-685
Volume 91–Episodes 686-690
Volume 92–Episodes 691-695
Volume 93–Episodes 696-700
Volume 94–Episodes 701-705
Volume 95–Episodes 706-710
Volume 96–Episodes 711-715
Volume 97–Episodes 716-720
Volume 98–Episodes 721-725
Volume 99–Episodes 726-730
Volume 100–Episodes 731-735
Volume 101–Episodes 736-740
Volume 102–Episodes 741-745
Volume 103–Episodes 746-750
Volume 104–Episodes 751-755
Volume 105–Episodes 756-760
Volume 106–Episodes 761-765
Volume 107–Episodes 766-770
Volume 108–Episodes 771-775
Volume 109–Episodes 776-780
Volume 110–Episodes 781-785
Volume 111–Episodes 786-790
Volume 112–Episodes 791-795
Volume 113–Episodes 796-800

Volume 114–Episodes 801/802-806*
Volume 115–Episodes 807-811
Volume 116–Episodes 812-816
Volume 117–Episodes 817-821
Volume 118–Episodes 822-827*
Volume 119–Episodes 828-832
Volume 120–Episodes 833-837
Volume 121–Episodes 838-842
Volume 122–Episodes 843-847
Volume 123–Episodes 848-852
Volume 124–Episodes 853-857
Volume 125–Episodes 858-862
Volume 126–Episodes 863-867
Volume 127–Episodes 868-872
Volume 128–Episodes 873-877
Volume 129–Episodes 878-882
Volume 130–Episodes 883-887
Volume 131–Episodes 888-892
Volume 132–Episodes 893-898*
Volume 133–Episodes 899-903
Volume 134–Episodes 904-908
Volume 135–Episodes 909-913
Volume 136–Episodes 913/914-
      919/920/921*
Volume 137–Episodes 922-926
Volume 138–Episodes 927-931
Volume 139–Episodes 932-936
Volume 140–Episodes 937-941
Volume 141–Episodes 942-946
Volume 142–Episodes 947-951
Volume 143–Episodes 952-956
Volume 144–Episodes 957-961
Volume 145–Episodes 962-966
Volume 146–Episodes 967-971
Volume 147–Episodes 972-976
Volume 148–Episodes 977-981
Volume 149–Episodes 982-986
Volume 150–Episodes 987-991
Volume 151–Episodes 992-996
Volume 152–Episodes 997-1001
Volume 153–Episodes 1002-1006
Volume 154–Episodes 1007-1011
Volume 155–Episodes 1012-1016
Volume 156–Episodes 1017-1021
Volume 157–Episodes 1022-1026

Volume 158–Episodes 1027-1031
Volume 159–Episodes 1032-1036
Volume 160–Episodes 1037-1041
Volume 161–Episodes 1042-1046
Volume 162–Episodes 1047-1051
Volume 163–Episodes 1052-1056
Volume 164–Episodes 1057-1061
Volume 165–Episodes 1062-1066
Volume 166–Episodes 1067-1071
Volume 167–Episodes 1072-1076
Volume 168–Episodes 1077-1081
Volume 169–Episodes 1082-1086
Volume 170–Episodes 1087-1091
Volume 171–Episodes 1092-1096
Volume 172–Episodes 1097-1101
Volume 173–Episodes 1102-1106
Volume 174–Episodes 1107-1111
Volume 175–Episodes 1112-1116
Volume 176–Episodes 1117-1121
Volume 177–Episodes 1122-1126
Volume 178–Episodes 1127-1131
Volume 179–Episodes 1132-1137*
Volume 180–Episodes 1138-1142
Volume 181–Episodes 1143-1147
Volume 182–Episodes 1148-1152
Volume 183–Episodes 1153-1158*
Volume 184–Episodes 1159-1163
Volume 185–Episodes 1164-1168
Volume 186–Episodes 1169-1173
Volume 187–Episodes 1174/1175-
      1179/1180*
Volume 188–Episodes 1181-1185
Volume 189–Episodes 1186-1190
Volume 190–Episodes 1191-1195
Volume 191–Episodes 1196-1200
Volume 192–Episodes 1201-1205
Volume 193–Episodes 1206-1211*
Volume 194–Episodes 1212-1216
Volume 195–Episodes 1217-1221
Volume 196–Episodes 1222-1226
Volume 197–Episodes 1227-1231
Volume 198–Episodes 1232-1236
Volume 199–Episodes 1237-1241
Volume 200–Episodes 1242-1245

## Special Notes

*Designated volumes contain one or more episodes with multiple numbers (The original ABC-TV numbering system assigned multiple numbers to certain episodes after a network pre-emption).

Volume 195 includes Lara Parker hosting a recreation of lost episodes #1219, utilizing the original audio and still-frame images from surrounding episodes.

Volume 200 includes the following bonus material: *Beyond the Shadows* (written by Sam Hall and narrated by Roger Davis), telling what happened to the characters, a music video containing Robert Cobert's non-soundtrack version of the *Dark Shadows* theme with clips spanning the entire series, an MGM *House of Dark Shadows* Miss American Vampire Contest trailer, Epilogue narrative by Jonathan Frid, and a preview of the MPI *Dark Shadows Collector's Series*

## MPI Dark Shadows Collector's Series Volumes

CS Volume 1–Episodes 1-5
CS Volume 2–Episodes 6-10
CS Volume 3–Episodes 11-15
CS Volume 4–Episodes 16-20
CS Volume 5–Episodes 21-25
CS Volume 6–Episodes 26-30
CS Volume 7–Episodes 31-35
CS Volume 8–Episodes 36-40
CS Volume 9–Episodes 41-45
CS Volume 10–Episodes 46-50
CS Volume 11–Episodes 51-55
CS Volume 12–Episodes 56-60
CS Volume 13–Episodes 61-65
CS Volume 14–Episodes 66-70
CS Volume 15–Episodes 71-75
CS Volume 16–Episodes 76-80
CS Volume 17–Episodes 81-85
CS Volume 18–Episodes 86-90
CS Volume 19–Episodes 91-95
CS Volume 20–Episodes 96-100
CS Volume 21–Episodes 101-105
CS Volume 22–Episodes 106-112*
CS Volume 23–Episodes 113-117
CS Volume 24–Episodes 118-122
CS Volume 25–Episodes 123-127
CS Volume 26–Episodes 128-133*
CS Volume 27–Episodes 134-138
CS Volume 28–Episodes 139-143

CS Volume 29–Episodes 144-148
CS Volume 30–Episodes 149-153
CS Volume 31–Episodes 154-158
CS Volume 32–Episodes 159-163
CS Volume 33–Episodes 164-168
CS Volume 34–Episodes 169-173
CS Volume 35–Episodes 174-178
CS Volume 36–Episodes 179-183
CS Volume 37–Episodes 184-188
CS Volume 38–Episodes 189-193
CS Volume 39–Episodes 194-198
CS Volume 40–Episodes 199-203
CS Volume 41–Episodes 204-208
CS Volume 42–Episodes 209-213
CS Volume 43–Episodes 214-218
CS Volume 44–Episodes 219-223
CS Volume 45–Episodes 224-228
CS Volume 46–Episodes 229-233
CS Volume 47–Episodes 234-238
CS Volume 48–Episodes 239-243
CS Volume 49–Episodes 244-248
CS Volume 50–Episodes 249-253
CS Volume 51–Episodes 254-258
CS Volume 52–Episodes 259-263
CS Volume 53–Episodes 264-268
CS Volume 54–Episodes 269-270;
    499;873;915

## Special Notes

*No episodes were assigned numbers 109, 110 or 131 due to holiday preemptions.

Episodes 1, 499, 873 and 915 in the MPI *Dark Shadows Collector's Series* include the original 1960s commercials as broadcast on ABC-TV.

The following *Collector's Series Volumes* contain bonus interview footage: *Volume 5*: Dan Curtis; *Volume 9*: Alexandra Moltke; *Volume 13*: Louis Edmonds; *Volume 17*: Nancy Barrett; *Volume 21*: Kathryn Leigh Scott; *Volume 25*: Clarice Blackburn; *Volume 29*: Diana Millay; *Volume 33*: Lela Swift; *Volume 37*: Dennis Patrick; *Volume 41*: John Karlen; *Volume 45*: Jonathan Frid; *Volume 49*: Jonathan Frid; *Volume 53*: Sharon Smyth.

## Compilations & Special Programs

*The Best of Barnabas*  (MP 6060, issued 1990)
*The Best of Dark Shadows*  (MP 5000, issued 1990)
*The Best of Dark Shadows 2*  (MP 6258, issued 1993)
*Dark Shadows 1840 Flashback*  (MP 6062, issued 1991)
*Dark Shadows Behind the Scenes*  (MP 6191, issued 1992)
*Dark Shadows Bloopers*  (MP 6293, issued 1993)
*Dark Shadows Music Videos*  (MP 6442, issued 1992)
*Dark Shadows 25th Anniversary*  (MP 6220, issued 1993)

*MPI commercial with Kathryn Leigh Scott on the Sci-Fi Channel.*

*Dark Shadows 30th Anniversary Tribute* (MP 7146, issued 1997)
*Dark Shadows Vampires & Ghosts* (MP 7051, issued 1995)
*Dark Shadows Video Scrapbook* (MP 7402, issued 1999)
*Scariest Moments From Dark Shadows* (MP 6061, issued 1991)

### Laserdisc

*Dark Shadows Behind The Scenes/Scariest Moments/Music Videos* (CLV 9800, issued 1992)

*Louis Edmonds and Alexandra Moltke during* Dark Shadows Behind the Scenes *video production (1991).*

### DVD

*Dark Shadows Special Edition* (DVD 7402, issued 1999)

## DARK SHADOWS MOVIES

The two MGM films based on the series were issued on MGM/UA Home Video in 1990.

*House of Dark Shadows* (M200437)
*Night of Dark Shadows* (M201195)

A double laserdisc release (ML 103972) of the two films was issued by MGM/UA in 1993, including the original theatrical trailers and TV commercials for both.

*1968 Hallowe'en ſun at the Dark Shadows studio with Jonathan Frid, Humbert Allen Astredo, Grayson Hall and Lara Parker hosting young visitors.*

*Jonathan Frid participates in a Hallowe'en 1969 UNICEF party at the White House.*

# Shadows Promotions

## A PARTIAL LISTING OF PROMOTIONAL ACTIVIITES

### Publicity Events

Traveling in a chartered Lear jet airplance, Jonathan Frid participated in a week-long *Dark Shadows* ten-city promotional tour in 1968. An itinerary follows:

Jonathan appeared at the airport in Atlanta, Georgia for photograph taking and autographs, followed by a press conference of approximately 35 high school newspaper editors at the Marriott Motor Hotel, in what local ABC-TV affiliate WQXI called a "Face to Fang Press Conference." (May 18, 1968)

Jonathan appeared at the airport in Charleston, South Carolina for photograph taking and autographs, including a high school newspaper press conference. A police motorcade to the Pinehaven Shopping Center followed, where Jonathan was mobbed by an estimated 3,000 anxious fans, causing a scheduled autograph session to be cancelled. Three police cars were called in to the rescue. (May 20, 1968)

Jonathan appeared at the airport in Little Rock, Arkansas. (May 20, 1968)

Jonathan appeared at the Lackey Field airport in Birmingham, Alabama for photograph taking and autographs on the runway. At City Hall, Jonathan was presented a key to the city by the mayor. (May 21, 1968)

Jonathan appeared at the Roscoe Turner Field airport in Indianapolis, Indiana for photograph taking and autographs. A high school newspaper press conference was held at Stouffer's Inn for Jonathan and twenty-five teenagers. (May 21, 1968)

Jonathan appeared at Baer Field airport in Fort Wayne, Indiana, for photograph taking and autographs, followed by an appearance at the Glenbrook Shopping Mall, where Jonathan was mobbed by an estimated 12,000 fans. The roads surrounding the area were jammed and Jonathan was rescued by police and security guards. He also rode in a motorcade for the Three Rivers Festival. (May 22, 1968)

Jonathan appeared at the airport in Grand Rapids, Michigan, where he was greeted by more than 5,000 screaming fans. He was driven in a hearse with police escort to a hotel, where fans followed. A press conference for high school newspaper editors was also held. (May 22, 1968)

Jonathan appeared at the airport in Flint, Michigan. (May 23, 1968)

Jonathan appeared in Washington, D.C. at the Washington Hilton Hotel for a high school press conference with eighteen editors. A press luncheon was held the next day at Paul Young's Restaurant. (May 23, 1968)

Jonathan (billed as "The cool ghoul Barnabas") appeared at the Devon Horse Show Country Fair in Philadelphia, Pennsylvania, where he was mobbed by enthusiastic fans and rescued by police. (May 25, 1968)

Jonathan appeared at the Palisades Amusement Park in New Jersey. (1968)

Jonathan Frid, Lara Parker, Humbert Allen Astredo, Joel Crothers and other cast members attended an ABC-TV Press Party at the Warwick Hotel in New York City. (1968)

Jonathan Frid held a press party at the Drake Hotel in New York with his mother, visiting from Canada, as a special guest. Among the attendees were Dan Curtis, Robert Costello, Kathryn Leigh Scott, Alexandra Moltke, Nancy Barrett, Joel Crothers, and David Ford. (1968)

Kathryn Leigh Scott appeared at The Birmingham Antique Show in Birmingham, Alabama. (April 27, 1969)

David Selby appeared at the I Am An American Parade in Baltimore, Maryland. (1969)

Jonathan Frid appeared at Marine World in Mission San Jose, California. (October 25, 1969)

Dark Shadows cast members Jonathan Frid, David Selby, Grayson Hall, Kathryn Leigh Scott, Don Briscoe, and others appeared in series costume at ABC-TV's Halloween Party for their daytime shows at Cheetah Night Club in New York. (October 29, 1969)

Jonathan Frid visited the White House for President Nixon's daughter Tricia's Halloween Party for underprivledged children. (October 31, 1969)

David Selby made a personal appearance at Harrisburg East Mall in Harrisburg, Pennsylvania, attracting an estimated 5,000 fans. The appearance was cut short due to the unmanageable crowd. (1969)

Jonathan Frid and Donna Wandrey appeared at the Minneapolis International Auto Show in Minnesota. (1970)

Jonathan Frid and Nancy Barrett appeared in person at the Palisades Amusement Park to award the Miss American Vampire Contest winner as part of a House of Dark Shadows promotion. (1970)

*David Selby in Baltimore for I Am An American parade (1969): Jonathan Frid and Marie Wallace at a press conference (1969).*

John Karlen appeared at the Brown Derby in Hollywood to help launch *Dark Shadows* reruns on local station KHJ-TV. (1975)

Jonathan Frid appeared at the Magique disco in New York City to promote *Dark Shadows* reruns on WNBC-TV. Fans in costume were admitted free. Proceeds were donated to the New York Blood Center. (June 10, 1982)

KDFI-TV sponsored a *Dark Shadows* Blood Drive at the Parkland Blood Bank in Dallas, Texas, and at Northlake College in Irving, Texas, to promote *Dark Shadows* reruns. Helpers were dressed as vampires and donors received a specially made *Dark Shadows* T-shirt. (October 31, 1983)

Kathryn Leigh Scott and Lara Parker appeared at Waldenbooks in a shopping mall in Cerritos, California to autograph copies of the book *My Scrapbook Memories of Dark Shadows*. (April 25, 1987)

Jonathan Frid and Kathryn Leigh Scott appeared at Waldenbooks in San Francisco, California on May 1, 1987 to autograph copies of the book *My Scrapbook Memories of Dark Shadows*. (May 1, 1987)

Jonathan Frid and Kathryn Leigh Scott appeared at Waldenbooks in Beverly Hills, California to autograph copies of the book *My Scrapbook Memories of Dark Shadows*. (June 5, 1987)

Lara Parker and Kathryn Leigh Scott attended a *Dark Shadows* Hallowe'en Party sponsored by KDOC-TV and held at Pinafini's Restaurant & Bar in Costa Mesa, California. (October 29, 1987)

Jonathan Frid appeared at the annual Video Software Dealer's Association convention in Las Vegas in August, 1989, to promote the launch of *Dark Shadows* episodes on MPI Home Video.

The *Dark Shadows* Festival sponsored by party at the Red Zone night club in Manhattan at 433 West 53rd Street, the former home of the *Dark Shadows* studio. Several hundred fans enjoyed dancing, cocktails, and hors d'ouvres with Jonathan Frid, Lara Parker, Kathryn Leigh Scott, Roger Davis, Marie Wallace, Diana Millay, Terry Crawford, and Sharon Smyth. (August 31, 1989)

A *Dark Shadows Companion Book* Signing Party was held at the Hollywood Studio Museum. Attending guests included Kathryn Leigh Scott, Lara Parker, Robert Rodan, Roger Davis, Lisa Richards and Sy Tomashoff. (November 18, 1990)

Jonathan also appeared in Barnabas costume on several TV programs to promote *Dark Shadows*. See TV publicity appearance listings.

A *San Francisco Examiner & Chronicle* article mentioned that Frid's personal appearances attracted as high as 20-50,000 fans.

# CONTESTS

## Magazines

"Have Dinner With Roger Davis"–Afternoon TV (1968)

"Win A Date With Vampire Jonathan Frid"–TV Radio Talk (December 11, 1968)

"Win A Date With Jonathan Frid"–Afternoon TV (December 1968)

"*Dark Shadows* Scrapbook Contest"–16 Magazine (May 1969)

"Win A Date With Jonathan Frid"–Modern Movies (December 1969)

"Meet Your Fav Contest–David Henesy"–16 Magazine (1969)

"Win Frid's Record"–(source and date unknown)

## Television

"Best Dressed Ghoul"–WZZM-TV, Atlanta, Georgia. (1968)

"*Win My Scrapbook Memories of Dark Shadows*"–KDOC-TV, Anaheim/Los Angeles, California. (1987)

"Best Barnabas Look-A-Like"–WNBC-TV/Magique Disco. (June 10, 1982)

"Win A Trip to the *Dark Shadows* Festival"–Kingston, NY.

Runner-up prizes: *My Scrapbook Memories of Dark Shadows* and subscriptions to *ShadowGram*. (1990)

## Miscellaneous

After becoming Miss Polish America of 1968, Bobbi Ann Woronko won the single Episode 632 role of Nurse Pritchett on *Dark Shadows* (1968).

"National Miss American Vampire Contest"–Sponsored by MGM in conjunction with *House of Dark Shadows*. Winner Christine Domaniecki played an 1840 barmaid in Episode 1126. (1970)

## Dark Shadows Festivals

Many of the Festival gatherings have offered charity raffles to win lunch with various *Dark Shadows* actors. Trivia contests have also been conducted in which winners receive prizes of *Dark Shadows* memorabilia.

Jonathan Frid hosts a 1968 party at the Drake Hotel in New York: (left) Nancy Barrett and Robert Rodan: (below left) Joel Crothers and Kathryn Leigh Scott; (below right) Lara Parker and Jonathan; (bottom) Alexandra Moltke and Jonathan.

More party shots: Jerry Lacy and guest;
Thayer David, guest, Orson Bean, Dan Curtis,
Grayson Hall; Joel Crothers, Jonathan,
Ron Sproat, and Rich Little.

*Jonathan Frid on* The Mike Douglas Show *(1968); Michael Stroka on* The Dating Game *(1969).*

## TV & RADIO APPEARANCES

### National Network, Cable & Syndicated Programs

*The Mike Douglas Show* (Joan Bennett: September 14, 1967)

*The Merv Griffin Show* (Joan Bennett: September 25, 1967)

*The Mike Douglas Show* (Jonathan Frid: July 16, 1968)

*The Dick Cavett Show* ABC-TV (Jonathan Frid: 1968)

*The Tonight Show* NBC-TV (Lara Parker: 1968)

*The Dating Game* ABC-TV (Robert Rodan: January 11, 1969)

*The Merv Griffin Show* (Jonathan Frid: March 27, 1969)

*The Ghost & Mrs. Muir Present the ABC Super Saturday Club Special*
   (Jonathan Frid, September 4, 1969)

*The Dating Game* ABC-TV (Michael Stroka: December 1969)

*The Dick Cavett Show* ABC-TV (Jonathan Frid: 1969)

*The Tonight Show* NBC-TV (Jonathan Frid: 1969)

*The Generation Gap* ABC-TV (Jonathan Frid: 1969)

*The Tonight Show* NBC-TV (Lara Parker: 1969)

*The Mike Douglas Show* (Joan Bennett: January 30, 1970)

*The Mike Douglas Show* (Joan Bennett: August 5, 1970)

*The Dick Cavett Show* ABC-TV (Jonathan Frid: August 1970)

*The Dating Game* ABC-TV (Joan Bennett: October 5, 1970)

*The Virginia Graham Show* (Jonathan Frid: October 1970)

*The Movie Game* (Joan Bennett: November 1970)

*The Virginia Graham Show* (Joan Bennett: November 1970)

*Girl Talk* (Jonathan Frid, Joan Bennett, Grayson Hall: 1970)

*What's My Line* (Jonathan Frid: 1970)

*The Virginia Graham Show* (Grayson Hall: 1970)

*The Tonight Show* NBC-TV (Jonathan Frid: 1970)

*The Tonight Show* NBC-TV (Lara Parker: 1970)

*The Joey Bishop Show* ABC-TV (Jonathan Frid: 1970)

*The Joan Rivers Show* (Joan Bennett: 1970)

*The Jerry Lewis Muscular Dystrophy Telethon* (Jonathan Frid: 1970)

*United Cerebral Palsy Telethon* (Jonathan Frid: 1970)

*The Jerry Lewis Muscular Dystrophy Telethon* (Jonathan Frid: 1971)

*United Cerebral Palsy Telethon* (Jonathan Frid: 1971)

*Entertainment Tonight* (Jonathan Frid: 1982)

*Soap World* (1983)

*Entertainment This Week* (Jonathan Frid, Kathryn Leigh Scott: November 16, 1986)

*Hour Magazine* (Jonathan Frid, Kathryn Leigh Scott: November 20, 1986)

*Entertainment This Week* (Jonathan Frid, Kathryn Leigh Scott: January 31, 1987)

*Showtime Showbiz* (February 1987)

*CBS Morning News* CBS-TV (Kathryn Leigh Scott, 1987)

*Showbiz Today* CNN (Kathryn Leigh Scott: 1987)

*Good Morning America* ABC-TV (Jonathan Frid, Louis Edmonds, Kathryn Leigh
    Scott: August 28, 1987)

*The Tom Snyder Show* ABC Radio (Jonathan Frid, Lara Parker, Kathryn Leigh Scott:
    March 2, 1989)

*View From The West* UPI Radio Network (Jonathan Frid, Kathryn Leigh Scott:
    March 1989)

*Entertainment Watch* VH-1 (August 1989)

*PBS Sneak Previews Goes Video* (October, 1989)

*Instant Recall* (Dan Curtis, Jonathan Frid, John Karlen, Kathryn Leigh Scott, Lara
    Parker: November 26, 1990)

*The Tom Snyder Show* ABC Radio (Jonathan Frid, Dan Curtis: January 7, 1991)

*Personalities* (Jonathan Frid: January 11, 1991)

*To Tell The Truth* NBC-TV (Lara Parker, Kathryn Leigh Scott: February 15, 1991)

*Inside Edition* (Jonathan Frid, 1991)

*Entertainment Tonight* (Lara Parker, Kathryn Leigh Scott)

*Rick Dees' Into the Night* ABC-TV (Jonathan Frid, Lara Parker, Kathryn Leigh Scott:
    June 27, 1991)

*Entertainment Tonight* (25th Anniversary Festival: 1991)

*Sci-Fi Buzz* Sci-Fi Channel (Halloween Festival: 1992)

*Sci-Fi Buzz* Sci-Fi Channel (1993)

*Pilot Playhouse* Sci-Fi Channel (Kathryn Leigh Scott: 1993)

*Pure Soap* E! TV (Louis Edmonds: July 28, 1994)

*E! Entertainment News* (August 1, 1994)

*E! Week In Review* (August 1994)

*Fifty Years of Soaps: An All Star Celebration* CBS-TV (Jonathan Frid, Lara Parker:
    October 27, 1994)

*The Sci-Fi Trader* Sci-Fi Channel (Kathryn Leigh Scott, 1994)

*The Sci-Fi Trader* Sci-Fi Channel (Lara Parker, 1994)

*Sci-Fi Buzz* Sci-Fi Channel (1994)

## Local Programs

*Dialing For Dollars Movie* WQXI-TV, Atlanta, GA (Jonathan Frid: 1968)

*Marsha Sicard Show* WPTA-TV, Fort Wayne, IN (Jonathan Frid: May 1968)

*Bozo's Big Top* WJRT-TV, Flint, MI (Jonathan Frid: May 23, 1968)

*The Morning Show* WZZM-TV Grand Rapids, MI (Jonathan Frid: May 23, 1968)

*The Vic Ames Show* KATV-TV Little Rock, AK (Jonathan Frid: May 1968)

*The Morning Show* WBRC-TV Birmingham, AL (Jonathan Frid: May 1968)

*Clair & Coco* WMAL-TV Washington, DC (Jonathan Frid: May 24, 1968)

*Jerry's Place* WFIL-TV Philadelphia, PA (Jonathan Frid: May 24, 1968)

*The Sally Starr Program* WFIL-TV Philadelphia, PA (Jonathan Frid: May 1968)

*The Ron Barry Show* WEST-AM Easton, PA (Jonathan Frid, Grayson Hall, Roger Davis, Humbert Allen Astredo, Robert Rodan, Don Briscoe: 1968)

*Prize Movie* WABC-TV New York, NY (Jonathan Frid: 1969)

*A.M. New York* WABC-TV(Jonathan Frid: 1970)

*The Morning Show* WXYZ-TV Detroit, MI (Kathryn Leigh Scott: August 1970)

*Dialing For Dollars Movie* WNAC-TV Boston, MA (Kathryn Leigh Scott: August 1970)

*5:00 News* KSD-TV St. Louis, MO (Kathryn Leigh Scott: August, 1970)

*One On The Aisle* KMBC-AM Kansas City, MO (Kathryn Leigh Scott, August 1970)

*News At Noon* KSD-TV St. Louis, MO (Grayson and Sam Hall: August, 1971)

*5:00 News* KMOX-TV St. Louis, MO (Grayson and Sam Hall: August, 1971)

*Live At Five* KNBC-TV New York, NY (Jonathan Frid: April 9, 1982)

*The Film Vault* KDFI-TV Dallas, TX (Jonathan Frid: 1986)

*Midday Live* WNEW-TV, New York, NY (Jonathan Frid, Kathryn Leigh Scott: 1986)

*Dark Shadows Introduction* WKPC-TV Louisville, KY (Roger Davis: October 1986)

*Dark Shadows PBS Pledge Spots* KETC-TV St. Louis, MO (Kathryn Leigh Scott: 1986-87; Jonathan Frid, 1987)

*KCBS News* KCBS-TV Los Angeles (Kathryn Leigh Scott, Lara Parker: 1987)

*Interviews, Promos & PBS Pledge Spots* WNYC-TV New York (Jonathan Frid, Joan Bennett, Kathryn Leigh Scott, Louis Edmonds, Nancy Barrett, Clarice Blackburn, Sharon Smyth: 1987)

*The Allan Colmes Show* WNBC-AM New York, NY (Jonathan Frid, Lara Parker, Louis Edmonds, Marie Wallace, August 18, 1988)

*Interviews, Promos & PBS Pledge Spots* WNYC-TV New York (Lara Parker, Roger Davis, Diana Millay, Marie Wallace, Terry Crawford: 1988)

*No Soaps Attitude* WMTV-TV Tampa, FL (Jonathan Frid, 1988)

*Hour 25* KPFK-AM Los Angeles, CA (Kathryn Leigh Scott, Lara Parker: February 27, 1989)

*Good Day* WNYW-TV New York, NY (Jonathan Frid, June 22, 1989)

*News* WMAQ-TV Chicago,IL (Jonathan Frid, 1990)

*A.M. Los Angeles* KABC-TV Los Angeles, CA (Jonathan Frid, Lara Parker, Kathryn Leigh Scott: June 27, 1991)

*5:00 News* WABC-TV New York, NY (Jonathan Frid: August 20, 1993)

*Interview* WCMH-TV Columbus, OH (Jonathan Frid: April 23, 1994)

*6:30 News* KABC-TV Los Angeles, CA (Lara Parker; 1998)


In addition, Jonathan appeared on numerous other interview programs for local ABC-TV affiliates during the network run of the series. He, Nancy Barrett, and Kathryn Leigh Scott also participated in additional television and radio promotions during the publicity campaign for *House of Dark Shadows*. He also also been seen in local television interviews in conjunction with performing his one-man shows and during the 1987-88 national tour of the Broadway production of *Arsenic and Old Lace*, in which he portrayed Jonathan Brewster.

During *Dark Shadows*, Jonathan taped several television public service commercials including spots for the New York Blood Bank and the Christmas Fund and State Fair in Indianapolis. He was also seen in several *Dark Shadows* promotional commercials on local stations (versions of two different Philadelphia spots appear on the MPI video releases *The Best of Barnabas* and *Dark Shadows Bloopers*).

A 1969 television commercial for the Milton-Bradley *Barnabas Collins–Dark Shadows Game* with Jonathan Frid and Terry Crawford on the Collinwood set is on MPI's. *Dark Shadow's Special Edition* DVD. A commercial for the *Dark Shadows* Horror Heads pillows can be seen on the MPI video release of *Dark Shadows Bloopers*.

During the Sci-Fi Channel's airings of *Dark Shadows*, Lara Parker and Kathryn Leigh Scott have appeared in several commercials to promote the MPI *Dark Shadows* video and merchandise releases, the *Dark Shadows Companion*, *Dark Shadows Resurrected*, and *Dark Shadows Almanac* books, and the *Dark Shadows* Festivals.

## DARK SHADOWS SPECIALS

While airing in reruns, *Dark Shadows* has been promoted on several local stations with the production of several special programs.

The *Dark Shadows Special* (New Jersey Network, January 24, 1985) A PBS fundraising special with a taped interview with Jonathan Frid, who also performed Edgar Allan Poe's *The Tell-Tale Heart* and William Shakespeare's *Richard III*. The program was repeated on June 10, 1985 with new live studio pledge wraparounds with Jonathan Frid co-hosting. A third special for NJN was announced for February 20, 1986, entitled *Jonathan Frid: On The Darkside*, but was never actually produced.

*Twenty Years of Dark Shadows* (KDOC-TV, November 24, 1986) A half-hour retrospective of clips and interviews with Jonathan Frid, Lara Parker, and Kathryn Leigh Scott.

*Behind The Shadows* (WNYC-TV, September 10, 1987) A full one-hour collection of interviews, series' clips, and footage of the 1987 Newark *Dark Shadows* Festival footage launches *Dark Shadows* reruns on New York's city-owned PBS station. Included are comments from Jonathan Frid, Joan Bennett, Kathryn Leigh Scott, Louis Edmonds, Nancy Barrett, Clarice Blackburn, and Sharon Smyth.

*Dark Shadows Introduction* (KLXI-TV, October 1988) A short introductory segment giving viewers a recap of the early Barnabas episodes, leading into the series' launch on KLXI midway through the first syndicated year of episodes. A heavy portion of material for this program was borrowed from WNYC'S *Behind the Shadows*.

*Dark Shadows Going Away Party* (WGTE-TV, January 7, 1989) When this PBS station concluded airing *Dark Shadows* reruns, it purchased the films *House of Dark Shadows* and *Night of Dark Shadows* to broadcast as a finale.

*Jonathan Frid and Lara Parker on* Fifty Years of Soaps: An All Star Celebration *(1994).*

# Awards & Nominations

"Outstanding Individual Performance–Daytime" (Joan Bennett)–Emmy
    Nomination (1968)

"Best Daytime TV Program"–*Afternoon TV* (1968/69)

"Favorite Actor" (Jonathan Frid)–*Afternoon TV* (1968/69)

"Favorite Actress" (Lara Parker)–*Afternoon TV* (1968/69)

"Best Daytime Serial–Runner Up"–*TV Picture Life* (date unknown)

"Best Daytime Serial Actor–Runner Up" (Jonathan Frid)–*TV Picture Life*
    (date unknown)

"Best TV Star Of The Year" (Jonathan Frid)–*16 Magazine* (1968)

"Most Popular TV Show"–*16 Magazine* (1968)

"Most Popular TV Show"–*16 Magazine* (1969)

"Best Instrumental Composition" (*Quentin's Theme*)–Grammy Nomination (1969)

"Most Popular TV Show"–*16 Magazine* (1970)

"Most Popular Move" (*House Of Dark Shadows*)–*16 Magazine* (1970)

"TV Radcliffe Award" (Jonathan Frid)–Count Dracula Society (1970)

"TV Radcliff Award" (Dan Curtis)–Count Dracula Society (1970)

"One Million Radio Performances" (*Quentin's Theme*)—Broadcast Music Incorporated
    (1990)

"Best Genre Television" (1991 Series)—The Academy of Science-Fiction, Fantasy
    and Horror (1991)

*1982 ShadowCon Cast Reunion: John Karlen, Jerry Lacy, Barbara Cason,
Denise Nickerson, Dennis Patrick, Michael Stroka and Jonathan Frid.*

# Fan Conventions

Back when *Dark Shadows* originally aired in the 1960s and early 1970s, the phenomenon of fan conventions had not yet been born. It wasn't until the *Star Trek* fan movement of the early 1970s that devotées of genre programs began organizing conventions. These gatherings allowed fans to share and enjoy their interests with other fans, and also gave fans a special opportunity to meet actors and other personnel involved with their favorite series.

The first *Dark Shadows* convention occurred in 1977 and was actually just a small get-together at a general science-fiction convention, Starcon, in San Diego, California. Two years later, in 1979, the first convention expressly for *Dark Shadows* was held—ShadowCon, became an annual event in Los Angeles through 1985. By that time, ShadowCon had moved away from *Dark Shadows* and focused on other science-fiction and fantasy topics. As a result, a new and more ambitious fan convention began in 1983 called the *Dark Shadows* Festival. The Festival debuted the weekend of September 30 in Newark, New Jersey—20 minutes by commuter train from *Dark Shadows'* point of origin, New York City.

With the emergence of the Festival, *Dark Shadows* experienced a renaissance period in the 1980s. Whereas many fans had not been aware of ShadowCon, the Festivals became high-profile media events that were heavily publicized and attended by thousands of fans from across the United States and beyond.

Dozens of *Dark Shadows* cast and production alumni have also reunited at the Festivals, enthusiastically answering questions and signing autographs for the show's legions of followers.

For a brief period, three other *Dark Shadows* conventions were independently organized. The *Inside The Old House* fanzine sponsored the Dallas *Dark Shadows* Convention at the Dallas Dunfey Hotel in 1983 and at the Twin Sixties Hotel in 1984. A New York based group held the Manhattan *Shadows* convention at Manhattan's Halloran House Hotel in 1983 and 1985, and 1986. In 1987 and 1988 a convention entitled *Dark Shadows* Fellowship Fair was coordinated by Louisville, Kentucky fans. The event was held at the historic Seelbach Hotel, owned by *Dark Shadows* actor and Louisville native Roger Davis.

The Festival remained the major *Dark Shadows* convention and became a support group for Public Broadcasting System stations, such as the New Jersey Network, that aired *Dark Shadows* reruns. The convention has also raised funds for other charities over the years, including The Actor's Fund of America, the American Foundation for AIDS Research, the Juvenile Diabetes Association and the National Trust for Historic Preservation.

## A HISTORY OF THE DARK SHADOWS FESTIVALS

1983
September 30-October 2; Gateway Hilton Hotel, Newark, NJ
October 30; Red Lion Inn, San Jose, CA
1984
August 3-5; Downtown Hilton Hotel, San Jose, CA (as part of Timecon)
November 9-11; Gateway Hilton Hotel, Newark, NJ
1985
July 26-28; Downtown Hilton Hotel, San Jose, CA (as part of Timecon)
October 4-6; Gateway Hilton Hotel, Newark, NJ
1986
July 25-27; Marriott Park Central, Dallas, TX
October 24-26; Gateway Hilton Hotel, Newark, NJ
1987
August 28-30; Gateay Hilton Hotel, Newark, NJ
October 30-November 1; Airport Marriott Hotel; Los Angeles, CA
1988
August 19-21; Vista International Hotel, New York, NY
1989
March 3-5; Airport Marriott Hotel, Los Angeles
September 2-3; Vista International Hotel, New York, NY
1990
July 6-8; Vista International Hotel, New York, NY
1991
June 28-30; Airport Marriott Hotel, Los Angeles, CA
November 30-December 1; Vista International Hotel, New York, NY
1992
October 31-November 1; Airport Marriott Hotel, Los Angeles, CA
1993
August 20-22; Marriott Marquis Hotel, New York, NY
1994
July ; Airport Marriott Hotel, Los Angeles, CA

1995
August 18-20; Marriott Marquis Hotel, New York, NY
1996
June 28-30; Airport Marriott Hotel, Los Angeles, CA
1997
August 22-24; Marriott Marquis Hotel, New York, NY
1998
July 10-12: MGM Grand Hotel, Las Vegas, NV
1999
August 21-22; Marriott World Trade Center, New York, NY
2000
July 7-9; Airport Marriott Hotel, Los Angeles, CA

## FESTIVAL EVENTS

In addition to the multiple-day gatherings at the hotels, the *Dark Shadows* Festival has also sponsored several special events, including bus trips to series and film locations in Newport, RI, Essex, CT, Scarborough, NY, Tarrytown, NY, Bridgeport, CT and Norwalk, CT.

The Festival held a private party for cast members and fans at the original *Dark Shadows* ABC-TV Studio 16 on September 1, 1989. The building had been converted into a nightclub called The Red Zone. The event included dancing, *Dark Shadows* related videos, 1960s music, and a tour of the former studio.

*1996 Dark Shadows Festival Cast Reunion: Conrad Bain, Donna Wandrey, Dennis Patrick, Denise Nickerson, Kathryn Leigh Scott, David Selby, Lara Parker, Michael Stroka, Diana Millay and Marie Wallace.*

# Dark Shadows TV Locations

Although each episode of *Dark Shadows* was videotaped in a Manhattan ABC-TV Studio, several outside locations were seen on the series through film footage and photographic slides.

The Collinwood exterior is a mansion called Seaview Terrace in Newport, Rhode Island.

Newport is also the home of the Blue Whale exterior, which in real life is the Black Pearl Restaurant.

The Old House exterior, which burned to the ground in 1969, was the Spratt Mansion on the Lyndhurst Estate in Tarrytown, New York.

The Collinsport Inn exterior is the historic Griswold Inn in Essex, Connecticut.

The Collinsport Train Station is the Scarborough, NY train station.

Essex is also the site for several other *Dark Shadows* locations seen during the first year of the series. This includes the Police Station exterior, main street, and waterfront around Roger's office at the Collins Cannery. The exterior for the Evans' cottage is also in the area.

Literature for a house called Thornfield Hall in Thompson, Connecticut falsely states that the structure was used on *Dark Shadows*. The building has a few features similar to Spratt House, but no portion of Thornfield Hall was ever seen on the series.

Other actual locations seen on *Dark Shadows* were taken from photographs and books. In the case of Rose Cottage during the 1840 storyline, the exterior was nothing more than the miniature model that David Collins and Hallie Stokes found in 1970.

## The Real Collinwood

Seaview Terrace, in Newport, Rhode Island, was used as the exterior for Collinwood. Several early publicity photos with Alexandra Moltke, Louis Edmonds and David Henesy were also taken inside the mansion.

The sixty-five room building, patterned after a French chateau of the Renaissance period, was constructed in 1928 at a cost of more than two million dollars. It is surrounded by seven acres of lawn and is located a few hundred yards from the shore of the Atlantic Ocean. The original owner was Edson Bradley, a distiller for Old Crow Whiskey, who built the mansion for his wife.

The building is made of hollow tile and concrete, and the roof is composed of copper and slate. There are marble, mosaic, and parquet-oak floors; statues; imported fireplaces; and 16th century stained glass windows. The mansion was built with several large chandeliers and 17th century oil-painting ceilings from Italy and France, as well as a collection of period antiques. One room features a ceiling of carved angel heads. A large flagstone terrace adjoins the building on the Atlantic Ocean side. The Architectural League of New York awarded Howard Greenley a prize for planning the home.

In 1951, Seaview Terrace was converted into Burnham-by-the-Sea, a non-profit summer school for girls, founded by Mrs. George Waldo Emerson. The building was later purchased by Martin Carey, and has been leased by Salve Regina College for classrooms and as a boy's dormitory.

*Vintage images of Seaview Terrace, aka "Collinwood."*

## FILM FOOTAGE

In 1966, prior to the start of production on *Dark Shadows*, Dan Curtis and a production crew went to Newport, Rhode Island, Essex, Connecticut, and Tarrytown, New York to shoot footage of some of the *Dark Shadows* actors that would be inserted into various shows.

The film material added an extra visual dimension to the series and prompted additional location shooting later in the year. The concept was innovative for a daytime drama, but as the series became heavily focused on the supernatural and the stories became more complicated, it was no longer cost-effective to do location filming. After the series went to color in August, 1967, the filmed segments were dropped. Instead, still-frame slides were used for exteriors of Collinwood, the Old House, and other outside locations.

Much of the location footage for *Dark Shadows* had actually been shot in color, but most of it was used only in the black and white episodes. Three exceptions were single exterior shots for Collinwood, Evans' Cottage, and the Blue Whale—these were the only location film clips seen after the series went to color.

Already existing stock footage was used a few times in the series. This included a scratchy film depicting lightning bolts, an equally scratched shot of waves crashing on jagged rocks, and still-framed images of a forest.

### Exterior Footage Highlights

Episode 1   The train carrying Victoria Winters is seen rushing by. Over Collinwood, the moon is shining. Victoria stands outside the Collinsport Train Station and gets into a taxi with Burke Devlin. The taxi arrives outside the Collinsport Inn.

Episode 2   Victoria walks on the terrace and grounds at Collinwood as well as the cliff at Widows' Hill, where she looks out at the ocean.

Episode 3   Roger Collins parks his car, a Ford Mustang, outside the Evans' cottage, walks to the front door, and leaves after knocking on the front door.

Episode 5   Victoria walks out of Collinwood.

Episode 13   Victoria walks on the Collinwood grounds to the entrance of Matthew Morgan's cottage. Later, she leaves the cottage, passes by the garage and enters.

Episode 15   Roger walks to his car in the garage area outside. David looks out a window from Collinwood as Roger drives away. Roger loses control of his car as he drives down a hill.

Episode 50   A dead man's body on the shore.

Episode 65   Victoria walks along the beach and finds a pen.

Episode 68   Roger walks on the pier outside his office.

Episode 70   David and Victoria walk up to the Old House. Matthew Morgan walks toward the Old House. Matthew, David and Victoria leave the Old House. The Ghost of Josette runs around the columns outside the Old House.

Episode 71   Victoria departs from Roger's office.

Episode 73   Sam Evans walks up to the police station.

Episode 80   Roger drives his car away from Collinwood. He walks along the shore, searching.

Episode 81   Matthew exits Collinwood entryway and later goes back in. A taxi arrives at Collinwood while Matthew trims bushes.

Episode 82   Roger drives car to Collinsport Inn.

Episode 83   Roger walks out of Collinwood.

Episode 85   Sam Evans walks outside the Blue Whale and enters.

Episode 96   Opening shot of Collinwood with rainfall

Episode 100   Victoria drives car to Collinsport Inn.

Episode 10   Roger walks into the Blue Whale. Roger walks inside Collinwood.

Episode 102   David walks up to Old House with flashlight. Matthew walks up to house with a lantern. Victoria walks outside Collinwood.

Episode 104   Roger drives car down the road and to Collinwood.

Episode 105   Sheriff Patterson's car outside Collinwood. Roger leaves Collinwood on the terrace.

Episode 107   Victoria walks outside Old House with flashlight. Matthew stands on roof of Old House and pushes urn off.

Episode 113   Film of Collinsport Inn with close-up on sign. David runs up to the Old House.

Episode 114   Victoria drives car to Collinsport Inn. David enters and departs the Old House.

Episode 115   David goes to the Old House. Victoria walks down the steps at Collinwood. Victoria goes to the Old House.

Episode 119   Roger drives to Collinwood.

Episode 120   David walks to Old House. Matthew leaves Old House and returns.

Episode 122   David leaves Old House.

Episode 127   The Ghost of Josette runs around the columns outside the Old House.

Episode 128   Sam walks inside Collinsport Inn.

Episode 130   David plays on swing outside Old House.

Episode 134   David looks out window at Collinwood.

Episode 139   Victoria and David walk in the woods.

Episode 143   Downtown Collinsport.

Episode 148   Boats in the Collinsport harbour.
Episode 153   Car drives down road.
Episode 162   Collinwood rear daytime. Old House daytime.
Episode 164   Collinsport Inn.
Episode 174   Phoenix, Arizona desert and city.
Episode 181   Downtown Collinsport.
Episode 183   Collinsport Inn.
Episode 193   Downtown Collinsport.
Episode 200   The Evans' cottage.
Episode 202   The Blue Whale
Episode 221   Collinsport Inn.
Episode 238   Victoria and Carolyn walk through the woods up to the Old House.
Episode 256   David plays on swing outside Old House.
Episode 262   Roger walks to the Old House.
Episode 263   The Collinsport wharf.
Episode 275   Carolyn walks along the shore.
Episode 295   The Blue Whale.

Note: A variety of film clips of Collinwood are used at the beginning of every episode. One of the opening film clips of Collinwood used in the early episodes was occasionally flipped the wrong way, such as the one seen at the start of episode 173.

Only two episodes of *Dark Shadows* began without a scene of Collinwood at the start. Episode 1 began with a shot of a train and episode 21 began with a shot of the ocean.

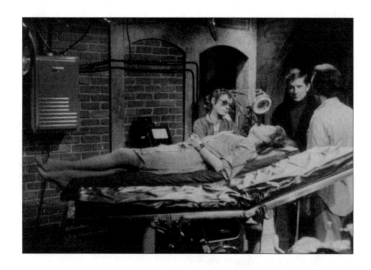

# Selected Bibliography

Hundreds of articles have been written about *Dark Shadows*, its stars, and its fans. This partial list focuses on some of the most significant articles which have appeared over the past thirty years. This select bibliography does not include the countless soap opera, teen, movie and television magazine features which appeared while the show was originally on the air.

*Variety*, "Dark Shadows" Review, June 29, 1966

*TV Guide*, "Giddy Gothic," December 3, 1966

*The New York Times*, "Out In Detergent Land: A Hard Day's Fright," July 30, 1967

*Newsweek*, "The Ghoul Show," August 21, 1967

*TV Guide*, "No Tears For Miss Bennett," August 26, 1967

*Wall Street Journal*, "Daytime Horror Show Lures the Housewives From Their Ironing," December 27, 1967

*TV Guide*, "A Vampire For All Seasons," July 13, 1968

*Time*, "Ship of Ghouls," August 30, 1968

*Variety*, "Monsters Making Good," September 18, 1968

*Famous Monsters of Filmland*, "Dark Shadows," October, 1968

*Saturday Evening Post*, "Can A 172-Year-Old Vampire Find Love And Happiness In A Typical New England Town?, November 1968

*New York Times*, "Vampires Are Voluptuous," December 29, 1968

*TV Guide*, *Dark Shadows* Review, February 1, 1969

*TV Guide*, "More Perils Than Pauline," May 31, 1969

*Famous Monsters of Filmland*, "Who's A-Frid of The Big, Bad Vampire?," November, 1969

*MacLean's*, "Bite Me, Barnabas–Bite Me!," December 1969

*New York Post*, "Afternoon of A Vampire," March 7, 1970

*Newsweek*, "Turned-On Vampire" April 20, 1970

*Ladies Home Journal*, "The Journal's Joyce Illig Emerges From *Dark Shadows*," August, 1970

*Variety*, "House of Dark Shadows" Review, September 2, 1970

*Cinefantastique*,"House of Dark Shadows" Review, Winter, 1971

*TV Guide*, "Out off The Shadows," January 23, 1971

*Famous Monsters of Filmland*, "House of Dark Shadows," February, 1971

*Variety*, "Night of Dark Shadows" Review, August 11, 1971

*TV Guide*, "Here's What Really Happened To Barnabas & Co.," October 9, 1971

*Cinefantastique*, "Night of Dark Shadows" Review, Winter, 1972.

*Famous Monsters of Filmland*, "Night of Dark Shadows," January, 1972

*Monsters of The Movies*, "Once Upon A Time There Was A Vampire," August, 1975

*Soap Opera Digest*, "Grayson Hall, Lady Of The Dark Shadows," May 1977

*Fangoria*, "Dark Shadows Revisited," #17, 1981

*Soap Opera Digest*, "Dark Shadows Has Risen Again!," July 20, 1982, August 3,
     1982, August 17, 1982

*TV Guide*, "He Was A Werewolf With A Ph.D," August 11, 1984

*Collectibles Illustrated*, "Dark Shadows On The Air," "Confessions of A Werewolf,"
     September/October 1984

*Soap Opera Digest*, "Dark Shadows Lives!," November 6, 1984

*Eastern Review*, "I Am A Cult," May, 1985

*Fangoria*, "Undead Soap," #44, 1985

*Dallas Morning News*, "Dark Shadows Draws Fans To Festival," July 29, 1986

*Soap Opera Digest*, "Dark Shadows–The Place Where The Dead Bodies Moved,"
     April 21, 1987

*Los Angeles Times*, "Dark Shadows Pumps New Blood Into PBS," November 3, 1987

*Theater Week*, "From Soap To Stage," September 25, 1988

*New Yorker*, "Shadows," June 26, 1989

*Bloody Best of Fangoria*, "As The Dark Shadows Turn," #8, 1989

*Hollywood Reporter*, "MPI Vid Scares Up Dark Shadows," August 2, 1989

*Detroit News*, "Tapes From the Crypt," October 25, 1989

*Newark Star-Ledger*, "Dark Shadows," January 21, 1990

*Cinefantastique*, "The Horror That Wouldn't Die," December, 1990

*Newsweek*," A Monster Revival," January 7, 1991

*Washington Times*, "The Show That Wouldn't Die," January 17, 1991

*People*, "As Dark Shadows Creeps Back To TV, The Old Show Still Haunts Its Cast,"
     January 21, 1991

*Soap Opera Weekly*, "The Vampire Who Conquered Daytime," January 29, 1991

*US*, "Dawn of The Dead," February 7, 1991

*Ladies Home Journal*, "The Show That Would Not Die," February, 1991

*New York Newsday*, "Gothic Romance," February 20, 1991

*Soap Opera Weekly*, "Lurking In The Shadows," November 3, 1992

Additionally, when the show was originally airing on ABC-TV, countless articles
appeared in magazines such as *Daytime TV, Afternoon TV, 16 Magazine, 16 Spec, Tiger
Beat, Fave, Flip, Photoplay, TV Photo Story, Modern Screen, TV By Day, All Day TV,
Hollywood Screen Parade, TV Radio Show, Starland, Screen Scene, TV Dawn to Dusk, TV
Picture Life, Who's Who In Daytime TV, TV Star Parade, TV Radio Movie Guide, Screen
Stars, TV & Movie Play, Outasite, Teen Life, Teen World, TV Star Annual, TV Movie
Spotlight, Teen Pinups, Yankee Magazine, Photo TV Land, TV Radio Mirror*, and others.

*Dark Shadows* is also featured in dozens of reference books pertaining to television,
horror, and soap operas.

*Dana Elcar; Gene Lindsey; John Harkins; Peter Turgeon; George Mitchell;*
*Michael McGuire; John Lasell; David Hurst; Mark Allen.*

# Actor Birthdays & Birthplaces

| | | |
|---|---|---|
| Humbert Allen Astredo | April 4 | Pasadena, CA |
| Conrad Bain | February 4 | Lethbridge, Alberta |
| Nancy Barrett | October 5 | Shreveport,LA |
| John Beal | August 13 | Joplin, MO | d. April 26, 1997 |
| Lee Beery | March 20 | Minneapolis, MN |
| Joan Bennett | February 27 | Palisades, NJ | d. December 7, 1990 |
| Chris Bernau | June 2 | Santa Barbara, CA | d. June 14, 1989 |
| Clarice Blackburn | February 26 | San Francisco, CA | d August 5, 1995 |
| Don Briscoe | March 20 | Yalobusha, MI |
| Barbara Cason | November 15 | Memphis, TN | d. June 18, 1990 |
| Kathy Cody | November 30 | Bronx, NY |
| Mary Cooper | December 4 | St. Joseph, MO |
| Terry Crawford | February 13 | Boston, MA |
| Joel Crothers | January 28 | Cincinnati, OH | d. November 6, 1985 |
| Keene Curtis | February 15 | Salt Lake City, UT |
| Thayer David | March 4 | Medford, MA | d. July 17, 1978 |
| Roger Davis | April 5 | Louisville, KY |
| Louis Edmonds | September 24 | Baton Rouge, LA |
| Elizabeth Eis | February 19 | Tacoma Park, MD |
| Dana Elcar | October 10 | Ferndale, MI |
| David Ford | October 30 | San Diego, CA | d. August 7, 1983 |
| Conard Fowkes | January 4 | Washington, DC |
| Hugh Franklin | August 24 | Muskogee, OK | d. September, 1986 |
| Jonathan Frid | December 2 | Hamilton, Ontario |
| Robert Gerringer | May 12 | New York, NY | d. November 8, 1989 |
| Timothy Gordon | January 3 | Lawrence, MA | d. September 28, 1993 |
| Anthony George | January 29 | Endicott, NY |
| Michael Hadge | June 28 | Greensboro, NC |
| David Henesy | October 20 | Glen Ridge, NJ |
| Grayson Hall | September 18 | Philadelphia, PA | d. August 7, 1985 |
| Tom Happer | October 15 | Miami, FL |
| Jered Holmes | February 15 | Parkersburg, WV | d. September 9, 1994 |
| Kate Jackson | October 29 | Birmingham, AL |
| John Karlen | May 28 | Brooklyn, NY |
| Daniel Keyes | March 1 | Concord, MA |
| Jerry Lacy | March 27 | Sioux City, KS |
| John Lasell | November 6 | Worcester, MA |
| Paula Laurence | January 25 | Brooklyn, NY |
| Michael McGuire | June 30 | Milwaukee, WI |
| Donna McKechnie | November 16 | Detroit, MI |
| Michael Maitland | August 27 | Fort Lauderdale, FL |
| Marsha Mason | April 3 | St. Louis, MO |
| Paul Michael | August 15 | Providence, RI |

| | | | |
|---|---|---|---|
| Diana Millay | June 7 | Rye, NY | |
| Alexandra Moltke | February 11 | Denmark | |
| Denise Nickerson | April 1 | Natick, MA | |
| Lara Parker | October 27 | Knoxville, TN | |
| Dennis Patrick | March 14 | Philadelphia, PA | |
| Christopher Pennock | June 7 | Jackson Hole, WY | |
| Addison Powell | February 23 | Belmont, MA | |
| Keith Prentice | February 21 | Dayton, OH | d. September 27, 1992 |
| Lisa Richards | May 5 | Brooklyn, NY | |
| Robert Rodan | January 30 | Newark, NJ | |
| Mitchell Ryan | January 11 | Cincinnati, OH | |
| Geoffrey Scott | February 22 | Hollywood, CA | |
| Kathryn Leigh Scott | January 26 | Robbinsdale, MN | |
| David Selby | February 5 | Morgantown, WV | |
| Craig Slocum | November 14 | New York, NY | d. September 12, 1978 |
| Sharon Smyth | November 29 | Philadelphia, PA | |
| Alex Stevens | January 6 | Harvard, CT | |
| James Storm | August 12 | Highland Park, IL | |
| Gail Strickland | May 18 | Birmingham, AL | |
| Michael Stroka | May 9 | Passaic, NJ | d. April 14, 1997 |
| Peter Turgeon | December 25 | Hinsdale, IL | |
| Virginia Vestoff | December 9 | New York, NY | d. March 2, 1982 |
| Abe Vigoda | March 24 | New York, NY | |
| Marie Wallace | May 19 | New York, NY | |
| Donna Wandrey | May 11 | Chicago, IL | |
| Elizabeth Wilson | April 4 | Grand Rapids, MI | |
| Richard Woods | May 9 | Buffalo, NY | |

## ACTOR'S REAL NAMES

John Beal was born John Bliedung
Kay Frye was born Kay Blume
Terry Crawford was born Terrayne Crawford
Thayer David was born David Thayer Hersey
Grayson Hall was born Shirley Grossman
Elaine Hyman was born Helen Hyman
John Karlen was born John Karlewicz
Dorrie Kavanaugh was born Dorothy Kirssker
Lara Parker was born Mary Lamar Rickey
Dennis Patrick was born Dennis Harrison
Robert Rodan was born Robert Trimas
Kathryn Leigh Scott was born Kathryn Marlene Kringstad
Lana Shaw was born Laura Shaw
Alex Stevens was born Alex Poulos

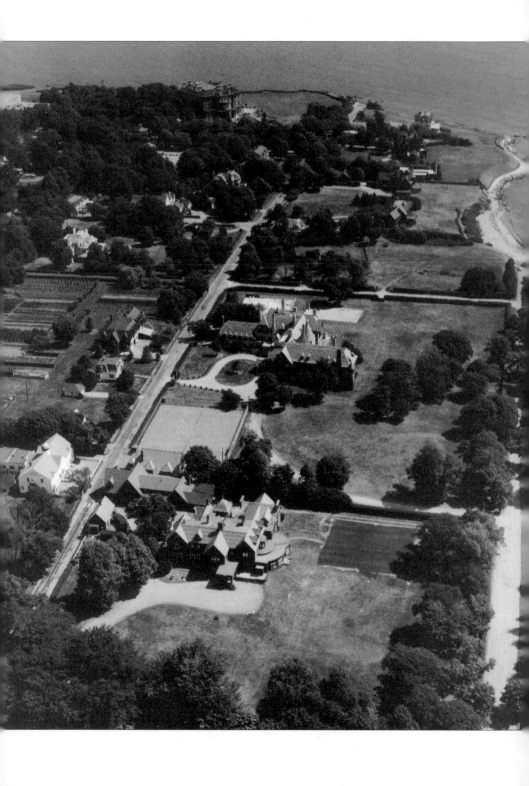

# 𝔅uilding 𝔖hadows

⸺ ◦•••◦ ⸺

## by Sy Tomashoff

ARK *SHADOWS* IS NEVER FAR AWAY FROM ME. A FEW YEARS AGO, I was at an anniversary party for *The Bold and the Beautiful* at the Bel Air Country Club. I had been the production designer on the show since its inception in 1987 until I retired in early 2000. One of the guests, a young man who works as a production assistant in the industry, approached me at the party and told me that I had been the one person he wanted to meet. He knew that I had been the scenic designer for *Dark Shadows* and the show had been a strong influence on him as a kid. Once again I am reminded of the tremendous impact the show has had.

It was back in 1966 that Bob Costello, the producer for series creator and executive producer Dan Curtis, asked me to be the art director of a new daytime drama to be called *Dark Shadows*. "I don't do soaps," was my reply.

I had been the designer on *Armstrong Circle Theatre* for two years when Bob was its producer in the early 1960s. Afterwards, I had worked on two filmed series, *East Side/West Side* with George C. Scott and *For the People* with William Shatner.

"Why don't we meet for dinner and catch up on old times anyway," Bob suggested. This seemed harmless enough and I accepted his invitation to renew our lapsed friendship. Dinner was at an elegant eastside restaurant and I recall that we celebrated with a couple of martinis. It had been about five years since we had seen each other.

The outcome of this dinner (or the martinis) was that I agreed to undertake the project for one year. And thus I became ensconced in the world of soap opera.

First, however, there was the matter of drawing up a contract with Dan Curtis Productions and that presented problems with my union. The freelance contract in those days included a clause which required the producer to pay the designer a fee for rebroadcast of any and all episodes. This created a stalemate in the negotiations and I found myself in the position of having already started designing, while at the same time my union insisted that if the production company did not agree to the conditions, I would be removed from the project. I pleaded with my business agent to allow me to stay on the job. Finally Dan Curtis said that he would agree to the conditions.

After all, Dan probably thought, "What chance is there that his show will ever be in reruns?"

That was the scuttlebutt at the time, so my contract was signed and I was permitted to work. It was Andy Clores, the union business agent, who had insisted on the enforcement of the rerun clause. I thank you, Andy!

As the fans know, Dark Shadows played in more languages and countries than you can shake a stick at. It was because of Andy's tenacity that I became, to my knowledge, the first scenic designer in broadcast history to receive residuals from a soap opera. The show that would never be rerun has been playing in some country or another almost all the time for the past 30 years.

However, when I first discovered that my contract committed me to five years I went ballistic! I had agreed to do the show for one year. I complained and Bob assured me that I was not going to be railroaded. Oddly enough, I couldn't imagine ever leaving once the show was rolling and actually stayed for its entire run.

We had too much fun. It was easily the most creative project I'd ever been associated with. So much for the guy who said, "I don't do soaps."

Dark Shadows was to be the second project for which I would be creating the designs from scratch. It didn't seem like a big deal to me then, but I soon realized that I had the opportunity to do a television project using all the knowledge and expertise that I had gained from the film medium. I had learned that real materials, such as wall paper and architectural moldings, had to be used rather than the simulated painted detail generally used in set construction that provided a flat two-dimensional surface.

In 1966, I wanted to explore sophisticated techniques using textures and materials thatwould look more convincing. Damask wall coverings

*Don Briscoe, Bobbi Ann Woronko and Sy Tomashoff on the set.*

would be actual damask rather than a painted substitute with a stenciled pattern. Wood would be real wood instead of painted canvas using a spatter drag technique. Even stone or brick walls would be conveyed with fiberglass or vacuform molds rather than a scenic artist's rendering of these materials. As fabulous as the scenic crafts were, these techniques were created for the stage and cannot stand up to the scrutiny of a camera closeup on screen. I felt that the textures we used should be capable of creating moods with shades, shadows and highlights. I was determined that I could improve the look of television, certainly on the soaps. The show originated from ABC's modestly-sized Studio 2 on 67th Street, premiering in June 1966 in glorious black and white. Among the first things we had to do was locate a house that would serve as the exterior for the Collinwood Mansion and a seaport village that would evoke the town of Collinsport. Where would we find such a town? I was elected to be the scout on this mission. It was decided that the best way to explore the Atlantic coastline would be in a Piper Cub, which I soon discovered was a very tiny two-passenger plane from which I could take photographs. That suited me fine.

My wife Naomi, who was pregnant with our third child Elizabeth, did not see it quite the same way. She thought it less than prudent for an expectant father to go flying in a wash tub under less than ideal conditions. "Sure," she said. "You can go up in a plane, but only if Mr. Curtis takes out a life insurance policy on you. Suppose something happens to you in the plane?"

I told Dan that I needed the protection of an insurance policy to give Naomi security. "No problem," said Dan, and so I was able to proceed on our adventure. (I never did find out how much I was insured for. I trust it was a goodly sum.)

"This seems to fit the bill," I remember thinking as we discovered the infamous seaport town of Essex—or should I say "Collinsport." We had spotted the village from the air at just the moment when I felt that our journey had been fruitless. I managed to lean out far enough to snap a roll of film which—to my surprise—turned out to be the pictures that transformed the town of Essex into the legend that it is today. Mission accomplished. Essex became the Collinsport location of the Collinsport Inn that housed the coffee shop where Maggie (Kathryn Leigh Scott) worked and where she befriended Victoria Winters (Alexandra Moltke) in the first episode.

"Here are the pictures of Essex from the air," I told Dan. "You will probably want to scout it by car to see if it satisfies all your needs."

Never happened. No survey. Dan and Bob took a camera crew up to Essex and filmed the scenes that were needed. A couple of weeks earlier, Dan, Bob and I had driven up to Newport, Rhode, Island, where we found the Gothic estate that would be used to portray Collinwood mansion, and I took pictures so that I would be able to match the set to our exterior.

As beautiful as the Newport estate was, the design of its interiors was totally inappropriate. Ultimately the only thing we matched was the front door, an intricate design consisting of multi-shaped paneled double doors. It was not an easy job, but copy them we did and no one ever doubted for one moment that those doors were the doors of the Newport estate.

How do you create a foreboding mood for a Gothic piece? We began with a staircase and a second floor landing where we could play some dramatic scenes and provide smooth transitions between scenes. We wanted a big fireplace in the drawing room. We built a secret panel in the rear wall of the drawing room not knowing at the time where it went or who would use it or even if it would be used at all. As it turned out the secret panel got more use than a subway turnstile! The *piece d'resistance* was the Gothic stained glass windows on the top stair landing in the entranceway. Those impressive windows gave the crowning touch to the foyer.

After a few weeks of designing most of the sets that would start the show, our director was brought into the scene. I remember sitting in Dan Curtis' office with Bob Costello when Lela Swift was introduced to me. She was a pioneering female director and had recently won an Emmy Award for her distinguished work.

"How can you design sets without the director being in on it? she asked, feeling a little exasperated. After I showed her the drawings and gave her a chance to study them, she felt more comfortable with them and we started a working relationship that would remain close and exciting. We always seemed to be in synch and shared a mutual admiration, personally and professionally. Lela, who went on to win further Emmys for her work after *Dark Shadows*, would say, "I don't ever want to work with any other designer but you." I did not win any Emmys for the show, but it wasn't that I didn't deserve one! It was simply that the *Daytime Emmy Awards* had not yet been established. Too bad, because I thought *Dark Shadows* looked wonderful. I have made up for it by garnering seven Emmys for daytime drama scenic design, beginning in 1981 for *Ryan's Hope*, followed by *Capitol* in 1986, and then five wins for *The Bold and the Beautiful* to date.

In the fall of 1966, while *Dark Shadows'* storyline still concerned the governess hired by the weird family in the spooky house, the show was moved from TV-2 on 66th Street to TV-16, a brand new studio on West 53rd Street. ABC had bought a lumber yard and renovated it to become the new home for *Dark Shadows*.

"You are going to have to cut two feet off the top of the foyer," I was told just as we were preparing to make the move. "The lighting pipes are too low to accommodate the height of the back wall."

"You're telling me I have to slice off part of the stained glass window at the top of the stairs?" I belched. "I've got a better idea."

"What?"

"You have to raise the pipes in that part of the studio."

Ta da! They did. And so we were all happy. The stained glass window remained intact.

A few months later, Dan Curtis decided that our story needed to move at a more dramatic pace and that perhaps it needed, well, maybe something darker. A dead ancestor or maybe a vampire! The appearance of the ancestor would follow the discovery of a portrait in the Foyer. I remember this sequence well because I was told we needed to see the portrait of Barnabas Collins before we were introduced to him. However, the role of Barnabas had not yet been cast! Bob Costello suggested that we better have the portrait artist start the picture with the appropriate period costume, the finger ring and the silver wolf head cane. His thought was that we could photograph anyone with the necessary accouterments and insert the face of the actor when he was cast. No one volunteered to sit for the picture so it was Bob who drew the short straw. I was assigned to be the photographer. As a vampire, Bob looked great! I wonder where that painting is today.

Finally our vampire was found in the person of Jonathan Frid and the rest is history. Jonathan's face was installed onto the painting for time immemorial.

Then, of course, there was the task of revealing the vampire and for those of you who don't know the circumstances of that horrendous event, the scenario went this way. Willie Loomis (John Karlen) was in search of the reported wealth of jewels that could be found in the Collins family mausoleum. In the studio, Dan dubbed me the "master builder of mausoleums."

When Willie discovered the mausoleum—and you can be sure it was a dark and foggy night—he saw three stone sarcophagi in a row inside the crypt. Certainly the jewels must be in one of these boxes, he figured. The lids were much too heavy for him to remove but he noticed that on the wall behind each of the sarcophagi was a tablet with the deceased's name on it and above each tablet was a decorative lion's head with a ring through its nose. This ring, Willie figured, could serve as a pulley system to help raise the lid. When Willie fastened the rope to the lid and through the ring in the lion's nose—you guessed it! The tug on the ring's spring device triggered the secret slab door to open into the inner chamber that housed a single wooden coffin. The coffin contained the vampire—the one and only, the infamous and lovable, the immortal Barnabas! Willie, of course, had been sure that in this coffin was the treasure he was seeking. Not quite! As Willie slowly raised the lid, a hand appeared and reached for Willie's throat in what appeared to be a death grip. End of episode! Shortly thereafter, there is a knock on the door at the Collins estate. Elizabeth Collins (Joan Bennett) answers the door to none other than Barnabas Collins, who presents himself as a long-lost cousin from England. From this point on, the storyline of *Dark Shadows* focused primarily on the reluctant vampire.

And where would our reluctant vampire live but at the Old House, with Elizabeth's blessings. We set about fixing up the old place a bit. We had the newly-painted portrait of Barnabas placed over the mantle. We put in curtains and drapes and provided enough candles to light up Transylvania at midnight.

ABC soon announced that our show was to be converted to color. It was inevitable. We couldn't stand in the way of technology; nor did we want to.

"What will you do now?" came the curious cry from many of the actors and crew. "You're going to have to redo everything." In those days color was a mystical thing.

"You know," I said, "maybe, just maybe, I designed it for color in the first place."

The fact is we did not have to modify a thing other than the lighting. What fascinated me was that while I had always thought of mystery being best photographed in black and white, color did enhance the imagery. The show still kept its suspenseful mood by virtue of Mel Handelsman's—and later John Connelly's—eloquent lighting. Our transition to color was truly glorious.

I venture to say that in all my experience I can't recall any time before or since when there was so much enthusiasm, creativity and innovation brought into play on a television show. We flashed forward and backward in time, creating settings and costumes from every historical time from the witch burnings in the 18th century to the apparent demise of Collinwood mansion at the end of the 20th century. We created effects with Chromakey (superimposing with the use of a blue screen). We created astral beings who could emerge from their own bodies. We created portraits that could bleed and characters who aged 100 years in a matter of days. Classic horror stories such as *The Pit and the Pendulum* and *Dr. Jekyll and Mr. Hyde* became our playground. The actors got the opportunity to perform roles in a repertory company playing characters from various walks of life in different centuries. A character could die in one century but be reincarnated in another with a completely different look and a totally different personality.

*The Collinwood drawing room.*

One marvelous sequence of events was the walling up of our dear and pious Reverend Trask. Who can forget the wonderful character conceived by our writers and played to the hilt by Jerry Lacy? The reverend could really get on your nerves. Finally Barnabas couldn't take it any longer and decided to put an end to the pious one. He escorted Trask down to the basement, chained him to the wall and ultimately sealed him up behind a new partition which he built slowly, brick by brick, not unlike the character in Edgar Allan Poe's *The Cask of Amontillado*. It was one of the show's most delicious moments for me, to see Barnabas butter each brick until the final brick sealed out the last ray of light Reverend Trask would ever see. Poe would have been proud.

During one of our periodic seances, the lovely Victoria Winters found herself transported back in time to 1795. While she inhabited this time period she was apprehended by the citizens of Collinsport because of her strange behavior and was brought to trial for witchcraft. Was it any wonder?

She knew too much because she was a product of the 20th century. She was found guilty and sentenced to be strung up on the gallows. What a great time we had planning that sequence! Victoria ascended the ladder to where a hood was placed over her head. The hangman then placed the noose around her neck. Then, on a signal, the hangman struck the ladder from under her feet and she hung there until the life was drained from her body. When the body was cut down and the hood removed, it was discovered, to the dismay of everyone present that the body was not Victoria's at all, but that of Phyllis Wick. Who would have known—and once again Victoria was spared.

There were many challenges we faced each week. Our production meetings became weekly think tanks. For example, we wondered how we could transform an abandoned room in Collinwood's west wing into a resplendent drawing room right before our eyes? (This is secret formula #84.) The answer was to lock a camera in place in the empty room, turn the camera on and then turn it off. The next step was to redress the set as the fully furnished drawing room, then come back to the camera and do a cut or dissolve to the now opulent room. The audience will gasp, just as we did when we saw the resulting sequence. Our meetings were attended by the producer, director, associate director, technical director, and prop master. It was at these meetings that we could thrash out the answers to all our challenges and problems.

How could we have the ghost of Josette emerge from her portrait? Her portrait originally hung in the Old House drawing room above the mantle until Barnabas had his own portrait placed there instead. Josette's portrait was moved upstairs to Josette's room. How can we forget the image of Josette descending from the portrait and floating eerily in the night air on the large portico? This feat accomplished by superimposing one camera taking a shot of the portrait of Josette over the fireplace and another camera taking a shot of Kathryn Leigh Scott walking down a black velour ramp in a black draped set. Follow that with the film of Josette wafting about on the porticos of the Old House on a breezy dark night and you have the chilling sequence that haunted our audiences. Did we see the full moon that night? I'm not sure. Ah, the Old House. It was there that Bob Costello decided to take the shot of the full moon. I remember it well. When Bob asked me to go with him to the Tarrytown location of the Old House, I suggested that he come to our house for dinner and then we would go take the pictures. Naomi and I were living in Hartsdale, a hop, skip and jump from Lyndhurst, the property on which the desolate Old House stood. After a delightful supper we left for the

Old House. My function, as I recall, was to count the seconds for the time exposures. This was as high tech as you could get in those days before automation in photography.

The slide that resulted became a much needed transition image for the heralding of visitations of our resident vampire, our beautiful phoenix, our werewolf or any other satanical creatures like the Leviathans or Nicholas Blair. What an assortment of demons and witches we had! What better way than the full moon to make a dissolve to the scene of a lurking predator, be it werewolf, witch or vampire? The Old House was indeed a tailor made image for *Dark Shadows*. The columns on the portico must have been three feet in diameter and soared to an intimidating height of at least three stories. Years later, and after the show had ended, I decided to visit the monumental Old House, only to discover it was gone. It had burned down and its remains cleared away like so much rubble. What a devastating disappointment.

At the time the Old House first appeared on the show, the set was used only on occasion and didn't seem to have any great significance. I don't think we knew that there was going to be such a thing as a vampire, or at least the writers didn't tell us. At first it was an exciting place for little David (David Henesy) to visit when he was off hunting for adventure. The set, covered in cobwebs, was kind of spooky, the kind of place we all loved as kids—at least I did!

I remember coming back to my office late one afternoon to the news, from another designer at ABC, that the Old House set was on the way to the dumps in New Jersey.

"You're kidding," I retorted.

"No," I was told. "If you're still going to use it, you'd better call the city dump."

Of course I made the call, but it was too late. I thought for about 20 seconds, went to the file drawer where I kept all my drawings and pulled out the original plan and elevations from which the set had been built. The shop would have to rebuild it. The story made a big splash in the newspapers and we rebuilt the Old House with all of its original decay.

In the summer of 1970, our story flashed forward to the year 1995, kind of like *The Time Machine*, which is one of my favorite movies. It is the story of a young scientist at the turn-of-the-century who builds a "time machine" and manages to travel forward and backward in time. *Dark Shadows* used the same trick in the form of the Parallel Time room and the stairway into time. When we arrived in the year 1995, Barnabas and Julia Hoffman (Grayson Hall) discovered that Collinwood was a deserted and abandoned mansion suffering from the ravages of neglect and the disintegrating effects of weather and time.

We decided that under these conditions the windows would have been demolished, the ceiling and beams would have tumbled down and plaster would have fallen off the walls and the ceilings. Leaves, dirt and debris would have created havoc on the inside. I decided that the best way to achieve this was to layer on top of everything the added elements that would have registered their effects on the interior of the foyer and the drawing room. I designed what looked like the overhead beams and chunks of old plaster and had the crew suspend them from the grid above. We created torn and shredded draperies and broken windows in place of the existing ones. We took the doors off their hinges and stood them askew. We exposed the brick that was beneath the plaster, even though there never had been brick there before.

The carpentry and paint shops had a couple of weeks to fabricate the various elements and ship them to the studio. I remember that it was a Friday night when the studio crew set everything in place in the drawing room and foyer. By midnight we had placed all the rubble and all but two of the eight hanging overhead sections of plaster and beams. The crew, who were by that time exhausted from a long and harrowing week of hard work, announced that whether I was done or not, they were going home. I really couldn't blame them and I was only too happy myself to call it a night. The episodes that followed certainly gave the show yet another look, which was what kept us percolating.

With the passage of time, sets fall into disuse and because new sets can be very costly, it is always wise to adapt the old adage of "waste not, want not." As an example of our recycling, Roger's office fell into disuse and we needed a bedroom for Barnabas that was set in an earlier time period. The office had been a jewel of a set and rather than lose it, I went about refurbishing it. The set did indeed translate itself into a marvelous bedroom. It just shows you what a little red damask will do.

We used the drawing room in at least six different time periods and for the most part created different looks by refurbishing. There were also different forms of lighting throughout the ages. We would use candles in the 18th century, oil lamps in the early 19th century, gaslight in the late 19th century and, of course, electricity in the 20th century.

In the years since *Dark Shadows* left the air, there have been great strides in scenery and its design. Add to that, working in Los Angeles, where I did *Capitol* and *The Bold and the Beautiful*, you can build sets in much larger units and they don't have to be shipped by truck. This affords the opportunity to create sets with much more reality and detail. For *The Bold and the Beautiful*, I created a set that reminded me very much of *Dark Shadows*. The storyline called for a dungeon to be found in a house which had formerly been owned, as legend would have it, by the famous magician Harry Houdini. What a great opportunity this was for me to delve back into my old bag of tricks. Twenty-five years later I had the chance to create yet another chamber of horror. This time we would use velvet drapes, a grand chandelier and elegant Victorian furnishings. The project made me feel like I had really come home again. We even included candles and cobwebs.

It seems to me that I have come full circle. For me, and for our audience, *Dark Shadows* will never die!

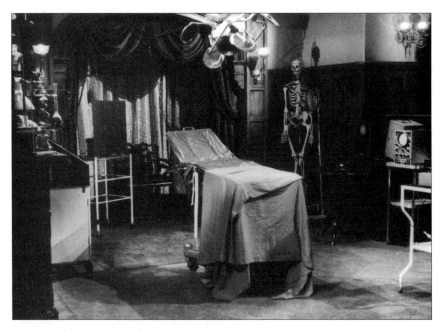

*Dr. Lang's laboratory.*

# Studio Kid

## by Richard Levantino

BEGAN WATCHING DARK SHADOWS SOMETIME IN 1968 AFTER MY SISTER told me all about it. It was the show that everyone in my high school dashed home to watch in the afternoon.

Growing up in Brooklyn, I was lucky to be able to visit the ABC-TV studio in Manhattan where the show was taped. I had read about it in a teen magazine and I was anxious to meet some of the *Dark Shadows* stars. So, in the summer of 1969 I went to the studio for the first time, especially hoping to see my favorite performer, Lara Parker. But she was not working that day, so it would be almost another year before my wish came true.

In late February, 1970, on a return excursion to the *Dark Shadows* studio, I was thrilled to finally see Lara as she left to go home at the end of the day. She had been off the show for a few weeks but said she would now be appearing more often again. In addition to playing Angélique, she would also portray a new character named Alexis, who ended up being her twin sister in "parallel time."

I learned Lara's upcoming schedule and returned the following week with flowers for her, the first woman I had done this for other than my mother! Lara's beautiful eyes lit up when I presented my gift. I took some great photos that day and it is a moment I'll never forget. I also asked if she had any professional glossy photos of herself and the next week she gave me a terrific publicity photo I still have in my collection.

I saw Lara several more times during the spring and summer of 1970. I was also privileged to get inside the studio and take photographs on the set. In June, on the day after I graduated from high school, I was treated to Lara,

*Lara Parker outside studio and with fan Richard Levantino in 1970 and 1994.*

Jonathan Frid and several other cast members signing my yearbook. That is a real treasure!

Another *Dark Shadows* favorite of mine is Jonathan Frid. Also in the summer of 1970, he asked a bunch of "studio kids," including myself, if we would like to help him process his enormous supply of fan mail. We got together at the studio on a Saturday and helped him sort it out the best we could. In return, Jonathan obtained passes for all of us to see a screening of *House of Dark Shadows* at the DeMille Theater. He also invited us to the Christmas party at the studio that year.

When *Dark Shadows* went off the air in the spring of 1971, I looked forward to the syndicated reruns, which took a few years to hit the air. Watching the show years later, I wondered if I would ever see Lara, Jonathan or any of the other cast members again. Happily, when the New Jersey Network PBS stations began airing the repeats in 1983, the *Dark Shadows* Festivals were born. Every year since then, fans have been fortunate to meet most of the actors in person and receive their autographs. It's always fun to see them again and I personally thank them for all the enjoyment they have given through *Dark Shadows*. 

# Child of the Shadows

## by Denise Nickerson

ET ME BEGIN BY SAYING HOW MUCH I ENJOYED PLAYING AMY JENNINGS and Nora Collins on *Dark Shadows*. All of the actors were terrific to work with and extremely talented. The crewmembers were always kind to me too—and I thought that Dan Curtis was the best.

But I must say that working with David Henesy was definitely the most fun aspect for me. We were about the same age, which was a treat since my acting career until then had mostly involved working with adults. David and I became good friends and had a lot of fun together.

I remember when we decided to open our own restaurant in the studio and sell lunch to the cast and crew. We had a hot plate to cook on and David's natural talent for cooking (he would later manage and own several respected eating establishments in New York) and his enthusiasm enabled us to thrive for several weeks. Everyone humored us by purchasing our daily "blue plate specials." We prepared quite a bit of David's favorite, tuna à la king. I remember one of the teen magazines did a piece on our little enterprise.

Another memory of mischief with David was sneaking into Joan Bennett's dressing room and smoking her cigarettes. (Although I don't recommend this to other kids.) We were able to do this undetected because Joan always wore heavy doses of Jungle Gardenia perfume, which masks any other odor for about six blocks!

While on *Dark Shadows*, its enormous popularity forced me to change my already unlisted telephone number numerous times. My home phone would constantly ring with girls calling to request Jonathan Frid's home phone number, which of course I never divulged.

I think that my favorite moment on the show was when David Henesy and I discovered the ghost of Quentin Collins. David Selby was so nice to us and *Quentin's Theme* is still a favorite of mine today.

Unfortunately, I had to leave *Dark Shadows* in the spring of 1970 to go to Germany to film the movie *Willy Wonka & the Chocolate Factory*. What I missed most were all my friends on the show. But I have wonderful memories, not to mention videotapes of the episodes, and it has been a real joy to see everyone at the *Dark Shadows* Festival cast reunions. ☞

*Denise Nickerson and David Henesy; Denise rehearsing with Diana Millay; Denise and David Selby.*

# 𝔗𝔯𝔦𝔟𝔦𝔞

*25th Anniversary Cast Reunion, 1991 Dark Shadows Festival, Los Angeles:
(from top) Roger Davis, Lara Parker, Robert Rodan, Diana Millay, Terry Crawford,
Donna Wandrey, Jonathan Frid, John Karlen, Marie Wallace and Dennis Patrick.*

## THE PORTRAITS OF BARNABAS

The original portrait of Barnabas Collins, dating from the 18th century, which hangs in the foyer at Collinwood, was posed for by producer Robert Costello. The face was not completed until Jonathan Frid was cast in the role. The portrait first appears in episode 205; on the front page of the script it is described as the "Jered Collins portrait in the foyer." In the same script, the name "Jeremiah" is crossed out and "Barnabus" (misspelled) is written in by hand. Even as late as episode 209, the script still lists the name of the character as "Jered," although "Barnabas" was always the name spoken on the show.

In 1967, Barnabas commissions the second portrait of himself, which is begun by artist Sam Evans in episode 222 shortly after Barnabas meets Sam's daughter Maggie in episode 221 and is struck by her resemblance to Josette. Sam later works on the painting at home and delivers it to Barnabas in episode 255. It is then hung over the mantel in the Old House. During the period in which Barnabas is chained in his coffin by Will Loomis in 1970 Parallel Time, this portrait is shown in most episode openings during the voiceover. In the 1967 painting, Barnabas is pictured in a pose similar to the 18th century portrait but in modern attire.

The third portrait of Barnabas closely resembles the original 18th century portrait. It was made to be used in the movie *House of Dark Shadows*, where it appears in the portrait gallery of Lyndhurst which serves as Collinwood in the film. It is shown in closeup at the beginning of the scene in which Barnabas presents Elizabeth Collins Stoddard with Naomi's original jeweled necklace.

During the time *House of Dark Shadows* was being filmed, the original 18th century portrait of Barnabas went missing from the television studio. Another portrait was made to resemble the original for use on the television series. During 1970 Parallel Time, this portrait of Barnabas is discovered by Amy and Daniel in episode 1003. It is rehung in the foyer in episode 1008.

In 1840, the portrait of Barnabas hangs in the room of Ben Stokes, Barnabas' faithful servant in 1795 who is still alive in 1840. After Ben dies, the portrait is rehung in the Collinwood foyer. In 1841 Parallel Time, the portrait of Barnabas does not hang in the foyer until the last episode. At the end of the final scene, the portrait is shown in closeup at the beginning of the final voiceover by Thayer David telling what happened to the characters.

## THE PORTRAIT OF JOSETTE

The Old House is first mentioned in episode 70 in 1966. David Collins and Victoria Winters visit it and see the portrait of Josette, which hangs over the drawing room mantel. At the end of the episode the ghost of Josette, played by Kathryn Leigh Scott, emerges from the portrait and walks around on the porch of the Old House. The portrait next appears in episode 102.

When Barnabas Collins moves into the Old House in 1967, the portrait of Josette is moved to Josette's room after its restoration by Willie Loomis. The portrait remains there until after Vicki goes back in time to 1795.

The first scene in Josette's room in 1795 occurs in episode 374. The portrait of Josette mistakenly hangs over the mantel, but it has been removed when the next scene takes place there in episode 377.

The portrait of Josette officially arrives in episode 402, during the 1795 story. Naomi Collins tells Barnabas a package has arrived for him; Riggs is requested to bring it to the Old House. There Barnabas unwraps the package to reveal the portrait of Josette, which from the accompanying letter is intended to be André duPrés' wedding gift to Barnabas and Josette. By episode 405, on Barnabas' orders, the portrait of Josette has been hung above the mantel in the drawing room of the Old House.

In 1897, it is erroneously revealed that an artist named Coswell painted the portrait of Josette in 1797. In episode 866, the portrait is shown with a prominent signature and date in red paint in the lower right-hand corner.

## CHANGE IN OPENING LOGO AND CREDITS

A change is made on the opening logo (where the name "Dark Shadows" appears on screen) beginning with episode 295, the first episode made in color. For black-and-white episodes, the logo is stationary and appears over three different films of waves and a silhouette of Collinwood. For the color episodes, the logo begins in a wavy manner, going to a stationary image when it is superimposed over Collinwood.

During the opening of the black-and-white episodes, films of three different waves appear. In the color episode openings, four different waves are shown. The second and third of the black-and-white waves are the same as the third and fourth color opening waves. The last wave is the only one in which the horizon appears.

The logo "DARK SHADOWS" is set in an unusual print style. The initial letters, "D" and "S" are set in Old English, but the remainder of the name, "ARK HADOWS" is set in Caslon Bold Condensed, but in capital letters, not in lower case print as might be expected.

## 1967 NABET STRIKE

Tuesday, October 3, 1967: Actors returned to work after meetings with Mr. Grott of AFTRA. Bob Gerringer and Daniel Keyes refused to cross picket lines. Bob's replacement was Peter Turgeon, and Dan's replacement was Peter Murphy. Executives were doing technical work. The NABET strike is still not ended, nor are they negotiating; there is no end in sight. Thursday, October 12, 1967: AFTRA gave the actors permission to return to work at 3:00 PM. Joan Bennett had been fined by the union for returning to work. October 12: Meeting at 7 PM with AFTRA officials; lawyer was George Gannantz. Two preliminary meetings with lawyer were held at studio. Still no NABET-ABC negotiations, meetings to start in Washington on Monday, October 30, 1967.

AFTRA Fines: Joan Bennett, $5400; Peter Turgeon, $3900; Alexandra Moltke, $3500; David Ford, $3500; Jonathan Frid, $3500; Grayson Hall, $3500; Louis Edmonds, $3500; Nancy Barrett, fine withdrawn; Anthony George, case adjourned but on November 17, $3500.

Claiming that the strike would kill *Dark Shadows*, Dan Curtis offered to pay the actors' fines if they continued to work during the strike. All of them obliged except for Robert Gerringer and Daniel Keyes, both of whom were replaced.

## SPECIAL ANNOUNCMENT ELIMINATES PART OF SCENE

The teaser for episode 251 is a repeat of the final scene from the previous episode, in which Maggie Evans almost stakes Barnabas Collins in his coffin using a tool left by Willie Loomis. The last frame is a closeup of Barnabas showing his fangs; he has not yet spoken to Maggie. On the original script, the first two pages of dialogue in Act I are marked "Not On Air—For Special Announcement" so that the start of Act I as televised begins, awkwardly, already in progress, with Barnabas remarking to Josette, "You still haven't answered my question." The unaired portion of dialogue from the start of the scene follows:

Barnabas:  What are you holding, Josette?

Maggie: (unable to get words out) I . . . I . . .

Barnabas:  Isn't that one of Willie's tools? Let me see it.  (He snatches it away from her)  What were you planning to do with this?

Maggie:  I . . .

Barnabas:  What's the matter?  Can't you speak?

Maggie:  Please -

Barnabas: Please what?  What are you asking me to do?

Maggie:  Don't . . .

Barnabas:  Don't? Don't . . . what?  I'm afraid you're not making sense, Josette.

Maggie:  (a fleeting moment of hope) Yes.  I . . . I am Josette.

Barnabas:  Of course. My bride.

Maggie:  Yes.  . . . your bride.

Barnabas:  And we're going to be happy together.

Maggie:  Yes . . .

Barnabas:  To the end of time.

Maggie:  Yes . . .

(On-air footage begins) Barnabas:  You still haven't answered my question.

The ABC-TV Special Announcement was made after a week of United Nations hearings on the Vietnam War which were carried on ABC stations instead of *Dark Shadows* in several time zones. To inform viewers of what they had missed, ABC gave storyline recap announcements over the opening credits of several episodes, as listed below. However, the announcement included at the start of episode 251 was too long and to accommodate it, ABC had to delete the first 45 seconds of Act I. That Special Announcement follows:

"For those who have missed the last few episodes of *Dark Shadows*: Elizabeth Collins, at Jason McGuire's insistance, has taken Vicki, Carolyn and Roger into the basement room and convinces them that it holds no mystery. They don't realize that beneath the flagstones on the floor is concealed the room's secret—the body of Elizabeth's husband Paul. Elizabeth, now realizing that the secret can never be told, announces to the family that she and Jason will be married. Maggie Evans escaped from Barnabas and attempted to get to her father, but was recaptured and told by Barnabas that unless she assumes the identity of Josette Collins, she will die. Realizing that she can never escape, Maggie attempts to destroy Barnabas."

Other special announcements from this part of the series include the following:

**Episode 247:** "In the last few moments of yesterday's episode Barnabas Collins discovered that Maggie has disappeared and sets out after her. In the meantime Maggie returns to the garden of her home and is seen by Sam through the window, but when he rushes out to find her she has vanished."

**Episode 249:** "In the Tuesday's and Wednesday's episodes Maggie runs away from Barnabas and appears outside her father's house. Sam sees her, but when he rushes out to her she has vanished. Barnabas finds Maggie and puts her in the family tomb. He warns her that she must believe she is Josette Collins or suffer the consequences. But Maggie cannot forget her identity and fears for her life."

**Episode 250:** "In Tuesday, Wednesday and Thursday's episodes, Maggie escapes, is recaptured, and her life threatened. Elizabeth Collins Stoddard allows the family to enter the locked room in the basement. To their surprise they find nothing, for the secret lies safely buried beneath the flagstone floor upon which they are all standing."

Note: It was later revealed that Paul Stoddard's body was not buried under the basement room and that Paul was, in fact, still alive.

## EMERGENCY LEVIATHAN EPISODE

Episode 915, in which actress Marsha Mason appears as Audrey, a Leviathan vampire, was a special episode created under emergency circumstances. During this time in the series, *Dark Shadows* fans complained about Barnabas Collins' return to evil ways. In an effort to appease viewers and to more clearly explain that the Leviathans were responsible for Barnabas' behavior, this episode was hastily written, produced and aired. The episode stands alone without affecting the continuity of the previous storyline.

At the end of the previous episode, the Leviathan child Michael tells David Collins that the suspicions of Doctor Julia Hoffman must be dealt with. In the opening scene of episode 915, Michael orders Barnabas to kill Julia. When Barnabas refuses, he is subjected to a dream in which the Leviathans Adlar and Audrey threaten him with a return to vampirism. Megan Todd appears, and Barnabas is just able to restrain himself from going for her neck. Then Adlar tells Barnabas that the Leviathans have Josette duPrés Collins in their power and will kill her unless he obeys. Reluctantly Barnabas promises to do their bidding.

Episode 916, which follows, takes up the plot from the end of episode, 913/914. Barnabas decides Julia must be made a Leviathan, but then learns she is immune to their power. As the story progresses, Michael turns against Maggie Evans, and Barnabas attempts to help Paul Stoddard. Barnabas learns that the Leviathans do not hold Josette under their power. After the special episode, Barnabas never again fully supports the Leviathan cause.

## SHADOWS SERVANTS

Female servants were in short supply on *Dark Shadows*, but they led exciting lives.

Victoria Winters, hired as governess at Collinwood in 1966, almost marries the wealthy Burke Devlin and eventually begins a new life in the eighteenth-century with her husband from the past, Peter Bradford.

In 1897, Beth Chavez takes care of Quentin Collins' mad wife Jenny and provides a contact with the woman who looks after Quentin and Jenny's twins. Beth believes Quentin plans to marry her but later becomes an ally of the evil Count Petofi.

Maggie Evans becomes governess at Collinwood in 1969 when Victoria leaves. After various harrowing adventures and narrow escapes, she departs with Sebastian Shaw for a rest cure at Windcliff Sanitarium.

Rachel Drummond is brought to Collinwood in 1897 by Edward Collins to look after his children, Jamison and Nora. She is later shot and killed by Judith Collins while under the influence of vampire Dirk Wilkins.

Angélique Bouchard arrives at the Old House in 1795 as maidservant to Josette duPrés. By using her powers as a witch, she ensures that her tenure as a servant is short. After she marries Barnabas Collins, Angélique never again appears as a servant except in a dream, when in 1897 Kitty Hampshire dreams of Angélique as a servant bearing gifts. Angélique is later revealed to have begun life as Miranda duVal, a servant in the 17th century who came under the influence of warlock Judah Zachery. In 1840 Judah takes away Angélique's powers, and she is shot and killed by Lamar Trask, who believes she is a witch.

Mrs. Sarah Johnson is hired at Collinwood in 1966 ostensibly to help Elizabeth Collins Stoddard with the housework, but she is actually a spy for Burke Devlin. Burke has convinced her the Collinses were responsible for the death of Bill Malloy, for whom Mrs. Johnson was a loyal and faithful servant for many years.

In 1795, Nathan Forbes schemes to win Millicent Collins and her wealth. Nathan's ally, Noah Gifford, delivers a note for Millicent hidden in a fan. Since Nathan plans to disguise Noah as Barnabas, Millicent receives the fan and note from a maid. The maid also appears later in the same episode, when she lets in Peter Bradford who has come to deliver a note to Natalie. Charlotte Fairchild plays the maid.

Magda Rakosi lives with her husband Sandor in the Old House when Barnabas arrives in 1897 By promising to reward her with jewels, Barnabas persuades

*Nathan Forbe's room at the inn.*

Magda to help him, although she strongly objects to his housekeeping standards. Magda sets the curse of the werewolf on Quentin but later attempts to lift the curse by using the mysterious powers of the hand of Count Petofi.

During 1970, the ghost of Daphne Harridge, who has been governess to Carrie Stokes and Tad Collins in 1840, haunts Collinwood. She attempts to counteract the evil influence of the ghost of Gerard Stiles. In 1840, Daphne arrives at Collinwood, having been hired by Quentin to look after the children. She has actually come to Collinwood for revenge against Quentin, blaming him for the death of her sister Joanna Mills. Later she falls in love with Quentin and discovers that the ghost of Joanna approves of their romance.

The first male servant seen on the series is Collinwood's surly, long-time caretaker, Matthew Morgan. Although Elizabeth Collins Stoddard tells Victoria Winters in 1966 that there are forty rooms in Collinwood, she admits there is only Matthew to do all the heavy work. Matthew is played by George Mitchell for three episodes; Thayer David assumes the role beginning in episode 38. Matthew tells Victoria he was retained by Elizabeth when all the other servants were dismissed eighteen years ago. He adds that before working at Collinwood, he had swept the floors in the cannery, and he has always been grateful to Elizabeth for rescuing him and giving him a good job and his own cottage home. Matthew admits he would do anything to help Elizabeth. When he learns that Bill Malloy intends to make trouble for Elizabeth in the name of justice, he causes Malloy's death. Matthew's paranoia grows after he kidnaps Victoria and threatens to kill her. The ghosts of Bill Malloy and Josette Collins join other ghosts in scaring Matthew to death.

Willie Loomis, Jason McGuire's drifter friend, causes trouble when he joins Jason as an unwelcome guest at Collinwood in 1967. In pursuit of the legendary

Collins jewels, he accidentally releases vampire Barnabas Collins, who immediately makes Willie his slave. Willie moves with Barnabas into the Old House and restores it under Barnabas' direction. Although at first he endures physical and mental abuse from Barnabas, Willie gradually becomes his loyal servant. Fearfully and reluctantly, Willie helps Barnabas and Julia Hoffman with Adam. Willie's unrequited love for Maggie Evans leads to much trouble for them both. In 1970, Willie is last seen in episode 1106, being dismissed from the room by Barnabas after having chained the coffin of the vampire Roxanne.

In 1795, Victoria meets Ben Stokes, a servant indentured to Joshua Collins. Barnabas has befriended Ben and taught him to read and write. Ben is enslaved by Angélique, who uses him to help with her schemes. Joshua frees Ben at the request of Barnabas just before Ben chains Barnabas in his coffin. Ben Stokes is still alive when Julia Hoffman arrives in 1840. She enlists his help in passing herself off as the sister of Barnabas Collins.

In 1795, Collins servant Riggs, played by Dan Morgan, guards Josette Collins in the hallway outside her room. He is unable to prevent her leaving through the secret panel inside. Earlier, Riggs and another servant carry out the body of Barnabas; the two servants are played by Tim Gordon and Tom Gorman.

Mrs. Johnson's son Harry Johnson, played by Craig Slocum, is enlisted by Carolyn Stoddard in 1968 to look after Adam, secretly hidden in Collinwood. Carolyn intervenes just in time when Adam is about to kill Harry. Harry is later enslaved by Nicholas Blair.

Dirk Wilkins, Collinwood caretaker in 1897, played by Roger Davis, is enslaved by the phoenix Laura Collins. After being attacked by Barnabas, Dirk dies and rises as a vampire who attacks Tim Shaw, Judith Collins and Rachel Drummond. Edward Collins stakes Dirk in his coffin.

Under a spell caused by Count Petofi in 1897, Edward Collins believes he is a servant, formerly employed by the Earl of Hampshire, who has come to Collinwood looking for work.

In 1970 Parallel Time, Mr. Trask is the butler for the Collinwood family headed by Quentin Collins. Trask is terrified that his part in the seance in which Angélique died will be discovered.

It is also revealed in 1970 Parallel Time that Buffie Harrington is a former servant at Collinwood.

In *Dark Shadows*' last episode, set in 1841 Parallel Time, writer Gordon Russell plays Harris, the second coachman, who carries in Melanie Collins Young and places her on the sofa in the Collinwood drawing room. All fear she has been attacked by a vampire, but it is revealed that an animal attacked her.

## DARK SHADOWS WEDDINGS

The first wedding planned on *Dark Shadows* never takes place. In 1967, Jason McGuire is about to marry Elizabeth Collins Stoddard, but at the last moment Elizabeth reveals her belief that she murdered her husband Paul with Jason as her accomplice.

Barnabas Collins kidnaps Maggie Evans in 1967 and attempts to turn her into his lost bride Josette, but with the aid of the ghost of Sarah Collins, Maggie escapes and is confined at Windcliff Sanitarium.

The wedding of Josette and Barnabas in 1795 is called off at the last minute when the bride disappears. Josette and Jeremiah are under a spell caused by Angélique; they are next seen on their wedding night when they realize they have betrayed their families.

Barnabas and Angélique are married in 1795 by Reverend Bland, played by Paul Giles. He also plays Reverend Brook who appeared only a short time before to marry Josette and Barnabas. In the script for episode 397, which includes the wedding, the full name of the bride is given as Angélique Fresne.

It is stated that the wedding of Suki and Nathan Forbes took place on April 8, 1792. In 1795, Nathan and Millicent are married off-screen, as are Roger Collins and Cassandra in 1968, shortly after the end of the 1795 time period.

In 1968, Victoria Winters and Jeff Clark (Peter Bradford) have a rocky road to the altar. Roger Collins dreams of their wedding being performed by a minister, played by Timothy Gordon, and wakes determined to stop it. Their real wedding is stopped when Eve gives Peter a note, after which he rushes off to find an empty grave. Victoria and Jeff are finally married, but shortly afterward Peter fades away, back to his own time. Victoria soon follows him.

In late 1968, Maggie Evans is dressed in her wedding gown, ready to marry Nicholas Blair; but instead he drugs her and attempts to perform the Black Mass so that they may be together forever.

Nicholas Blair (Humbert Allen Astredo) performs the Black Mass with Maggie Evans (Kathryn Leigh Scott).

In 1897, Judith Collins and Gregory Trask are married in town, as are Samantha Collins and Gerard Stiles in 1840. Both marriages lead to disaster for the bride and to the eventual death of the groom.

In 1970, Carolyn Stoddard first marries Leviathan leader Jeb Hawkes at the Leviathan altar with Nicholas presiding. During the ceremony, Jeb smashes the Leviathan box and altar. Later he and Carolyn are married in the Collinwood drawing room by Reverend Brand with Elizabeth as a witness.

*Nicholas Blair (Humbert Allen Astredo) performs the Black Mass with Maggie Evans (Kathryn Leigh Scott).*

During 1840, at the close of episode 1194, Quentin appears a moment too late to prevent the wedding of Daphne Harridge and Gerard Stiles. Daphne has been placed under a spell caused by Gerard. The ceremony is performed by Reverend Johnson.

In 1841 Parallel Time, Bramwell Collins interrupts the wedding of Catherine Harridge and Morgan Collins. Later Catherine and Morgan are married off-screen in the village. Bramwell and Daphne Harridge are subsequently married, also off-screen in the village, just before Catherine tells Bramwell she is pregnant with his child. Melanie Collins and Kendrick Young are later married off-screen in the village. At the end of *Dark Shadows'* last episode, the voice-over by Thayer David reveals that Catherine marries Bramwell, who becomes master of Collinwood.

## SHADOWS MISCONCEPTIONS

Over the years, several soap opera and televison publications, reference books and fan publications have featured incomplete and inaccurate *Dark Shadows* articles and cast lists. The following are some commonly printed mistakes.

Humbert Allen Astredo never played a character named Balberith or Diabolos. Balberith was the original name for the 1968 character of Diabolos (who was supposed to be the Devil), played by Duane Morris in Episodes 628 and 629. But the name of Balberith only appeared on the scripts and was changed to Diabolos when the episodes were produced and aired. The *Dark Shadows* Viewmaster

Jerry Lacy.

reels issued in 1969 added to the confusion by erroneously calling the character Balberith. The mistaken identity with Humbert Allen Astredo likely resulted from the fact that he portrayed a warlock, Nicholas Blair, who was very much the devil's desciple.

Clarice Blackburn did not play the good witch Bathia Mapes in the 1795 storyline. That role was played by Anita Bolster.

Betsy Durkin, who took over the role of Victoria Winters when Alexandra Moltke left the series, did not play Victoria in the 1700s. She only appeared in late 1968 present day episodes. Carolyn Groves replaced her for the final two Victoria episodes in the 1796 storyline.

Nancy Barrett did not play a character referred to as "The Woman In White." That character, mentioned in the 1841 Parallel Time storyline, was never actually seen on screen.

Grayson Hall did not appear as the Ghost of Harriet Collins in 1840. That single appearance was by Gaye Edmonds, who later played Stella Young in the 1841 Parallel Time story.

Jonathan Frid played two roles on the series: Barnabas Collins and Bramwell Collins. He did not portray Abraham Howell in the 1897 story. Philip Cusack appeared as Abraham.

## FANG MAIL

Jonathan Frid commanded an intense army of devoted fans, particularly female ones, during the run of *Dark Shadows*. These women were passionately attracted to the romantic aspects of Barnabas.

Besides writing him thousands of letters each week, some of the most enthusiastic followers would gather at Jonathan's personal appearances.

When Jonathan appeared on the *Merv Griffin Show* in 1969, Merv refers to "The Frid Girls" waiting for Jonathan outside of the studio. There was also a fan group entitled "The Fanatic Followers of Frid" (aka The 3-F Society.)

Jonathan heard from devoted fans of all ages. During *Dark Shadows*, Jonathan often averaged 15,000 letters a week with 4,000 during peak periods. Eventually, Jonathan recruited local fans to help him sort his mountains of mail and send replies.

## THE ENGLISH CONNECTION

In 1967, when Barnabas Collins first introduces himself to the present-day Collins family in episode 212, he describes himself as a cousin from

*Jonathan Frid and his secretary answer fan mail.*

England, the last of his line and a direct descendant of the Barnabas Collins in the foyer portrait.

Later Burke Devlin forces Barnabas to reveal that he lived with his cousin Niall Bradford on the outskirts of London. Burke investigates the story and learns that Niall Bradford died one-hundred-and-thirty years earlier, but Victoria Winters persuades Burke to stop his investigation of Barnabas.

When Barnabas meets the Collins family in 1897, in episode 703, he tells Judith Collins and Quentin Collins that the original Barnabas went to England in 1797 and established the English branch of the family. Quentin insists there is no English branch of the family, but Barnabas is able to persuade him that this did in fact exist.

Barnabas is preceded in 1840 by Dr. Julia Hoffman, who conspires with Ben Stokes to pass herself off as the sister of Barnabas Collins, whom she plans to meet at Collinwood. She and Barnabas pretend to be the children of the original Barnabas, who allegedly went to England in 1797. After Barnabas arrives, he meets the family in episode 1117 and claims that he lived in Cadogan Square in London.

In the movie *House of Dark Shadows*, Barnabas also introduces himself as a descendant of the original Barnabas, who supposedly moved to England and settled in Coventry. Barnabas says that the family place was destroyed during the war. When he mentions he lived in Cadogan Square in London, Professor Stokes asks Barnabas if he knew the Bramwells in number 33, but Barnabas uncomfortably turns away without replying.

Cadogan Square was built upon in the middle of the 19th century. It was part of the development of Belgravia, a socially desirable part of London. Coventry is a city of some antiquity, best known for the legend of Lady Godiva who rode naked through the streets on a white horse, her nudity covered by her long blonde hair. Coventry is also known for having suffered exceptional bomb damage during World War II, which would have inspired the comment made by Barnabas.

The name "Niall Bradford" must be a precursor of Peter Bradford, who had not yet appeared when the name was mentioned; and Stokes' query about the "Bromwells" presages the character named "Bramwell" played by Jonathan Frid in 1841 Parallel Time.

Jonathan Frid studied at the Royal Academy of Dramatic Arts in London in 1949 and then toured Britain briefly until the outbreak of the Korean War in 1950. Because the British had difficulty in pronouncing his surname, he changed it to Fridd, the name by which he was then known on stage there.

## THE PETOFI BOX

The box in which the Hand of Count Petofi is kept in 1897 appears in several time periods during *Dark Shadows*. In the present time, it is usually located on a table in the upstairs hall at Collinwood. The hall is first seen in episode 4 with the table, on which the Petofi box sits.

The most prominent view of the Petofi box in the present time is in episode 339. Dr. Dave Woodard, deeply suspicious of Dr. Julia Hoffman's activities, secretly enters her room hoping to find her notebook. While he searches, Mrs. Johnson, outside in the hallway, dusts around the Petofi box on the table.

The Petofi box is moved during the 1795 time period. First shown on the table in the drawing room at Collinwood, it appears in the bedroom of Barnabas Collins in the Old House while he is dying from the effects of a bat bite. The box then is seen on the table in the upstairs hall at Collinwood and later moves back to the table in the drawing room. It makes one appearance on the drawing room table just beyond the doors, in episode 238, but then returns to the front table, where it is shown during the opening voiceover in episode 458, shortly before Victoria Winters returns from the past.

During 1968, the Petofi box is shown back on the table in the upstairs hall in episode 650.

The Petofi box stands on the mantel of the drawing room in Collinwood when Barnabas arrives in 1897. Magda Rakosi brings the box containing the Hand of Count Petofi to the Old House in episode 778. She describes the box: "This is no ordinary box. Every one of these carvings has a meaning. Ancient as the gypsies. This box is very precious, Barnabas." Magda then opens it to reveal the Hand and tells Barnabas how the Hand will lift the curse of the werewolf from Quentin Collins. Unless the Hand is in action, it is kept in this box until it is reunited with Count Petofi in episode 814. After this, the box returns to the table in the upstairs hall in episodes 924 and 956.

In 1840, in episode 1171, the Petofi box can be seen in Rose Cottage. The box appears on the table in the Collinwood drawing room in 1680 Parallel Time, during episode 1231, for its final appearance.

## DARK DOCTORS

Dr. Julia Hoffman was originally meant to be Dr. Julius Hoffman. He is described in the script at the start of episode 265: "Dr. Hoffman, a man in his sixties, spare, ascetic, fine bones, with piercing eyes, is watching Maggie closely."

However, Dr. Hoffman is not *Dark Shadows'* only doctor with identity problems. Dr. Woodard, first played by Richard Woods, is twice referred to in the technical list for episode 229 as "Dr. Faulkner," although the script itself correctly refers to him as "Dr. Woodard." An actor named Alex was supposed to play an intern summoned by the nurse who discovers Maggie Evans missing at the end of episode 235. Instead Woodard, now played by Robert Gerringer, was obliged to appear in that scene as well as earlier in the episode. With the advent of a new actor, Dr. Woodard was given the first name of "Dave." After Maggie is sent to Windcliff, Sam inquires about her by phone to Dr. Woodard, whom he calls "Bill" in the script for episode 263. The script was changed to "Dave" before the show was taped.

## COLLINSPORT COPS

Although it was a small town, Collinsport was well supplied by law enforcement personnel, mostly in the present time. They were constantly called upon to investigate murders, attempted murders and mysterious disappearances.

Constable Jonas Carter appears in episode 23 to investigate the car crash in which Roger Collins was injured. He wears a shoulder badge that says "Sheriff" and is called "Sheriff" beginning in episode 28. Played by Michael Currie, he appears in five episodes. Elizabeth Stoddard Collins covers up David Collins' involvement, and the case is closed in episode 32.

Sheriff George Patterson, first played by Dana Elcar, is Collinsport's longest serving policeman. Beginning in episode 55, he investigates the murder of Bill Malloy.

Lieutenant Dan Riley, of the State Police, played by John Connell, appears in episode 143, looking into the supposed death of Laura Collins in Phoenix. Beginning in episode 148, Vince O'Brien plays Lieutenant Riley, who is joined in Phoenix by Lieutenant Costa, played by John Harkins, in episode 174.

In episode 219, Sheriff Patterson reports to Roger that cattle have been dying mysteriously. By episode 237, the sheriff has begun to investigate the disappearance of Maggie Evans. The sheriff also listens to the confession by Elizabeth that she murdered Paul Stoddard. A deputy, played by Ed Sauter, brings in Jason McGuire after his attempt to escape. The sheriff later searches for David when he is accidentally locked in the secret room of the Collins Mausoleum.

Beginning in episode 319, Sheriff Patterson helps activate Maggie's plan to pretend that her memory has returned. When Sam Evans, supposedly drunk, carries out the plan in the Blue Whale, Willie Loomis overhears and goes to warn

Maggie about Barnabas Collins. In episode 322, Willie is shot by the police who guard her. Ed Crowley and Theodore Beniades play the two policemen. In the following episode they are joined by Deputy Dennis Johnson and the Sheriff.

In episode 328, while Willie lies near death, Sheriff Patterson, now played by Vince O'Brien, searches Willie's room. Later, Deputy Dennis Johnson arrives to inform the sheriff and Barnabas that Willie is coming out of his coma. Episode 329 opens with a repeat of the same scene, but with Dana Elcar returning to replace O'Brien as the sheriff.

In episode 341, Sheriff Patterson, now played by Angus Cairns, accompanies Sam Evans when they discover that Dr. Woodard has been murdered. The investigation continues in episode 342, but the sheriff is played by Vince O'Brien. No constables are present during the episodes set in 1795.

Sheriff Patterson, still played by Vince O'Brien, returns in episode 503 to investigate the strange and frightening creature known as Adam. In the next episode, Adam is jailed; and James Shannon plays a policeman. Clifford Pellow, described in the script as a "Red-Necked Jailor," plays a sadistic deputy who taunts Adam in jail. Adam overpowers him and escapes. In episode 505, the Sheriff, Deputy Shannon and two other deputies, played by Tom Murphy and Angie Brown, watch as Adam jumps off Widows' Hill. After Adam's return, Sheriff Patterson continues his investigation. In episode 556, an unnamed deputy investigates the disappearance of Tom Jennings.

When Joe Haskell becomes the victim of Angélique as a vampire, he attempts to kill Barnabas. Sheriff Patterson, now played by Alfred Sandor, investigates in episode 615. In episode 658, Sheriff Patterson, played again by Vince O'Brien, questions Joe, who hallucinates and is taken away to Windcliff Sanitarium. Sheriff Patterson is seen for the last time when he investigates the murder of Carolyn Stoddard's friend Donna Friedlander in episode 675.

The character of Sheriff George Patterson is played by four actors, more than play any other character: Dana Elcar, Vince O'Brien, Dana Elcar again, Angus Cairns, Vince O'Brien again, Alfred Sandor, then Vince O'Brien yet again. Vince O'Brien also plays Lt. Riley, not to be confused with actor Ed Riley, who plays Sheriff Davenport, mistakenly listed on two scripts as Sheriff George Patterson. In the movie *House of Dark Shadows*, Sheriff George Patterson is played by Dennis Patrick, who plays both Jason McGuire and Paul Stoddard in the television series, each of whom is investigated by one of the sheriffs.

During 1897, three policemen are involved in capturing and guarding Quentin Collins: John Miranda in episode 786, Paul Vincent in episode 787, and Robert Warlock in 790.

During the Leviathan storyline, Deputy Davenport, played by Ed Riley, investigates the curious case of Paul Stoddard in episode 917. By episode 934, Riley has become Sheriff Davenport and continues investigating Paul's death. In episode 935, he, Julia Hoffman and Philip Todd meet Jeb Hawkes for the first time. At the end of the episode, the sheriff takes a call from someone he calls "George," possibly George Patterson, and is then killed by Jeb. Jeb raises Sheriff Davenport as a zombie in episode 939, and the sheriff is destroyed by the werewolf in episode 961.

While searching for Maggie Evans, Barnabas talks on the phone to Joseph Scofield in episode 942 and then describes him as a special investigator from the state capital. In episode 949, Lawrence Guthrie, Maine State Police investigator, played by Jered Mickey, questions Philip and Jeb and is later killed by the Leviathan creature.

In 1970 Parallel Time, Detective Frank Paxton, played by Stanley Grover, questions Cyrus Longworth about John Yaeger in Episode 989. After Yaeger kills Sabrina Stuart, a policeman played by Phillip R. Allen arrives to question Longworth in episode 1034. Later, Inspector Hamilton, played by Colin Hamilton, questions Quentin Collins in episode 1040 about the death of Angélique, then arrests him for the murder of Bruno Hess, but Quentin escapes. Hamilton questions everyone about the seance at which Angélique died. After the death of Angélique* posing as Alexis, Hamilton arrests Quentin in episode 1056. He and Barnabas search for Julia Hoffman in Episode 1057 after she has been hidden by Angélique.

In 1995, Barnabas and Julia attempt to learn what caused the destruction of Collinwood. The sheriff, played by Don Crabtree, suggests to Julia and Barnabas that they leave town. Later the sheriff investigates the death of Carolyn. Barnabas kills the sheriff when he finds his secret has been discovered.

In episodes 1156 and 1157, set in 1840, Constable Jim Ward, played by Roger Hamilton, arrests Quentin for the murder of Randall Drew.

## NAME CALLLING

Actors made some interesting mistakes in speaking names. "Barnabas" presented special difficulty. Quentin Collins calls him "Barnabas Cousins" in episode 710, and Sam Evans calls him "Barnabas Conrad" in episode 255. Lamar Trask refers to him as "Barnabas Collums" in episode 1172, and Hallie Stokes says "Doctor Barnabas" in episode 1081, perhaps referring back to the scene in which Willie Loomis comes out of his coma and Barnabas confirms Willie's suspicions that he is indeed a doctor. Willie calls him "Barnus" in episode 560, as does David Collins in episode 767. Elizabeth Collins Stoddard calls him "Barnass" in episode 281, and Doctor Dave Woodard calls him "Barnabies" in episode 337. In episode 288, Doctor Julia Hoffman calls him "Barnas-bas."

Victoria Winters is called "Miss Collins" by Peter Bradford in episode 433, by Doctor Eric Lang in episode 466, and by Judge Hanley in episode 452. Nicholas Blair calls her "Miss Monte" in episode 523. Carolyn Stoddard is called "Carolyn Collins" by Joe in episode 512. Barnabas calls Carolyn "Barrett" in episode 659, calls her "Vicki" in episode 553, and calls Chris Jennings "Car-Chris" in episode 944. Carolyn's friend Donna Friedlander, in her first speaking line, calls Carolyn "Don-carolyn" in episode 674.

David calls Dr. Woodard "Dr. Hoffman" in episode 318, and Burke does the same in episode 335. Elizabeth refers to "Dr. Kaufman" in episode 571.

Joshua Collins speaks of "Reverend Task" in episode 383, and Barnabas does the same in episode 1179/80, but referring to Lamar Trask, who is not a reverend, in 1840.

Edward Collins refers to Dirk Wilkins as "Wilson" in episode 712. Naomi Collins speaks of "Peter Brandon" in episode 434. Barnabas refers to "Professor Strokes" in episode 498. In episode 1154/5, in 1840, Edith Collins speaks of "Randolph" referring to Randall Drew. In episode 1048, Barnabas calls Inspector Hamilton "Doctor Hamilton." Cyrus Longworth speaks of the body of Larry Chase, combining it with that of Horace Gladstone by calling it "Horace Chase." In episode 669, Maggie Evans speaks of Chris Jennings when she means Tom Jennings.

Bruno calls Sky "Jeb" in episode 974; Joshua calls Naomi "Millicent" in episode 452; Amanda Harris calls Quentin "Tim" in episode 847; Edward calls Laura Collins "lawyer" in episode 730; Count Petofi calls Edward "Charles" in episode 834; Julia calls Maggie "Julia" in episode 608; Carolyn calls Joe Haskell "David" in episode 311; and Judith calls Carl Collins "Dirk" in episode 771.

In episode 456, in a scene between Vicki and Naomi, each refers to Daniel as "David." Barnabas calls Amy "Carolyn" in episode 667 and calls Sebastian "Quentin" in episode 1108. In episode 20, Sam calls Burke "Roger."

## THE OTHER SEAVIEW

Victoria Winters' dream house, a typical New England saltbox, is named Seaview, the same name given to the actual New England mansion which serves as the exterior of Collinwood.

After Vicki raves about the house, she goes with Barnabas Collins and Burke Devlin to explore it in episode 294. They find it deserted but in perfect condition. Barnabas goes upstairs and returns with a handkerchief which bears the initials F McA C. He presents it to Vicki, who is fascinated, wondering to whom it might have belonged.

Burke asks Elizabeth Collins Stoddard to sell him Seaview, part of the Collins real estate holdings. In episode 298, Burke, Elizabeth and Carolyn Stoddard visit it. Elizabeth agrees to sell it to Burke but then learns of a legal impediment. In episode 335, Liz reveals that its last owner was Caleb Sayers Collins, whose will stipulated that only a Collins could live in the house for one hundred years after his death. Elizabeth cannot break the will but plans to present the house to Burke and Vicki when the time is up in five years. Meanwhile Elizabeth offers the West Wing as a place for them to live. But Burke's death in a plane crash in Brazil prevents these plans from coming to fruition. Neither the handkerchief nor Seaview is ever mentioned again.

## SHADOWS BITS

✝ Joan Bennett, a top motion picture actress of the 1930s-1950s, was one of the first major film performers from Hollywood's Golden Era to join daytime television.

✝ Henry Baker, who played the gypsy Istvan during 1897, had a featured role in Seizure, the Oliver Stone film starring Jonathan Frid which was made in Quebec soon after *Dark Shadows* finished its run.

✝ Episode 497, which occurs during the dream curse, was taped the day before it was broadcast. The episode includes David Collins' dream, and a note on the script reads, "Too long—cut one door for David."

✝ A telephone is visible in the Old House only during 1970 Parallel Time. In episode 1034, it is on the tall desk in the drawing room, and in episode 1051 it is on the small table in the foreground of the drawing room.

✝ In 1966, Kathryn Leigh Scott wears a short, light wig in episode 1 when she greets Victoria in the Collinsport Inn restaurant. She continues to

Joan Bennett began her career as a blonde and then went brunette. One of her famous co-stars— from Green Hell—was Douglas Fairbanks, Jr.

wear this wig in episodes 3, 7 and 12, but beginning in episode 20, the wig is discarded, and she appears thereafter in her own long brown hair.

✢ Although *Dark Shadows* was set in Maine, no snow is shown, nor are trees seen without leaves. No character speaks with a New England accent. Thunder and lightning are constantly present, but rain is shown only in one early sequence: while driving back from Bangor, Roger Collins' car is caught in bad weather and is abandoned by Victoria Winters and Roger, who take shelter in a deserted shack.

✢ Two perfumes feature prominently in the *Dark Shadows* storyline. The ghost of Josette was fond of Jasmine, whereas Daphne's ghost preferred the sweet aroma of lilacs.It was also established in Episode 657 that lilac was Victoria Winters' perfume.

✢ In episode 20, in the Evans Cottage, Sam Evans finds a sketch of Collinwood. Looking at it, he is inspired to get up early the following morning and go to the cliffs at Collinwood to paint. In episode 48, the same sketch of Collinwood, now attributed to David Collins, is described by Victoria Winters as being "good enough to show to a real artist." David tears it up when Vicki reveals she showed it to Roger Collins.

✢ When Laura Collins appears in 1966 to reclaim her son David Collins, it is gradually revealed that she is a phoenix who dies in flames every one-hundred years. At that time it was stated that in the 18th century, she was Laura

The portrait of Laura Collins and her son David.

Murdoch Stockbridge, 1740-1767; in the 19th century, she was Laura Murdoch Radcliffe, 1840-1867; and in the 20th century she was Laura Murdoch Collins, who died in flames in 1967. However, she does not adhere to this sequence when she reappears during the 1897 storyline later in the series.

✛ At the beginning of 1970, David Henesy's leg got jammed in a door at the studio. For four episodes, David appears in his own leg cast, seated in a wheelchair. It is explained that Jeb Hawkes, the Leviathan leader, punished David by making him fall off a bicycle, as a warning. David's shows in the cast and wheelchair are, episode 937, taped January 8, 1970; episode 942, taped February 3, 1970; episode 958, taped February 13, 1970, and episode 959, taped February 6, 1970. He is out of the wheelchair on his next show, episode 979, taped March 12, which is his first appearance in Parallel Time as Daniel Collins. Kathy Cody is seen wearing an arm sling in the 1970 storyline involving the haunting of Collinwood by Daphne and Gerard. Kathy had been hit by a car outside the *Dark Shadows* studio.

✛ The bartender, played by Bob O'Connell, is seen during most early scenes set in the Blue Whale, beginning with episode 2. The character was originally named "Andy" in the scripts for episodes 33 and 63, and he was called by this name in episode 33. In episodes 58 and 63, Joe Haskell calls him "Pudgy," and in episode 58, Sam Evans calls him "Mike." Apart from these early episodes, the character is not named until episode 319, on September 14, 1967. During the events which lead to Willie Loomis being shot, the bartender Bob Rooney discusses Maggie Evans' memory loss with Sam and Sheriff Patterson.

✛ As part of its Haunted Dungeon attraction, New Orleans' Musée Conti Museum of Wax has featured figures of Barnabas battling the werewolf with Collinwood in the distance and a modern day Angélique preparing to stake Barnabas in his coffin.

✛ At one point during the original daytime run of *Dark Shadows*, ABC-TV considered moving the show to its nighttime schedule.

✛ The title "Dark Shadows" was previously used for a September 15, 1950 episode of CBS-TV's dramatic anthology *Suspense*, and for a three-issue horror anthology issued in 1957-58 by Steinway Comic Publications.

✛ The Dan Curtis collection of original *Dark Shadows* scripts is on file at the University of Southern California at Los Angeles in the Fine Arts Research Library. A donation from the *Dark Shadows* Festival enabled the entire set to be preserved on microfilm, which is available for viewing by the general public.

✝ The Barnabas wolf's head cane seen on the series is a traditional design. Made of silver sterling with nickel, it is sometimes referred to as a "dog's head" cane and is available from companies specializing in canes.

✝ When it came to its depiction of vampirism, witchcraft, and other supernatural folklore, *Dark Shadows* did not always follow the rules. For example, vampires are not supposed to be seen in mirrors, yet when Angélique was a vampire she was prominently featured in a laboratory mirror. The legend of the phoenix revolves around a 100-year cycle, yet Laura Collins did not follow that pattern. When she returned in 1967, it had only been 70 years since her last appearance, in 1897.

✝  Many *Dark Shadows* viewers aren't aware that the kitchen at Collinwood was actually featured on the show. In the 1966-67 episodes, characters were seen dining and discussing in the breakfast room/kitchen. Carolyn even ironed clothes in the kitchen in episode 5. The kitchen was last seen in episode 204, shortly before the introduction of Barnabas. Another set essentially took its place—the Collinwood study, which first appeared in episode 196.

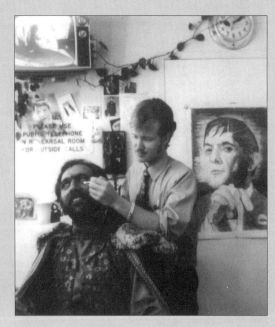

*Dennis Eger applies makeup to Paul Michael as King Johnny Romano.*

# In Memoriam

Syd Andrews
Frank Bailey
Bil Baird
Katharine Balfour
John Baragrey
John Beal
Joan Bennett
Chris Bernau
Clarice Blackburn
Ed Blainey
Anita Bolster
Angus Cairns
Barbara Cason
Joel Crothers
Thayer David
Ronald Dawson
John Devoe
David Ford
Ivor Francis

Hugh Franklin
Robert Gerringer
Paul Kirk Giles
Timothy Gordon
Tom Gorman
Grayson Hall
Lloyd Harris
Jered Holmes
Isabella Hoopes
House Jameson
Joseph Julian
Dorrie Kavanaugh
James Langrall
Gene Lindsey
Vincent Loscalzo
Patrick McVey
Kenneth McMillan
George Mathews
Everett Melosh

Edward Melton
George Mitchell
Sho Onodera
Arthur Ornitz
Rudy Piccirillo
Keith Prentice
Ed Riley
Jane Rose
Gordon Russell
Stanley Simmons
Ross Skipper
Craig Slocum
Thomas Spratley
Fred Stewart
Michael Stroka
Francis Swann
K.C. Townsend
Virginia Vestoff
Art Wallace

*Chris Pennock and Nancy Barrett playing around on the Lyndhurst grounds during a* Night of Dark Shadows *promotional photoshoot.*

# Dark Shadows Information

For fan club and convention information:

*DARK SHADOWS* FESTIVAL
P.O. Box 92
Maplewood, NJ 07040

For newsletter information:

*SHADOWGRAM*
P.O. Box 1766
Temple City, CA 91780

For home video and merchandise:

MPI MEDIA GROUP
16101 South 108th Ave.
Orland Park, IL 60467
(Toll free: 1-800-323-0442)
(In IL, call: 708-460-0555)
www.mpimedia.com/darkshadows

# Other Books by Pomegranate Press

Charlie's Angels Casebook
The Bunny Years
Entertainment 101
Dark Shadows Companion
Dark Shadows Comic Strip Book
Dark Shadows Music Book
Dark Shadows Collectibles Book
Dark Shadows Movie Book
Dark Shadows Program Guide
Dark Shadows Resurrected
Shadows on the Wall
The Fugitive Recaptured
The Night Stalker Companion
The Rockford Files
Maverick
Michael Landon: Life, Love & Laughter
Following the Comedy Trail
Hollywood At Your Feet
Hollywood Goes on Location
Hollywood's Chinese Theatre
Lobby Cards: Classic Comedies
Lobby Cards: Classic Films
Fiction: The Art and Craft of Writing and Getting Published
Rupert Hughes: A Hollywood Legend
Coya Come Home
Word of Mouth—Voice-over book and audiocassette

## For a Free Catalog:

POMEGRANATE PRESS, LTD., P.O. Box 17217, Beverly Hills, CA 90209
Check our website: www.pompress.com